How the Scots Won the English Civil War

How the Scots Won the English Civil War

The Triumph of Fraser's Dragoons

Alisdair McRae

The History Press

Cover illustrations. Front: The Battle of Marston Moor. (By Cooper Abraham/Harris Museum and Art Gallery/The Bridgeman Art Library) The Declaration of Arbroath. (Alisdair McRae)

First published 2011 by Dragoone Books

The new edition published 2013, 2020
by Spellmount, an imprint of

The History Press
97 St George's Place, Cheltenham,
Gloucestershire, GL50 3QB
www.thehistorypress.co.uk

British Library Cataloguing in Publication Data.
A catalogue record for this book is available from the British Library.

ISBN 978 0 7524 9860 7

Typesetting and origination by The History Press
Printed in Great Britain by TJ International Ltd, Padstow, Cornwall.

Contents

Introduction

I WAS TOLD RECENTLY by a very reputable publisher that English Civil War projects are increasingly difficult to sell and that there is not considered to be a large enough market for them. There are certainly a host of books available on the subject, but upon investigating, I find the same subjects and the same points of view expounded time and again. I suspect also that the same markets have been targeted time and again, leading to a saturation point being achieved.

This book is aimed at finding, and being of some interest to, a different market – perhaps the title might intrigue the Scottish reader (among many others, I hope), for whom, to date, the English Civil War has played no part in their educational curriculum, no part in their national psyche, and no part in their consciousness, with the possible exception of the 1970 film *Cromwell*, memories of which boil over with historical inaccuracies and Alec Guinness's toe-curling portrayal of Charles I; or perhaps the BBC's saccharine '80's television series *By the Sword Divided*.

The purpose of this history of the Scots in England from January 1644 is to argue the case that the English Civil War was won by the decisive campaigns in the north of England, that the entry into the war and participation of the Scottish Army of the Covenant was such a decisive factor within those campaigns that it can be likened to the Americans entering the two world wars, perhaps only after the conflict had started, but bringing with them an overwhelming force and standard of troops that they tipped the balance of conflict so there could only be one conclusion, at the same time bringing the war to an end far sooner than would otherwise have been the case.

The English Civil War divides into three components – the first, from 1642 to 1646, when Charles I came over to the Scots at their camp outside Newark; the second, from 1648 to 1649, comprising a series of uprisings in England and Scotland, the English rebellion being put down after a series of skirmishes and the Scottish invasion being crushed at the Battle of Preston, after which further uprising Charles was put on trial and executed; and the third, from 1649 to 1651, brought to a close at the Battle of Worcester in September of that year.

This volume focuses primarily on the first of these periods, following the Army of the Covenant as a whole and one regiment in particular – Colonel Hugh Fraser's Regiment of Dragoons; the only dragoon regiment out of twenty-one regiments which made up Lord Leven's Scottish Army, and a unit which appears time and again at key points throughout the history of the Scots' campaign.

It also takes the occasional glimpse at the better-documented actions of the Marquis of Montrose on behalf of his royal master against Scots Government troops at home. These successes led to a cavalry strike force, including Fraser's, returning from England to deal a crushing blow to the Marquis at Philiphaugh, ending the unbroken succession of victories which inspired such fear in his foes. The account touches briefly upon the later dissolution of the Scottish regiments, including Fraser's, the shift in the north towards the Royalist cause which erupted into the second civil war, and the death of Hugh Fraser in somewhat ambiguous circumstances prior to the fate of the Scots' and Royalists' causes being sealed in the third civil war at the battles of Dunbar and Worcester.

The Scots' campaigns were dominated by foul-weather marches, protracted sieges, illness, malnutrition and an ongoing battle for arrears of pay, subsistence, food and quarters. While Scots units were, compared to their English counterparts, very well equipped, had excellent training and battle experience, were politically highly motivated and acquitted themselves well in the main, there is little or no 'glory of war'. Punishment for infringement of military discipline was of necessity brutal, and death was just as likely to come in the form of malnutrition or disease as it was to be found marching under the colours of the enemy.

Finally, when reading about a war which spanned so many years, it is all too easy to lose sight of the human element – the death, the wounds inflicted on individuals which were very likely to become infected and turn septic, the effect on morale of years of fighting, and of the frequent breakdowns of pay and provisions which would lead to a rapid deterioration in relations between occupying forces and the locals on whom the unwelcome quartering of such armies was imposed. So while looking at military actions spanning a vast geographical area and many years, there is an attempt to keep a focus on the individual participants on both sides of a war which ripped Britain apart for years. I hope that in reading this you discover a new take on a period of our history that is a complex tangle of subtle differences in stance between the various factions, their further shifts in political and ideological position as the conflict progressed, and the huge gulf in the social, religious and cultural laws and mores which dictated life 400 years ago, when compared to the present day – this last reinforcing my belief that history is both another time, and another place.

Alisdair McRae DA

Prologue: The Background to War in Britain – War in Europe

The Root Causes of Conflict in Europe

We must first go back fifty years or so before the beginning of the seventeenth century to understand the causes of the Thirty Years' War in Europe and the subsequent political and military context of the conflict in Britain.

Religious tensions were strong in Europe from the second half of the sixteenth century while the rulers of the Holy Roman Empire[1] and Spain sought to restore the power of Catholicism.

In the Cologne War (1583–88), Spanish troops had expelled the prince-archbishop of that city who had converted to Calvinism, and replaced him with Ernst of Bavaria, a Roman Catholic. This had forced Lutheran residents to choose between conversion and exile.

By 1600, two camps had emerged in Europe; France and the United Provinces on one side, and Spain and The House of Habsburg on the other. Phillip III of Spain had sought to continue the foreign policy of his father, Phillip II, by keeping Spain on a war footing after the revolt of the Spanish Netherlands – when the Dutch had rebelled against Spanish domination, waged a protracted war of independence, eventually ended by truce in 1609 – the southern provinces of the Spanish Netherlands (the 'Obedient Provinces') having remained loyal to Spain, arranging the truce with the United Provinces (today's Holland). No one however believed Spain would give up this valuable region that included Amsterdam and its lucrative merchant industry.

After her success against the Spanish, the United Provinces had built up a powerful navy and established itself as a powerful commercial and colonial power. The most obvious and vulnerable overseas colonies for it to focus on however belonged to Spain, a fact Phillip III and his advisors were all too aware of. As early as 1618 Madrid had decided to renew the war against the United Provinces to eliminate this threat and re-occupy the region, gaining access to the large sums of money being made in the state.

However, the defeat of the 1588 Spanish Armada had shattered Spain's morale and any fleet she was to attempt to send through the channel to the United

Provinces would never be tolerated by England while anti-Catholic feeling was still so widespread after the 1605 Gunpowder Plot. Any military venture by the Spanish therefore would have to be carried out overland.

The only option was what the Spanish called the 'Spanish Road'. This ran along the French border to Luxembourg and the Obedient Provinces. While the Catholic north Italian states would not feel threatened by the Spanish taking this passage; and similarly south German states, also Catholic, would not be alarmed by the movement of Spanish troops, France did fear movement along her border by Spanish troops due to a centuries-old rivalry between France and Spain. Despite both nations being Catholic, for years France had been apprehensive of Habsburg encirclement. With Spain on her southern border and the Spanish Netherlands on her north-east border, France had actively helped the rebels during the revolt despite religious differences. With the success of the Dutch rebels, France would not tolerate any attempt by the Spanish to re-assert her authority in the area.

France was also eager to exert its power against the weaker German states; this dynastic concern overtook religious ones and would lead to Catholic France's participation on the otherwise Protestant side of the war.

Spain too was interested in the German states because the Spanish Netherlands sat on their western border.

Sweden and Denmark, Lutheran kingdoms, looked to help the Protestant cause in the Empire, and also sought political and economic influence in the north German states bordering the Baltic.

Religious tensions broke into violence in the German free city of Donauwörth in 1606 when the Lutheran majority barred Catholic residents from holding a procession, provoking a riot. This prompted foreign intervention by the Catholic Duke Maximilian of Bavaria. After the violence ended, Calvinists in Germany (who remained a minority) felt the most threatened. They banded together to form the League of Evangelical Union in 1608, under the leadership of the Palatine elector Frederick IV (whose son, Frederick V, married Elizabeth Stuart, daughter of James I of England). The establishment of this League prompted the Catholics to form the Catholic League in 1609, under the leadership of Duke Maximilian.

By 1617 it was clear that Matthias, Holy Roman Emperor and King of Bohemia, was going to die without heir, with his lands going to his cousin Archduke Ferdinand II of Austria, heir-apparent and Crown Prince of Bohemia.

Ferdinand, educated by Jesuits, was a staunch Catholic who wanted to impose religious uniformity on his lands. This made him highly unpopular in Protestant Bohemia. The added insult of the nobility's rejection of Ferdinand triggered the Thirty Years' War in 1618 when his representatives were thrown out of a window into a pile of horse manure. This act of defiance became known as the Defenestration of Prague – (Defenestration meaning the act of being tossed out of a window). Bohemia was in open revolt, and had foreign Allies. Ferdinand II of Austria, a staunch supporter of the German Catholic League, a ruler of vast Habsburg monarchy demesnes, and soon to be elected Holy Roman Emperor, was quite upset by this calculated insult, but his intolerant policies in his own lands had left him in a weak position. Had the Bohemian rebellion remained a local conflict, the war could have been over within a couple of years. However, the death of Emperor Matthias emboldened the rebellious Protestant leaders, who had been on the verge of a settlement. The weaknesses of both Ferdinand (now officially on the throne after the death of Emperor Matthias) and of the Bohemians themselves led to the spread of war into western Germany. Ferdinand was forced to call on his nephew, Philip of Spain, for assistance.

The Bohemians, desperate for allies against the emperor, applied to be admitted into the Protestant Union, which was led by their original candidate for the Bohemian throne, the Calvinist Frederick V, Elector Palatine. The Bohemians hinted that Frederick would become King of Bohemia if he allowed them to join the union and come under its protection. However, similar offers had been made by other members of the Bohemian Estates to the Duke of Savoy, the Elector of Saxony, and the Prince of Transylvania. The Austrians, who seemed to have intercepted every letter leaving Prague, made these duplicities public. This unravelled much of the support for the Bohemians; however, they were soon joined in their revolt by much of Upper Austria, whose nobility was then chiefly Lutheran and Calvinist. Lower Austria then revolted and in 1619, Count Thurn led an army to the walls of Vienna itself. In the east, the Protestant Prince of Transylvania led a spirited campaign into Hungary with the support of the Ottoman Sultan. The emperor, who had been preoccupied with the Uzkok War, hurried to reform an army to stop the Bohemians and their Allies from entirely overwhelming his country.[2]

In 1621, the Dutch-Spanish conflict restarted. As was common at the time, those states that could afford to use mercenaries did. The Dutch could afford to do so. To ensure that the focus of the Habsburgs was split, the Dutch encouraged the growing problems in Bohemia. The United Provinces became a focal point of all anti-Habsburg feeling and Spain could not avoid getting involved in a conflict which involved them moving more troops along the sensitive 'Spanish Road', which in turn further antagonised the French, who gave more and more help to the Dutch. The result was a war that would tear Europe apart. Principally fought in Germany, the conflict gradually developed into a general, political and religious war involving most European powers. The major impact of the conflict, fought mostly by mercenary armies, was the extensive destruction of entire regions, denuded by foraging armies. Famine and disease slashed the populations of the German states, the Low Countries and Italy, while bankrupting most of the combatant powers. So great was the devastation that the reduction of population in the German states has been estimated at between 15 per cent and 30 per cent. In Brandenburg, losses amounted to half, while in some areas an estimated two-thirds of the population died.

The male population of the German states was reduced by almost half. The population of Czech lands declined by a third due to war, disease, famine and the expulsion of Protestant Czechs. The Swedish armies alone destroyed 2,000 castles, 18,000 villages and 1,500 towns in Germany – one-third of all German towns.

By the end of the 1620s Habsburg power seemed more threatening than ever. Spain now wielded great influence in German affairs; and in the war with the Dutch, she was making some headway. The Holy Roman Emperor Ferdinand II seemed about to give the German world effective leadership and central control, something it had lacked for centuries. France, the traditional counterbalance to Habsburg power, was still weakened by the rivalries of noble factions and the autonomy enjoyed by the Huguenots, the French Protestants. Militarily she was still hardly a match for Spain, while England, militarily a third-rate state, had squandered her limited resources during the 1620s in brief and completely ineffective hostilities with both Spain and France.

This situation was dramatically changed by the landing of Swedish forces in north Germany in 1630. In 1629 a truce with Poland ended a long and largely unsuccessful war which Gustavus Adolphus, the warlike King of Sweden, had been waging in Livonia since 1621. This allowed him, backed by French money, to give free reign to the alarm which the growth of Habsburg and Catholic power in north Germany had now aroused in Stockholm. In 1631, at Breitenfeld, near Leipzig, he inflicted one of the most decisive military defeats in European history on the army of the Catholic League.

When in 1635 France at last declared war on Spain, the way was opened for an eventually successful assault on the position of both the Austrian and the Spanish branches of the family. This took time to develop: Spain, in spite of growing economic exhaustion, was still a great power capable of remarkable military and financial efforts. It took a treaty in 1659 to end almost a quarter of a century of Franco-Spanish struggle. The failure of the Austrian branch of the dynasty came quicker. Ferdinand III, who succeeded his father as emperor in 1637, soon found himself deserted by his German allies, while the Swedes now held a dominant position in much of north and central Germany. When in 1648 a series of agreements – which made up the Peace of Westphalia – at last brought peace to an exhausted central Europe, Swedish forces had briefly held Prague and were threatening Vienna itself.

A growth in the size and cost of armed forces already discernible during the sixteenth century continued during the first half of the seventeenth. While the French Army during the 1620s cost on average about 16 million livres tournois a year, after 1635, with the declaration of war against Spain, this figure rose sharply to over 33 million. After 1640 it climbed to over 38 million: in two decades it had more than doubled. In Spain, already much the greatest military power in Europe during the 1620s, the change was less marked. Nevertheless the plans for an attack on France in 1635 involved coordinated action by two fleets and four armies. It demanded field forces totalling 100,000 men and has been described as the most ambitious military conception of early modern Europe. The example of increasing military numbers which most impressed contemporaries was probably the startling growth in the forces controlled by Albrecht von Wallenstein, the Bohemian nobleman who in the 1620s became the supreme example of the military entrepreneur. From 62,000 in 1625 they had risen to 150,000 at their peak only five years later. Both in its size and still more in its control by a man who was, for all his power and wealth, still a private individual, this great army was something new in the history of Europe.

By March 1632, Gustavus Adolphus, then at the height of his success, had under his command 120,000 men (of whom only 13,000 were Swedes). In England, a highly unmilitary country, the transformation which came in the 1640s with the Civil War was perhaps more striking than any continental development. Before the war there were fewer than 1,000 men in the military service of Charles I, including those employed in the Ordnance Office and the Tower of London. Even if English subjects fighting on the continent in foreign armies, and the strengthened army in Ireland (which was largely Welsh and later native Irish) are added, the figure hardly exceeds 10,000. Yet within a year of the beginning of the conflict, both sides were actively pressing men into service and there were probably in all over 110,000 under arms in Britain. This was a ratio of soldiers to civilians – achieved very quickly – substantially higher than anything reached in France, and a striking illustration of the new scale of military effort which it was now possible to evoke in European societies. Almost two decades earlier, England had shown that she had the capacity to become a serious military power. Between the middle of 1624 and the beginning of 1628, for the pathetically unsuccessful expeditions to Cadiz in 1625 and La Rochelle in 1627–28, about 50,000 men, some 2 per cent of the entire male population, had been recruited for the army, often by highly oppressive means.

This growth in military numbers was not unbroken or universal. In Germany the remarkable increase of the 1620s and early 1630s was not maintained. As much of central Europe became increasingly exhausted, it became more and more unfeasible to feed, clothe and pay forces of the size Wallenstein and Gustavus Adolphus had controlled.

Moreover large armies very often could not be brought to bear as unified forces at any one point, even for a decisive battle. Although there were during most of the English Civil War well over 100,000 men in all engaged on the two sides, 5,000 constituted a respectable field force and 12,000 was considered an exceptionally large one. It is doubtful whether the Royalists ever had as many as 20,000 operating at any time as a single force. Also the most formidable army, if there were serious difficulties in paying and feeding it, might shrink with disconcerting speed through desertion.[3] It might also find its fighting efficiency sharply reduced as discipline collapsed and starving soldiers became increasingly difficult to control. The armies which fought the Thirty Years' War, made up mainly of mercenaries and lacking any national or linguistic unity, were particularly vulnerable. Thus in May 1631, when Gustavus Adolphus was on the brink of his greatest triumphs, a Swedish official wrote of his army that:

> I can give you no adequate idea of our miserable condition. The foot are fifteen pays in arrear, and both officers and men mighty discontented, so that I never heard such grumbling, both public and private. The foot desert by thousands, and some 600 have gone off in this camp alone. The cavalry do as they list; it is not safe to ride a mile outside the camp. They plunder the land to the bare bones, provoking complaints and curses fit to make you shudder.

Nonetheless, the general picture of Europe during these decades is one of growing military effort, of a remorseless tendency for armies to become bigger than ever in the past. Bigger meant more expensive. More men meant more money; and the increase in the financial burden was often greater than the mere increase in numbers indicated. This was because war as waged by the Dutch, the French and the Spanish, was now, as it long continued to be, very much a matter of sieges. This was most strikingly the case in the Netherlands, densely populated and thickly studded with cities whose fortifications had been becoming stronger and more elaborate since the 1570s.

A siege ate up money, materials and men in a way that the greatest battle hardly ever did. To some observers it seemed that a predominance of siege warfare was a mark of advanced civilisation. It was, after all, a systematic and technologically demanding way of fighting. It called for planning and organisation.

A great siege was, with the possible exception of the building of a great canal, the biggest engineering operation of the age. Normally a besieging army protected itself against attack from any relieving force while the siege was in progress by building elaborate defensive lines that often enclosed a very large area. These, coupled with the siege-works proper, the digging of trenches and mounting of batteries or exploding of mines to breach the defences, were an immense undertaking.

In 1629, for the siege of the fortress of s'Hertogenbosch, Prince William Henry built defensive lines that took 11 hours to walk around. They included six entrenched camps, nine forts and a dozen hornworks (a smaller form of fortification). He used 116 guns, most of them heavier than would have been employed on the battlefield, to attack the walls at four different points. These operations involved the damming of two rivers. War of this sort meant expenditure of men and money on a potentially crippling scale.

Any reliable calculation of the money-cost of a great siege is hard to make; but that of the Huguenot stronghold of La Rochelle by the French Army in 1627–8 (admittedly a long one: it lasted for fifteen months) was believed to have cost 40 million livres. Then, a bushel of wheat cost a livre and an agricultural worker's daily wage was 10–12 sous (at 20 sous to the livre). Therefore the siege may have cost 40 million bushels of wheat or 70 million days of labour. A long siege could also be expensive in men to the besieging army. Supply problems might become acute, the disease fostered by the concentration of large numbers of soldiers for a long period in poor sanitary conditions may take a heavy toll; boredom and frustration might intensify the ever-present threat of desertion. Thus in 1622 the Spanish commander Spinola lost 9,000 men (1,900 of whom deserted to the besieged garrison) during his unsuccessful attempt to take Bergen-op-Zoom.

Gustavus Adolphus

IN 1627 GUSTAVUS ADOLPHUS, the 'Lion of the North', had compared the revived Roman Catholic Church to the sea: 'as one wave follows another in the sea, so the Papal deluge is approaching our shores.' Gustavus Adolphus saw himself as the protector of Protestantism in Germany, and if north Germany was safe then so was Sweden. Gustavus Adolphus was an accomplished soldier and with the help of Catholic France, by the end of 1629, controlled much of the east Baltic coast and effectively controlled Baltic trade.

Cardinal Richelieu of France wanted an alliance with Gustavus Adolphus to form a counter-weight to Habsburg power in Europe. If he could enlist the help of Maximillian of Bavaria and the Catholic League then so much the better. Both Gustavus Adolphus and Richelieu were pragmatists. Though they held opposite views on religion, they both realised that they needed each other if they were to form a realistic opposition to Ferdinand.

When Gustavus Adolphus landed on Peenemunde in Pomerania in June/July 1630 with 4,000 men, no alliance had been made. This worried Richelieu, as he had no control over what Gustavus Adolphus might do. Gustavus Adolphus captured Stettin and the Neumark area in Brandenburg, securing his communication lines with Sweden. He could then push further into Germany. His task was made easier by the five year Treaty of Barwalde signed with France in 1631, giving Sweden a million livres a year to fight her war while Sweden agreed to provide the men to do the fighting. Richelieu was happy with this arrangement; Gustavus Adolphus' army was far enough away not to threaten France; Ferdinand's army would have to track Gustavus Adolphus', keeping the emperor's army away from the French border.

Not all of Germany's northern princes welcomed Gustavus Adolphus. John George of Saxony and George William of Brandenburg saw his position in northern Germany as a threat to their own possessions. Both men called for a Protestant conference to be held at Leipzig in 1631 where Protestant princes were persuaded to raise their own independent army. This they duly did and put it under the control of Hans George von Arnim – an able soldier who had served under Wallenstein but had since left his services. Gustavus Adolphus had a problem. What would happen if the Protestant force allied itself to the Catholic League in defence of German liberties? Would he have to fight two forces?

The situation was resolved before any Protestant agreement could be signed. The Catholic League, led by Tilly, besieged and destroyed the city of Magdeburg – a great Protestant centre and its freedom guaranteed by Gustavus Adolphus. Tilly's troops massacred the population and razed many of the houses by fire, causing anger throughout Protestant Europe. The Dutch made an agreement with Sweden to supply the army of Gustavus Adolphus, and with this assistance, Gustavus Adolphus marched on to Berlin, from where he completed his occupation of Pomerania. Gustavus Adolphus conquered Mecklenburg, where he restored the dukes whom Wallenstein had expelled and replaced with himself. His actions did much to restore Protestant confidence that had been weakened after Magdeburg.

Tilly found it very difficult to react to this as Maximillian of Bavaria had signed a secret treaty with France, in which he promised not to aid the enemies of France while France recognised his Electoral rights. As Sweden was a recognised Ally of France via Barwalde, Tilly (his master was Maximillian) could not attack Gustavus Adolphus, as this would aid the enemies of France.

Tilly was in a dangerous position. His army was quartered in the Duchy of Friedland – land owned by Wallenstein. He was short of supplies and Wallenstein deliberately withheld them, as he hoped that Tilly's failure could lead to his own return to power. To escape from his predicament, Tilly mistakenly attacked Saxony. There was a reason for him to do so – the area was well stocked with food and provisions. His excuse for the attack was two-fold: John George had refused to enforce the Edict of Restitution, which Tilly claimed was an insult to Ferdinand. He had also defied the emperor by raising an army after Leipzig.

Leipzig quickly fell and John George was forced into seeking an alliance with Gustavus Adolphus. Their combined forces heavily defeated Tilly at the Battle of Breitenfeld in September 1631, Adolphus' army standing at 24,000, while John George had 18,000 soldiers in the field, facing Tilly's force of 35,000 men. Tilly lost all his artillery and nearly 18,000 men. He could only retreat towards Bavaria.
With nothing to stop him, Adolphus occupied the Lower Palatinate, Mainz, Bamberg and Wurzburg, while the Saxon force marched into Bohemia and captured Prague in November 1631.

After Breitenfeld, no decent army stood in the way of Gustavus Adolphus. The speed and extent of his victories alarmed Richelieu, who had considered Adolphus and Sweden the junior partner in their alliance. German princes in general were alarmed at the success of the Swedish king, especially when he spent 1631–32 wintered in Germany and treating the area he had conquered as his own. Gustavus Adolphus doled out land rewards to his successful generals, and Oxenstierna was made governor-general of the region.

Gustavus Adolphus was the master of Germany. Maximillian rejected claims by Richelieu that Bavaria was safe and openly sought the protection of Ferdinand. He also asked for the re-instatement of Wallenstein as he saw this as the only way to counter Gustavus Adolphus. This reinstatement took place in December 1631, Wallenstein accepting the Catholic Emperor's offer to raise a new army for him.

Gustavus Adolphus used Mainz as his capital and planned the invasion of the rest of the Holy Roman Empire. Richelieu could do nothing to stop him. After the devastating victory at Breitenfeld, Ferdinand considered fleeing to Italy.

Wallenstein saw the situation as an opportunity to extend his own power. In April 1632, he was promised regular subsidies from Ferdinand and Spain under Phillip III; he was confirmed as Duke of Mecklenburg; he was given financial compensation for his help and he could make peace with any prince when he felt like it – except the Duke of Saxony (this had to be vetted by an Imperial Diet). The one caveat was that Wallenstein could not use Spanish or Catholic League troops without permission.

During March 1632 the Swedes under Adolphus had started their invasion of Bavaria and gradually gained control of the south-western part of the Empire. In April there was a battle between the Swedes and Tilly's troops, where the Swedes effected a forced crossing of the river Lech near Rain. At this battle Tilly was fatally wounded and the Holy Roman Empire lost one of its most experienced generals. This was followed swiftly by Gustavus taking Augsburg and Munich and returning to the central regions of the Empire. However, this was to be the peak of his achievements and power.

After the fall of Munich, Gustavus Adolphus failed in his attempt to take Regensburg, and in May, Wallenstein's new army had driven the Saxons under Arnim out of Bohemia. To aid John George and also fearful that he might join the forces of Wallenstein; Gustavus Adolphus marched north, ending his projected drive towards Vienna.

In the summer of 1632, Gustavus Adolphus published plans for a German settlement. His idea was to create two Protestant leagues – the *Corpus Bellicum* (responsible for military affairs) and the *Corpus Evangelicorum* (to run the civil administration). His aim was to preserve the existing structure of states in Germany and to confirm the security of Protestants in Germany. He did not envisage himself as the head of a Protestant empire.

For Sweden he wanted to keep the territory gained in the south Baltic from the Vistula to the Elbe. This would give Sweden future security and the profits from port revenues, and the expansion of Swedish trade would help pay for the huge outlay Sweden had made in assisting northern Germany against the Holy Roman Emperor. Ferdinand had no interest in the plan, which could only succeed if Gustavus Adolphus continued to be successful at a military level.

Wallenstein had placed himself in a strategically very strong position – the Alte Feste at Zirndorf Castle near Nuremburg. In September 1632, Gustavus Adolphus launched an unsuccessful attack on the Alte Feste. This failure led to many mercenaries deserting the Swedish force. Wallenstein then marched north to Saxony and Gustavus Adolphus could do nothing about it. Wallenstein captured Leipzig – though the attack on the city was merely bait to attract Gustavus Adolphus to him.

Wallenstein planned to make his winter quarters at Lutzen, and Gustavus Adolphus attempted to make a surprise attack on the Catholic forces there. On the 16 November 1632, the relatively indecisive Battle of Lutzen took place. This was no surprise attack, as Wallenstein had succeeded in his plan of drawing Gustavus Adolphus out into a full-scale battle. However, Wallenstein still suffered a defeat at this battle and had to retreat into Bohemia. The cost of this victory was Sweden losing 15,000 men, and a more disastrous blow was struck to the morale of the Protestants and their cause when Gustavus Adolphus died in the midst of action.

Without their figurehead, the Protestant forces seemed to lack direction. Count Horn and Bernard of Weimar took over supreme command of the Protestant forces – but their names did not have the aura of Gustavus Adolphus.

After Lutzen, many wanted a peace settlement. War had dragged on with no obvious results for all those who had been fighting in it. Adolphus was dead; Queen Christina of Sweden supported a peace plan; John George of Saxony wanted one. Even the original cause of the problem – Frederick of the Lower Palatinate – had died in November 1632. So why was there no settlement?

Oxenstierna still feared a resurgent Habsburg force and used his influence to call for a meeting of Sweden, the Lower Saxon Circle and Saxony itself to discuss matters. They met in Heilbronn in March 1633 and the end result was a defensive alliance – the Heilbronn League – which existed to defend Protestantism in north Germany. John George did not join as he had reverted to supporting the Holy Roman Emperor. Catholic France and Protestant Sweden became joint protectors of the new organisation. In November 1633, the Heilbronn League had its first victory when it invaded Bavaria and captured Regensburg – something that Gustavus Adolphus had failed to do.

Wallenstein by now had started to exceed his authority within the Holy Roman Empire. He started secret negotiations with France and Sweden, which was outside his jurisdiction. There were those in Vienna who disliked Wallenstein, and when news reached the capital of the Holy Roman Empire of what Wallenstein was doing, it confirmed to them that he was unstable and unpredictable. For example: when Wallenstein had defeated the Swedish at Steinau he had released the captured generals in exchange for some fortresses in Silesia. Swedish troops were good but they needed decent commanders. Here was Wallenstein releasing their generals in exchange for castles!

Wallenstein then ordered one of his generals to Bavaria to help Regensburg and Breisach but the general, Aldringen, was ordered not to fight the Swedish Army there. This greatly angered Aldringen, as the Swedes were the enemy of the Holy

Roman Empire. In fact, Aldringen disobeyed his command and took on the Swedes. Disquiet about Wallenstein was not only being heard in Vienna – it was also spreading to his army.

It is difficult to account for Wallenstein's actions in 1634. He had gout and depression, which may have affected his decisions. He may also have been playing a complex strategy game that no one else understood. In January 1634, Ferdinand ordered Wallenstein's arrest. This order was made redundant when Wallenstein and part of his entourage were murdered in Eger, Western Bohemia by some of his officers in February 1634. At the time of his death, he had only 1,500 men loyal to him.

The command of the Imperial Army went to Ferdinand, the son of the emperor. He was married to the Spanish Infanta – thus bringing both houses of the Habsburgs even closer together. Ferdinand the son had also cultivated a friendship between himself and the brother of his wife – the Spanish Infante. He was the nominal head of the Spanish Netherlands. Both men were able military leaders and their friendship regenerated the Austrian-Spanish alliance. Both men were dedicated to turning back the tide of Protestantism in Europe.

In September 1634, both Catholic armies joined at Nordlingen. They were opposed by the Protestant army under Horn. Horn's plan was to break both armies into two separate parts and take each one on singularly. It was a disaster. The Swedes were heavily defeated and Horn was captured. This one victory re-established Ferdinand in Europe. The Heilbronn League was in total disarray; the Protestants had no army while the Catholics had two armies in the field that had already proved themselves to be a potent force. By the spring of 1635, all Swedish resistance in the south of Germany had ended. A peace package which had been started in 1634 ended with the Peace of Prague signed on 30 May 1635,[4] between the Holy Roman Emperor, Ferdinand II, and most of the Protestant states of the Empire. It effectively brought to an end the civil war aspect of the Thirty Years' War. However, the war still carried on due to the continued intervention on the German soil of Spain, Sweden, and, from mid-1635, France.

In April 1635 a French and Swedish alliance was concluded, with the 'Eminence Gris', Cardinal Richelieu, acting as a mediator in the truce of Stuhmdorf: extending the truce between the Swedes and the Poles, and allowing the Swedes to concentrate all their efforts on their military campaigns in Germany. In November the Swedish Army was victorious at Domitz, Mecklenburg, and in October of the following year Swedish troops under the command of Johan Baner beat the Imperial and Saxonian armies at Wittstock in Prussia.

Ferdinand II, the Holy Roman Emperor, died of natural causes in Vienna in February, so in December, Ferdinand III was elected king of the Romans, heir apparent to the Imperial throne. In the years that followed, however, the Empire suffered a series of defeats at the hands of Bernard of Saxe-Weimar until he died of the plague in 1639 and his troops entered the French service.

Through the 1640s, the Swedes and the French conducted their campaigns against the Spanish and Bavarian forces with mixed success, while the principal players at the outset of the wars – Baner, Richelieu, Louis XIII – successively died off, often from natural causes.

In July 1644, peace negotiations were arranged at Westphalia, which dragged on until September 1646 when the Imperial ambassadors finally rejected the Swedes' proposals on religious issues. However, after the Spanish and Dutch made peace at Munster in January 1648, the French inflicted a crushing defeat on the Imperials in May 1648 and the Swedes besieged Prague in July of the same year, before the Treaty of Osnabruck finally ended the war.

***

Before ending on the war in Europe altogether, it may be worth touching briefly on the practicalities of life for the soldiery within the various armies, whatever their religious or political persuasion, and their struggle to survive or whether or not their enemies were actively trying to snuff out their existence.

A soldier whose pay was months and sometimes years overdue was driven to look elsewhere for money. Money was required because normally he had to find much or all of his own food, buying it from the regimental sutlers and butchers – all civilians – and from the traders – often women – who brought it to camps and garrisons for sale. All these were part of the network of ancillaries – dealers, prostitutes and hangers-on generally – which accumulated around every army. Without money, the soldier might be hard-pressed to live even if food itself were in good supply. One of the many Scottish officers in the Swedish Army recalled during the long siege of Hameln in 1633, that, 'my best entertainment was bread and water, abundance of the last, but not so of the first; but this proceeded from want of money, for the leager [i.e. the camp] was plentiful enough.' To unpaid men the main alternative source of money was some form of plunder. Even if they had been paid more regularly, many of them would still have been strongly attracted by possibilities of this kind, for the chance of at least temporary and relative wealth through looting, or through the capture of a prisoner who could be ransomed for his release, was sometimes a substantial inducement to enlist. The Thirty Years' War, because of the anarchy it produced throughout much of the country, and the increasing poverty of many of the governments whose forces fought there, saw plundering carried to a pitch unique in the history of modern Europe. From the highest-ranking commanders to the humblest private soldier, armies were involved in the seizure or extortion of money and goods from the civilian population. New recruits, at first too ignorant or burdened by scruples to take advantage of their opportunities, soon learned the facts of this aspect of military life. After the first stages of his service, wrote one of them, 'I had learnd so much cunning, and become so vigilant to lay hold on opportunities, that I wanted for nothing, horses, clothes, meats, nor moneys; and made so good use of what I had learned, that the whole time I served in Germanie, I suffered no such miserie as I had done in the first yeare and a halfe that I came to it.' In the highest ranks looting was possible on a much greater scale and could be correspondingly more profitable. An outstanding example is the capture of Mantua by the Habsburg commanders Gallas and Aldringen in 1630: the contents of the Ducal Castle were estimated at 18 million scudi, the greater part of which went to the victorious generals. Another is the capture in 1648 of part of Prague, a great city still little touched by the war, by the Swedish. Some contemporaries argued that too successful looting was bad for an army, not so much because of its effects on discipline, as because men would fight well only under the spur of want. One claimed that the disastrous defeat of the Catholic League commander Tilly by the Swedes at Breitenfeld in September 1631 was caused partly by the 'richesse of his souldiers', especially the cavalry, from the booty taken when they captured Leipzig only two days before. The result was that 'loth to loose so soon their richesse with their lives, many Troops of horse went from him, even when they were to goe to fight'; which emphasises the maxim, 'A rich souldier will never fight well'.

Plundering and extortion were not the only means by which impoverished armies could maintain themselves and soldiers hope to grow rich. A wealthy or important prisoner could be made to pay a ransom or have one paid for him by his superiors. The ransoming of prisoners was a practice as old as recorded history, and the right to a ransom a well-established form of property. In practice, a valuable prisoner taken by a common soldier was usually sold at once to a superior, often to the colonel of the regiment, who might in turn sell him to someone higher in the hierarchy. It was, therefore, again a practice which tended to benefit officers, particularly high-ranking ones, rather than privates or NCOs, (though of course it was also high-ranking officers who might, if taken, find themselves in their turn compelled to pay heavily for their freedom). By the 1630s efforts were being made to assert the principle that prisoners were the property of an army as a whole rather than of the individuals who had taken them; but until the second half of the century ransoms remained an element in the maintenance of armies which, although secondary, was occasionally significant. The Swedes, for example, are said to have made 120,000 thalers from the prisoners taken when they defeated the imperial and Bavarian forces at Jankau in 1645.

There were more direct means, and very important ones, by which soldiers made demands on civilian society. Every army demanded 'contributions' from the population of the areas through which it marched and in which it fought, payments in money and kind, in food, fodder, clothing etc., which were enforced by the threat of burning villages and seizing livestock. These gave scope for a great deal of extortion, corruption and dishonesty. A district might pay not to have troops quartered on it, or to have them march through it as quickly as possible, or merely for a promise that good discipline would be observed when the army was on the march. Towns and villages regularly offered bribes to have the amount of the contribution demanded from them reduced. A neutral area unable to defend its neutrality by force might pay to have it observed or at least infringed in a not too destructive and expensive way. All these devices were seen in their most developed and widespread form in Germany in the terrible generation from the 1620s onwards; but all of them were prevalent and taken for granted throughout Europe. For the areas affected by them they were a greater burden, and one imposed more ruthlessly than even the heaviest normal taxation.

In England the growth during the Civil War of considerable armies on both sides, and of corresponding demands on the civil population, produced incidents such as the violence of the peasant movement known as the Clubmen, which affected the West Midlands and parts of the West Country in 1645. It was inspired mainly by a bitter dislike of soldiers of all kinds, whatever the cause for which they professed to be fighting. Moreover just as peasants hated soldiers indiscriminately, so soldiers despised all peasants. French soldiers defending Burgundy against attack from the Spanish forces in neighbouring Franche-Comte often showed more fellow feeling with the enemy than with the French peasants they were allegedly protecting.

Towns, though less exposed than villages, also often suffered severely. Sometimes their capture by a besieging army produced an orgy of murder, looting and devastation. The outstanding example is the destruction of Magdeburg by Tilly's army in 1631, an event which shocked even so hardened an age, and generated a huge pamphlet literature of condemnation; but even in Britain, Bristol was looted for two days after it was taken by the Royalists in 1643, Montrose loosed his Irish upon Aberdeen for three days in 1644 and two-thirds of Taunton was destroyed in the siege of 1645.

Even within a town or village, war and its demands might affect individuals in markedly different ways. Some groups such as innkeepers and shoemakers could, under favourable conditions, benefit at least for a time from a strong demand for what they sold and from the resulting higher prices, even when those around them were suffering badly. It must be remembered that much of the money extracted by soldiers from civilian society was returned to it very quickly in payment for such goods and services.[5]

Finally, as an insight into officer training and attendance, it must be noted that in these armies the most basic forms of professionalism were still far from complete. Hardly anywhere could there be found any real effort to train officers, while for the rank and file training was still absolutely elementary. Officers were still, by the standards of later ages, scandalously lax in the performance of their duties. In France an ordinance of 1629 commanded colonels to spend at least three months of the year with their regiments, captains four months, lieutenants five, and so forth.

1. The Lead Up to Scotland's Involvement in the Civil War and the Mystery of Fraser's Beginnings

The Scots in Europe

As a career, the option of becoming a professional soldier was an important and perhaps essential outlet for young men who might otherwise have found it very difficult to wring a living from the land and who may have become a threat to domestic peace and stability. Military service allowed areas such as Scotland to export their poverty to wealthier regions better able to cope with it. Sometimes this export was on a spectacular scale: from 1626–32, the most critical and dramatic years of the Thirty Years' War, about 25,000 Scots went to fight in Germany. This meant that a tenth of the entire male population of Scotland was given employment in this way.

Professional armies acted as a social safety valve; and this ensured them some tolerance from the respectable citizens who paid for them. An army recruited largely from the margins of society, often including a significant element of foreigners, and only interfered with normal life, all going well, through its financial demands. It was therefore acceptable to the ordinary taxpayer, to whom war was a matter for rulers and governments and not one in which he wished or expected to play any more direct part. The early seventeenth century saw protests, sometimes serious ones, against the increasing cost of armies, but little criticism of the principle of professional and mercenary forces.

It has been said of Gustavus, 'the lion and the bulwark of the north', that without his Scottish regiments and leaders he would hardly have gained his victories and saved the cause of Protestantism in Germany. He was an unusually brilliant general and strategist, whose fame rapidly spread over the civilised world; and a great number of the Scottish officers, many of them of noble rank, who enlisted in the Swedish Army did so in order to go through the 'high school' of military training. The Swedish formation of arms was, effectively, the cutting edge of the technology of the day – ammunition was for the first time made up into cartridges, regiments were formed into right and left wings, with pikes centred to guard the colours.

Gustavus formed his ranks six deep as opposed to Wallenstein's thirty – all this would prove the ideal training for the conflict to come, and Scotland was undoubtedly the country in which by far the most numerous levies of soldiers for the 'lion of the north' were raised.

On the whole, reports of these Scottish mercenaries are good. It was said of them, 'no troops could be better fitted, morally as well as physically, for desperate undertakings, than these Scots. They proved hardy, frugal and sober soldiers'. The same praise is bestowed upon them by an old wood engraving preserved in the British Museum. Dating around 1641, it represents four highlanders, three in kilts, the fourth in a sort of trunk-hose. Above it, in German, are the words 'In such dress the 800 highlanders (lately) arrived at Stettin walk (about)'. Beneath is written 'They are a strong, hardy race, contenting themselves with little food, if they have no bread, they eat roots and carrots; in case of necessity they are able to walk twenty German miles[6] in a day; they have besides muskets, their bows and quivers and long knives'.

Under Colonel Hepburn, the Scots earned great praise for their bravery, and whenever an enterprise of a particularly daring character was to be undertaken it was usually Hepburn who was chosen for it. In 1630, the Scots whom Colonel Lumsden had brought to Germany – the corps of Hardgate and McKay's highlanders – were united into one brigade, bearing the name of the Green, or Hepburn's Scottish Brigade.[7]

The exploits of the united Scottish Brigade, such as the taking of the fortresses Frankfurt-on-the-Oder and Landsberg, their march to Leipzig in 1631, Marienberg, the march against Mainz (one of the strongest fortresses in the whole seat of the war), and many other similar adventures are recounted elsewhere but, combined, paint a glittering picture of often incredible and always hard-fought successes of the Scots for the Swedish and Protestant cause. Several points are, however, worth highlighting.

In 1626 on 6 November, 500 of Munro's highlanders were ordered to defend to the last Colberg, a half-ruined castle and town on the coast of Pomerania. He threw up redoubts, barricaded the approaches, and before long the place was under attack by 8,000 Imperialists led by the famous Count de Monteculculi, under whom were the splendidly accoutred regiments of Goetz and Sparre, Charles, Wallenstein, Isolani, and Colorado. Three troops of Cuirassiers in white armour led the van, with three of Croats and a thousand arquebussiers, all of whom were hurled back in confusion by the steady highland fire. On being summoned to treat for the surrender of the post, Munro replied, 'The word *treaty* has been omitted in my instructions; thus I have only powder and ball at the service of the Count de Monteculculi'.

A dreadful strife ensued. The whole town was laid in ashes. Lord Reay's Regiment retired into the castle and, despairing of success, the count drew off into the night under cover of a mist, admitting that 500 highlanders could repel sixteen times their number of Germans.

A contingent of 6,000, reinforcements from Britain under the Marquis of Hamilton, set out for Germany, made up of Scots from Leith and English from Yarmouth. However, there was soon only Scots left of this contingent as the English all perished on the march between Wolgast and Werben, by overeating themselves with 'German bread; which is heavier, darker and sourer than their own; they suffered too by an inordinate fondness for new honey; nor did the German beer agree with their constitutions'.

Scots fought throughout most of the Thirty Years' War, on both sides of the conflict. James Turner, going out in 1632 to seek his fortune, wrote:

> I was not seventeen years old when I left the schools where, having lightly passed through that course of philosophy which is ordinarily taught in the universities of Scotland, I was commanded by my father and grandfather to commence master of arts at Glasgow, much against my will, as never intending to make use of that title, which undeservedly was bestowed upon me, as it was on many others before me, and hath been on too many since. I stayed a year after with my father at Dalkeith, applying myself to the study of humane letters and history, in both of which I always took delight. I did read also the controversies of religion between us and the Roman Catholics (for the Presbyterians at that time made little noise) whereby I might be enabled to discern the truth of the Protestant persuasion and the fallacies of the Popish one or any other, that so I might not, in traversing the world, be carried away with every wind of doctrine. But before I attained to the eighteenth year of my age, a restlessness entered my mind, to be, if not an actor, at least a spectator of those wars which at that time made so much noise over all the world, and were managed against the Roman Emperor and the Catholic League in Germany, under the auspicious control of the thrice famous Gustavus Adolphus, King of Sweden. Sir James Lumsden was then levying a regiment for that service: with him (my nearest friends consenting to it) I engaged to go over to his brother, Robert Lumsden, eldest captain.

Turner's first march may have gone to the song Monro quotes which Sir Walter Scott was to borrow for Dugald Dalgetty:

> When cannon are roaring and colours are flying
> Our lads that seek honour must never fear dying.
> Then, stout cavaliers, let us toil our brave trade in,
> And fight for the Gospel and bold King of Sweden.

Monro gives many pictures of the wars in Low Germany. Here is the sortie of Lord Spynie's Regiment from Stralsund (1628):

> Here also was killed the valorous Captain MacDonald. Divers also of their officers were hurt, as Captain Lindsay of Bainsho, who received three dangerous wounds, Lieutenant Pringle, who was hurt also, and divers more. They being made to retire, their powder being spent, to make their retreat good falls up Captain Mackenzie with the old Scottish blades of our Regiment to suppress the enemy's fury. They keeping faces to their enemies while their comrades were retiring, the service went on afresh. Where order is kept, as in this retreat was done by that noble spark, all things flourish and thrive.

One famous defence was that of the sconce at Boizenburg. The town was on the confluence of the Boize and the Elbe, and barred the chief road into Denmark, so Tilly marched against it with a large column. Major Dunbar threw up a sconce on the Luneburg side of the town, to cover the crossing, and manned it with 800 highlanders.

> [The enemy] lay down within a cannon shot of the sconce and having begun his lines of approach, the first night the Major made an outfall where having bravely shown their courage and resolution returned again without great loss. The enemy longing to be repaired of this their bravado, resolved to storm the sconce at all quarters, but finding resolution joined with valour against them, after long fighting in vain he is beat off from the walls and forced to retire at that time, with the loss of five hundred men at least. But having redoubled his forces the next time, sets on with greater fury than before, but is beat off the second time also, with loss: the third time he adventures, and as was reported, the Scots defenders, as is well known, believe themselves so well, that the enemy storming the walls, the defenders, for want of powder, threw sand in their enemies' eyes, knocking them down with the butts of muskets. Having been divers times pell mell through hither, at last the enemy is forced to retire without effectuating anything.

There was also a Scottish gentleman under the enemy, who coming to scale the walls said aloud, 'Have with you, gentlemen. Think not now you are on the streets of Edinburgh bravading.' One of his own countrymen thrusting him through the body with a pike, he ended there. On the Danish March, by the waters of the Elbe, Monro remarks that the four companies who held the sconce were the poorest-looking of the regiment, but the affair sent their fame through Germany … and may have caused the barbarous treatment of Major Dunbar's dead body later on by their enemies. The Scots had opportunities to experience the less pleasing sides of the North German mind. Recalling the grim retreat from Rappen to Ivismar on the Baltic, Monro remarks, 'I did observe first here that the towns of Germany are but friends ever to the masters of the field, in flattering the victorious and in persecuting of the loser, which is ever well seen in all estates.'

During this period the Scots had sent some 40,000 men to fight on the continent. Bear in mind that this huge figure is to be set against a Scottish population estimated at a little over one million at the end of the seventeenth century (England and Wales totalling around 5.2 million at the same time). The defence of the honour of the House of Stuart was a major reason for their participation in the European conflict, and gave the Scots an opportunity to demonstrate their particular degree of loyalty to the House of Stuart through their endeavours in the defence of Princess Elizabeth, younger sister of Charles I and wife of Frederick V, Elector Palatine (whose younger son was to be Prince Rupert of the Rhine – opponent of the Scots' cavalry at Marston Moor). The war also ensured that Europe was replete with experienced and disciplined Scottish soldiers more zealous than their fellow Stuart subjects from England and Ireland in pursuing the anti-Habsburg cause. The number of these men was instrumental in ensuring that the evolution of the Scottish identity that took place in the seventeenth century would continue to have a strong martial component, as it had done in previous centuries.

The loyalty of the Scots was complex and steadfast. It was directed very much towards the House of Stuart first and only secondly to those European leaders prepared to fight against the Habsburgs in defence of the Protestant cause – a way of attempting to restore the Palatinate in the eyes of the Scots.

A contemporary observer, the Venetian Ambassador, concluded that [one regiment] 'included a larger number of Scots than English and of better quality', presumably explained by the Scots being motivated, not as mercenaries, but in defence of Queen Elizabeth and her family in particular, and of the honour of the House of Stuart in general. Loyalty to their country and king was undoubtedly strong – the Scots were not willing to fight under anyone's banner without thought for or consultation with their own monarch.

The apparent contradiction of the change of heart in those same Scots soldiers, from a defence of the House of Stuart, to an attack against it on their return to Scotland, may have been because their monarch demonstrated by his actions that their loyalty to him was misplaced. When Charles tried to interfere with the integrity of their country, they re-evaluated their personal loyalty to him. This resulted in a shift away from allegiance to the king and a strengthening of Scottish national identity. The problem for the Stuart king lay in the fact that the Scots, unlike the monarchy, were now in possession of a professional military organisation to support their position. The professional soldiers returned to their officer, imparted experience and gave strength to their countrymen in their preparation to defend the integrity and polity of the nation.

While the war in Europe – which had for decades been sapping the lifeblood of the western continent – was by now regarded by many as simply a fact of life (and was to rage on for almost a decade further), events in Britain too were turning bellicose. When Charles I had travelled north to be crowned before the Scots parliament in 1633 he had directed the Scots to ratify an Act of Revocation which empowered the Crown to recover possession of all lands which had been owned by the Kirk prior to 1540. This alienated large and influential elements of society, while not yet resulting in all-out rebellion. But at a time when radical changes were being imposed on religious practice and ministers were dismayed by the apparently imminent destruction of Presbyterian worship, common cause was found between them and the lairds who saw themselves losing their feudal superiorities, and the seeds of rebellion were sown. This opposition to Charles arranged to elect members to 'the Tables' – committees representing lairds, burgesses and ministers, and the forerunner of the Committee of Estates, which would exercise executive power in Scotland during the Civil War. In 1638 the National Covenant was drafted to bind the country to the defence of the Protestant religion. The Covenanters, as the Tables became known, became the leading political and religious force in Scotland after they succeeded in dominating the Glasgow Assembly the following November. With neither king nor Covenanters prepared to compromise their religious convictions, a military solution to the crisis became inevitable.

First Bishops' War, 1639

Preparations for war began in January 1639. The Covenanting Lords Argyll, Montrose, Rothes, Balmerino and others met in Edinburgh to co-ordinate strategy. Instructions were issued to Scottish shires to start recruiting and training for war and an appeal was issued calling upon Protestant Scots serving abroad to return and fight for the Covenant. Among those who responded was Alexander Leslie, who was appointed commander of Covenanter forces. Meanwhile, King Charles proclaimed his intention of raising an army against the Scots and summoned his nobles to attend him in arms at York in April. The king planned an ambitious campaign: he would raise an army of 20,000 men to attack Edinburgh; the Earl of Antrim would invade western Scotland with troops from Ireland, while the Marquis of Hamilton would command a naval expedition to land troops behind enemy lines on the east coast. With Royalist clans attacking from the highlands, it was expected that the Covenanters would be quickly overwhelmed. However, the king's preparations proceeded slowly, hampered by a lack of funds. There was little enthusiasm in England for the war, where most Puritans were sympathetic to the Covenanters' cause.

In March, the Covenanter forces mustered at Aberdeen, at which time their clothing and equipment was described:

> In order of battle they came, well armed both on horse and foot, each horseman having at least five shot, with a carbine in his hand, two pistols by his sides and

> other two by his saddle, the pikemen in their ranks with pike and sword; the musketeers in their ranks, with musket, staff, bandolier, sword, powder, ball and match; each company both of horse and foot had their captains, lieutenants, ensigns, sergeants and other officers and commanders, all for the most part in buff coats, and in good order.

Here it is noted that few or none of this army wanted (was without) a blue ribband … called the *Covenanters' Ribband* by the haill (whole) soldiers of the army.[8]

Militia soldiers equipped at Aberdeen a short while later in the 1640s, wore as part of their uniform shirts of 'harden' (a coarse cloth), and 'blue bonnets on their heads with feathers waving in the wind'. From the same town comes the anecdote:

> the country round about was pitifully plundered, their meal gurnals broken up, eaten and consumed; no fowl, cock, or hen left unkilled, the whole house dogs, messens, and whelps within Aberdeen killed upon the streets, so that neither hound, messen or other dog was left alive that they could see; the reason was this, when the first army came here, ilk captain and soldier had a blue ribband about his craig (neck), in despite and derision whereof, when they removed from Aberdeen, some women of Aberdeen (as was alleged) knit blue ribbons about their messens' craig (dog's head), whereat their soldiers took offence, and killed all their dogs for this very cause.

Each soldier was also furnished with two sarks, coat, breeks,[9] hose and bonnet, bands and shoes, a sword and musket, powder and ball for some, and for others a sword and pike, according to order. All twelve of them had a baggage-horse, a stoop, a pan, a pot for their meat and drink, together with their hire or levy or loan money.

An example of a captain's clothing (from the Earl Marischal's regiment) includes a fashionably low-crowned broad brim demi-beaver hat and band; four dozen silk buttons, buckskin gloves, silk stockings, 9yd of silver and silk ribbon, 6yd of satin ribbon, 4½ dozen gold and silver buttons, all costing £15 05*s* Sterling.[10] The Scots were still in the habit of equipping their forces with lances – described as pike-staves[11] – and amongst equipment for the artillery were luntstanes or portfires, and Lombard paper for cartridges.

Tents were used in the Scottish armies. When Leslie camped on Duns Law in 1639 Baillie described the Scottish camp: 'The crowners (Colonels) lay in kennous (canvas) lodges, high and wide, their captains about them in lesser ones; the soldiers about all in huts of timber covered by divot (turf) or straw.' An English account describes the Scottish soldiers as lodged in 'dry and handsome huts'. In 1640, when the second war began, Leslie was to provide tents for the rank and file, as well as for the officers. According to Baillie, this was for political reasons, so that the friends of the Scots in England should have no cause to complain.

> Because it would be troublesome to these of England, who were much delighted with their planting, if our army should cut down timber for bigging (building) of our huts, they prayed that the honest women [of Edinburgh] might be tried what webs of harding or sheets they might spare, that every four soldiers might be accommodated in a tent of eight ells.[12] Thanks to an inspiring sermon from Mr Rollock, the women of Edinburgh zealously furnished nine thousand ells of canvas and harden to be tents and pavilions. This was enough for as many as 1,125 tents, for up to 4,500 soldiers, out of an army totalling some 20,000 plus 10,000 baggage men.[13]

During March 1639, the Covenanters moved swiftly to secure major ports and strongholds. General Leslie secured Edinburgh Castle, Lord Rothes seized the king's arsenal and the Scottish crown jewels at Dalkeith; the port of Dumbarton was captured against the possibility of Royalist reinforcements arriving from Ireland. Support for the king was concentrated in Aberdeenshire, where the Marquis of Huntly rallied his forces at Kintore. In mid-February, however, Huntly withdrew from a potential confrontation with several hundred Covenanters assembled at Turriff. The Earl of Montrose (then with the Covenanters) occupied Aberdeen unopposed at the end of March, after which Huntly virtually abandoned his leadership of the Scottish Royalists and allowed himself to be arrested at Edinburgh in April. Sir George Ogilvy of Banff and other Royalist lairds drove the Covenanters out of Turriff and briefly occupied Aberdeen during May, but Ogilvy's men dispersed when Montrose concentrated Covenanter forces in the region.

The king rode for York in March to lead the main English Army against the Scots in person. With no standing army to call upon, a special levy of 6,000 foot and 1,000 horse was raised, then another 4,000 troops were recruited by mobilising the Trained Bands of the northern border counties. King Charles also revived the medieval practice of summoning his nobles to attend him in person, each accompanied by a troop of armed horsemen, which caused further resentment amongst the nobility. Although by June the English Army was 18,000 strong, it was mostly made up of raw conscripts. The Earl of Arundel, earl-marshal of England and lord-general of the army, had no previous experience of war. His second in command, the Earl of Essex, was demoted in favour of one of the queen's courtiers, the inexperienced Earl of Holland. Veteran soldiers like Sir Jacob Astley, commander of the infantry, despaired at the English Army's lack of training and equipment – many of the northern Trained Bands being armed with bows and arrows.

While the king marched north from York, the Marquis of Hamilton's fleet sailed from Yarmouth with 5,000 men, most of whom were completely untrained. Hamilton anchored off Leith in the Firth of Forth early in May but the Covenanters' control of the region made landing impossible. The Marquis of Huntly's younger son, Viscount Aboyne, went north with some of Hamilton's ships to occupy Aberdeen and lead the Royalist Gordons early in June. From Aberdeen, Aboyne marched to Stonehaven. He intended to advance further south but was driven back by Covenanter forces on 14 June and took up a defensive position at Brig of Dee which guarded the approach to Aberdeen. Montrose mounted an artillery bombardment of Brig of Dee on 18 June. The Royalists were driven from the town the following day.

In mid-May, King Charles issued a proclamation announcing that he would settle all Scottish grievances as soon as order was restored in the kingdom. He would not invade Scotland, providing the Covenanter army remained at least 10 miles north of the border. The king joined his army near Berwick on 30 May, a few miles to the west at a place called Birks on the English side of the River Tweed. Things were far from good. Most of the troops were badly prepared, food was scarce, and disease had broken out. All were tormented by lice, known in the grim humour of the camp as 'Covenanters.' When the weather turned bad few had any shelter, and for miles there were no trees from which to build huts. Smallpox was an ever present hazard; desertions were frequent. Thomas Windebank, son of the king's Secretary of State, carried his own frustrations to an explosive extent. The only thing that kept out the cold and the wet, he wrote,

> ... was the hope of; Rubbing, fubbing and scrubbing those scurvy, filthy, dirty, nasty, lousy, itchy, scabby, shitten, stinking, slovenly, snotty-nosed, logger-headed, foolish, insolent, proud, beggarly, impertinent, absurd, grout-headed, villainous, barbarous, bestial, false, lying, rougish, devlish, long-eared, short-haired, damnable, atheistic, puritanical crew of the Scottish Covenant.

It was not to be, however. Lord Arundel led a detachment across the border to Duns to issue a proclamation pardoning all rebels if they submitted within eight days. In response, the Covenanter army advanced to Kelso, well within the 10 mile limit. The Earl of Holland's cavalry advanced to probe the Scottish position and although the Covenanter army was still undermanned and short of money, horses and provisions, the professionalism and discipline of its officers overawed Holland, who retreated to Berwick. When General Leslie advanced to Duns, morale in the English camp collapsed amid rumours that the Scottish Army overwhelmingly outnumbered the English. The king decided to negotiate with the Covenanters.

Treaty negotiations opened at Berwick in June. The Covenanters' demands were that the king ratify all acts of the Glasgow Assembly including the abolition of Episcopacy; that all ecclesiastical matters in Scotland would in future be settled at the General Assembly, and all civil matters in parliament; that all forces sent against Scotland would be recalled; that all 'incendiaries' who had caused the troubles should be returned to Scotland for punishment (i.e. the excommunicated bishops who had tried to introduce Laud's reforms).

Although the king apparently conceded that church matters should in future be governed by assemblies, he was adamant in his refusal to ratify the Glasgow

Assembly of 1638. The Covenanters were aware that their military position was not as strong as was widely believed and, after a week of legalistic wrangling, they too agreed to modify their position. A treaty was signed on 19 June 1639. The king agreed to authorise a General Assembly of the Kirk at Edinburgh in August, to be followed by a meeting of the Scottish parliament. Both sides agreed to disband their armies. Other controversial issues were left deliberately vague or as verbal agreements only. The treaty was poorly received in Edinburgh, where Covenanters complained that the commissioners had made too many concessions.

During the following weeks, relations between the king and the Covenanter leaders deteriorated. In an atmosphere of mutual mistrust, King Charles left Berwick and returned to London in July.

Second Bishops' War, 1640

King Charles was still determined to subdue the Covenanters by force and summoned Sir Thomas Wentworth from Ireland as an adviser. Wentworth was created Earl of Strafford in January 1640. He coerced the Irish parliament into granting funds to raise an Irish army for service against the Scots, and advised the king to summon a parliament in England to raise further funds. When the Short Parliament refused to grant funds for the war, the king appealed for a loan from Spain, while the queen appealed to her brother the King of France and even to the Pope. The appeals were unsuccessful. The king was on his own. The northern militia from the First Bishops' War was disbanded and a new levy raised in the south. Untrained and poorly-disciplined, many of the southern levies deserted on their march north. Others were prone to mutiny: two officers found to be Catholics were lynched by their own men, who then dispersed. Violent disorders were reported from all parts of England that the levies passed through. By August 1640, the king's forces had mustered in Yorkshire and Northumberland, most of them poorly-armed, unpaid and underfed. Strafford's Irish Army was not ready in time to take part in the campaign against Scotland.

In Edinburgh, the Scottish parliament appointed the Committee of Estates to direct the defence of Scotland. In February 1640 the Lovat Frasers and Mackenzies seized Inverness for the Covenant. Earl-Marischal William Keith occupied Aberdeen for the Covenanters in May, while Major-General Robert Monro invaded the lands of the Royalist Gordons in the north-east. In June, the Earl of Argyll was granted a commission of 'fire and sword' and led 5,000 Campbells in a six-week expedition to pillage and burn the lands of Royalist clans in the highlands. Once the Scottish Royalists had been subdued, Argyll besieged Dumbarton as a precaution against the possibility of Strafford's Irish Army landing in western Scotland.

Several regiments of the Covenanter army had remained in arms after the First Bishops' War and, with another war imminent, new levies were quickly raised.

By early August, the Covenanter army massed on the English border was 20,000 strong with an artillery train of sixty guns. The English Army was concentrated in two areas of assembly: one in central Yorkshire awaiting the king, the other in Northumberland. The Earl of Northumberland, appointed commander-in-chief of the English Army with the rank of Captain General, did not want to go to war, and feared that his estates in northern England would be occupied during the hostilities. As such, he was entirely defeatist about the prospect of vanquishing the Covenanters militarily and was happy to let illness prevent him from joining the army in the field. The commander of the northern army, Viscount Conway, concentrated on building up the defences of the border town of Berwick and seems to have disregarded the mustering of the Covenanters until it was too late.

Faced with the difficulties of keeping the Covenanter army supplied while it remained on the defensive, the Committee of Estates unanimously decided to mount a pre-emptive invasion of England. On 20 August 1640, General Leslie crossed the River Tweed at Coldstream and marched into England. Leslie thwarted Conway's defensive preparations by simply bypassing the well-defended town of Berwick and marching straight for Newcastle and the rich coalfields that supplied London with coal. As the king hurried north to York, the Scots arrived at the outskirts of Newcastle on 27 August.

The Battle of Newburn, August 1640

RATHER THAN ATTACK THE strongly-fortified northern approach to Newcastle, Leslie marched west along the Tyne to Newburn Ford, the first crossing over the Tyne a few miles upstream from the city. He intended to secure control of the northern and southern banks of the Tyne and then encircle Newcastle.

Viscount Conway sent 1,500 horse and 3,000 foot to reinforce the troops guarding the ford. Two improvised earthwork forts had been constructed on the south bank of the Tyne, each garrisoned by four artillery pieces and 400 musketeers. However, the forts were poorly placed and Leslie's artillery officer Alexander Hamilton deployed his guns on higher ground on the north bank of the Tyne; even hoisting light cannon to the top of Newburn church tower to dominate the English position.

Leslie then sent a messenger to Conway saying that he did not wish to fight but only wanted free passage to petition the king. Conway had no option but to refuse. The first wave of Scottish cavalry advanced towards the ford in the early afternoon of 28 August 1640, but was driven back by gunfire from the English entrenchments. In the ensuing artillery duel, Colonel Lunsford was unable to restrain his raw defending troops, who deserted the earthworks and fled. The Covenanters poured across the ford to take possession of the undefended river bank. Henry Wilmot, commander of the English cavalry, led a gallant charge to try and drive them back but was overwhelmed as disciplined Covenanter musketeers were posted to secure the position. Most of the English infantry fled in panic towards Newcastle. Colonel Monck managed to retain control of his regiment and retreated in good order with the English artillery.

General Leslie ordered his troops not to pursue the fleeing English to avoid causing ill feeling by inflicting unnecessary casualties. To the amazement of the Scots, Viscount Conway decided that Newcastle could not be defended and withdrew the garrison to Durham. On 30 August, the Covenanters marched unopposed into Newcastle.

The morale of the English Army in Yorkshire collapsed after the defeat at Newburn. Charles had to summon a Great Council of Peers at York which almost unanimously advised the king to negotiate a truce with the Scots and summon another parliament in England. While the Council of Peers continued to sit in York, English and Scottish commissioners met to negotiate a treaty.

The Treaty of Ripon was signed on 14 October. A cessation of hostilities was agreed. Negotiations for a permanent settlement were to be negotiated and ratified by a new parliament to be summoned in London. Meanwhile, the Scottish Army was to occupy Northumberland and Durham, exacting an indemnity of £850 a day from the English Government for its quarter; furthermore the Scottish Government was to be reimbursed for its expenses in prosecuting the war against England.

In desperate need of money, Charles was obliged to summon the Long Parliament, which assembled on 3 November 1640. A week later, the Scottish commissioners arrived in London to finalise the treaty. Despite King Charles' denunciation of the Scottish Army as rebel invaders, the commissioners were welcomed by the Puritans of London and the king retracted his remarks.

The negotiations between the Scottish and English commissioners continued through the spring and summer of 1641. Against a background of civil unrest in London and the impeachment by parliament of the king's principal ministers Strafford and Laud, Charles was anxious to settle the treaty quickly and therefore made a number of unexpected concessions: the resolutions of the General Assemblies that banished Episcopacy from the Scottish Church were ratified; the royal castles at Edinburgh and Dumbarton were to be used for defensive purposes only; no Scots were to be censured or persecuted for signing the Covenant; the Scottish 'incendiaries' regarded as responsible for creating the crisis were to be prosecuted in Scotland; Scottish goods and ships captured during the war would be returned; all books, publications and proclamations published against the Covenanters would be suppressed. It was also agreed that the Scots would receive the sum of £300,000 as recompense for the wars, which parliament regarded as 'brotherly assistance'.

The Treaty of London was signed on 10 August 1641.[14]

Scots continued to return from the continent in droves, believing that opportunities for betterment in the military in their own country were greater than in the service of the Swedes, or that service to their country suited them better than serving abroad for an alienated king.

Amongst this legion of troops, Hugh Fraser emerged from the mists of continental warfare to return to Scotland in December 1640, with the rank of major, having fought with distinction in Europe and acquired a considerable fortune. With this money he had already bought a number of properties around Inverness-shire and he now continued his land acquisition on his return to Scotland[1].

His whereabouts and actions during the conflict remain shrouded in mystery. What we do know is that he was the youngest son of a landed father, also called Hugh Fraser, of Culbokie and Guisachan – territories south and west of Inverness – and was probably born shortly after the beginning of the seventeenth century.[15] Hugh's father expanded his estates in 1616 when he acquired the town and lands of Drumchardiny, which were incorporated into the Barony of Drumchardiny. He died in 1634.[16] Not long after his father's death, Hugh, like many other young Scots of the period, travelled abroad, and from January 1637 saw considerable service on the continent as a soldier with the Swedish Army, his four years of military service standing him in good stead for the affairs at home in which he was all too soon to become embroiled.

***

In a situation marked by mutual distrust and paranoia, Charles' failure to bring the Bishops' Wars to a quick end made other discontented groups feel that force could serve to get them what they wanted.

In Ireland tensions had begun to mount. Charles' Lord Deputy, Thomas Wentworth, had antagonised the Irish Catholics by repeated initiatives to confiscate their lands and grant them to English colonists. He had also angered Roman Catholics by enforcing new taxes but denying them full rights as subjects. This situation became explosive in 1639 when Wentworth offered the Irish Catholics the reforms they had desired, in return for them raising and paying for an Irish army to put down the Scottish rebellion. Although plans called for an army with Protestant officers, the idea of an Irish Catholic army enforcing what many saw as tyrannical government horrified both the Scottish and the English parliaments, who in response threatened to invade Ireland.

Alienated by Protestant domination and frightened by the rhetoric of the English and Scottish parliaments, a group of conspirators launched the Irish Rebellion of 1641, ostensibly in support of the 'King's Rights'. The rising led to widespread assaults on Protestant communities in Ireland, some culminating in massacres. Rumours spread in England and Scotland that the killings had the king's sanction and that this would be their own fate if the kings' Irish troops landed in Britain. The English parliament therefore refused to pay for a royal army to put down the rebellion in Ireland and instead raised their own armed forces. The king did likewise, rallying those who believed that loyalty to the king outweighed other political principles.

When Charles approached parliament to pay for the campaign against the Scots, they had refused, declaring themselves to be permanently in session and putting forward a long list of civil and religious grievances that Charles would have to remedy before they approved any new legislation. On 1 December 1641, parliament issued the Grand Remonstrance to Charles, seen as a direct challenge to the king's authority. Charles refused to address the grievances raised and in 1642 he entered the House of Commons to arrest five 'traitors'. The news of this assault on parliament caused uproar in London. Charles left the city in fear for his life. In his absence parliament passed the Militia Bill, seizing control of the London arsenal and placing the trained bands and militia under its authority. Charles retaliated by appointing individuals to take control of other regional militias. With both sides actively raising troops and gathered munitions, the English Civil War was under way.

The Raising of Fraser's Dragoons

THE CLAN FRASER HAD its own varied family affairs to keep it busy in the far north of Scotland. In April 1642, Lord Lovat's son Hugh Fraser, Master of Lovat[17] married Anna, daughter of General Alexander Leslie, Earl of Leven and former field marshal in the army of Sweden,[18] at Holyrood House.[19]

At the end of August 1642 young Thomas Fraser, the Laird of Strichen – a parish in north Aberdeenshire owned by the Frasers of Saltoun – along with his lady, Lord Pitsligo's daughter, came north for a visit. His party included the old laird and his lady, who took hospitality at Moniak, while Simon Fraser of Inverallochy stayed at Bunchrive and Culbokie – belonging to Major Hugh Fraser's eldest brother – at Drumchrie, with many more of the retinue residing near Lovat and all 'maintaining a charming correspondence'.

In September, the young master of Lovat travelled to Stratharick to divert his young lady with hunting, taking with him both the Lairds of Strichen, Simon, Laird of Inverallochy; his uncle Sir James Fraser of Brea (tutor of Lovat), then living at Beauly; William Fraser of Culbokie, his brother Major Fraser[20] and many more. They went on to the forest of Killin to hunt fallow deer and have 'such princely sport as might alleviate the dullest spirit, and such as perhaps most of them had never seen before' and fed that night on fish and venison.

They continued to Abertarff where the M'ranalds waited for the master and welcomed his huge party royally, inviting them all to take sport in their fields, where abundant deer and roe, hart and hare for hunting were to be had. After a short stay the party, replete with fine foods and all the successful hunting to be had in the place, returned to Inverness and to Lovat in October, where Lord Lovat waited to welcome them.

This short-lived picture of idyllic plenty amidst pastoral splendour bore stark comparison to the meagre existence of the common local folk and to the bloodshed of the bitter religious wars being waged across Europe. Closer to home, conflict in England was already underway, and Major Fraser's task was soon to accept a colonelcy and raise the only dragoon regiment in the Army of the Covenant. His acquaintance-ship with Alexander Leslie in all likelihood meant that Hugh was not only aware of Scotland's future role in the then English war, but was active in the planning of raising the country's armed forces.

The recruiting area of the dragoon regiment that Fraser raised during 1643 is unknown, although there is evidence as to the composition of the unit. Somerville speaks of Fraser's as 'four complete companies, wherein they confided much, as they had good reason, these afterward being made up a regiment, being commanded by Colonel Frizell [Fraser], and were known, with Lawers regiment of foot, to be the stoutest regiment in the Scots army.' A large number of its field officers were veterans out of Europe; so the four companies may have been brought back from Europe by officers returning to Scotland. The standard of the day was for a regiment to be raised by a laird or gentleman who furnished the finance required, and gave his name to the regiment, and who therefore became its colonel, with a veteran of the European conflict serving as lieutenant colonel and second in command to provide the experienced military leadership required. Beneath him would be a greater or lesser number of seasoned field officers, while junior officer posts were filled by the sons of lairds and the like. The rank and file would be built around this core, raised within the county or parishes within the sphere of influence of the colonel. Of the twenty-one regiments forming the Army of the Covenant, all were formed on this basic model, only two, other than Fraser's, having the additional benefit of a colonel who had seen service in Europe. If indeed Fraser's Dragoons were built around 'four complete companies' returned from continental service, this would go a long way to explain the reputation quickly built up by the unit of being reckoned the 'stoutest' in the army.[21]

Dragoon Formation

Dragoons were the cheapest form of cavalry, or mounted infantry. According to the Duke de Rohan in France, 'they ruined the infantry, every man desiring to have a nag so that he might be the fitter to rob and to pillage', and during the English Civil War, both parties raised large numbers – no garrison being considered complete without a company of them. They cost little to equip for, as they usually fought on foot, any sort of horse that could carry a man was good enough for them. In Lacy's old troop a Royalist officer rebukes some of his comrades for their plundering habits. 'Rascals', says he, 'did I not know you at first to be three tattered musketeers, and by plundering a malt mill of 3 blind horses, you then turned dragooners?' Even in the New Model Army, while the horse of the ordinary trooper in a cavalry regiment cost £8 or £10, half that sum was enough to provide a nag for a dragoon.

In the earlier seventeenth century there had been two kinds of regular cavalry troops: cuirassiers and arquebusiers.

The cuirassier was protected from head to knee with plate armour. His arms were protected by pauldrons, couters and vambraces, and his hands by gauntlets. His thighs were covered with tassets. The breastplate was designed to withstand not only a pistol shot but also a ball fired from the more powerful musket. The cuirassier wore high, leather riding-boots with spurs and wore a backsword by his side, designed as a piercing as well as slashing weapon. Cuirassiers were divided into subgroups according to ordnance, the first armed with two wheel lock pistols carried in holsters fastened to the front sides of the saddle, while the second group also had heavy cavalry-type lances, although these had already begun to disappear by this time – lances of lighter weight surviving only in some irregular cavalry units. The arquebusiers, sometimes called carabiniers, wore only the breastplate and the morion helmet. Their ordnance was limited to a short wheel lock handgun or arquebus and one or two pistols. Like the cuirassiers, they also had a side weapon. The arquebus was carried slung from the bandolier by means of a snaphook and the pistols were in holsters like those of the cuirassiers.

As a rule, cuirassiers and arquebusiers fought mounted, using mainly their firearms, the arquebus and pistol, in combat.

Dragoons also rode horses but their mounts served only to carry them to the battlefield. In the early seventeenth century the dragoons' task was similar to that of regular infantry and therefore dragoons were not ranked among the regular cavalry. As a rule they dismounted and fought on foot, one out of every ten men remaining behind the firing line to hold the horses. When he was armed with the matchlock musket it was absolutely necessary to dismount, because it was difficult, if not impossible, to fire it on horseback.[22] If he had a firelock he could use it on foot or horseback as he chose.

In the Scottish Covenanter Army under Lord Leven which was to enter England in 1644, of twenty-one regiments, only Fraser's was a dragoon regiment. As cheaply armed as he was mounted, like the musketeer, he wore no defensive armour generally, although descriptions of the Scottish Army make a number of references to buff coats. It is also probable that they wore hats or bonnets rather than helmets.

Their standard offensive arms included a sword and a musket[23] or firelock – unlike the regular cavalry they had no pistols except perhaps for the officers. Colonel Hugh Fraser is recorded as having been advanced 2,000 merks[24] 'for firelocks and pikes', by that other Hugh Fraser, Lord Lovat – a man who 'obliged every gentleman and tenant when he came to the age of eighteen to have arms suitable to his rank' and who described Colonel Fraser as his consanguineous. The firelock was lighter, more reliable and more mobile than the matchlock. In the matchlock era, two other forms of ignition were known and were called firelocks in most surviving records, though now known as the wheel lock and flintlock. One type of firelock however retained slow match – it used a trigger which moved a serpentine holding a burning wick of match to the touchhole, allowing the firer to hold the weapon with both hands and make an aimed shot. This could fire a round every 2–3 minutes. It would appear that the regiment was issued with the serpentine firelock evidenced by the quantities of matchcord which was to be supplied to Fraser's throughout the war (see end tables).

As mentioned, dragoons were to serve on foot, and in all likelihood wore closed shoes or shorter and lighter boots than the regular cavalry.[25] In similar fashion, while the cavalry trooper's saddle, with furniture, was bought for the horseman of the new model in July 1645 for example, at 16*s* or 16*s* 6*d* (Sterling),[26] dragoon saddles – lighter and of inferior workmanship – cost (at the same date) 7*s* 10*d*.[27] We can build up a picture of the clothing of the common soldier from 1639 onwards, including, in all probability, the dragoon during the period 1643–46 – clad in a coarse, ill-fitting buttoned doublet[28] and breeches[29] of pre-shrunk cloth, perhaps faced and bound in a contrasting material (the 'regimental colours'), a rough shirt, either the Scottish 'sark', distinctive from its English counterpart, being almost full length – more like a night shirt as we might picture it,[30] or a short linen shirt. Shoes with cockers or light boots may have been more common than the heavier and more expensive cavalry 'bucket' boots, with spurs and butterflies,[31] and a blue bonnet[32] provided some colour to relieve the drab 'hodden' grey of the tunic. If leather buff coats were worn, they would serve more as a defense against the cold than an enemy. According to lists of arms and ammunition received by the regiment, Fraser's would have been laden down with muskets, swords, bandoliers, flasks of powder, sacks of musket ball and yards of slow match.[33] It is likely that their full-length or near full-length serpentine muskets would have been slung from the bandoliers by a snaphook, in a fashion similar to the arquebusiers from earlier in the century, while the officers will have received pistols too, for self defence.

In Wallenstein's marches 'the dragooners with their muskets, shovels, and mattocks[34] (with which they still rode during the conflict of Britain) were ever sent before "to make good the passes".'

Sir James Turner also sets out the special services which dragoons were expected to perform. In an advance they were sent ahead of the army to secure passes or bridges until the infantry could come up. In a retreat they were to hold defensible positions and cover the retiring army in the same way. When the fighting was in enclosed country they were employed to line hedges and ditches and possess enclosures. In open country they might be called on to dismount and co-operate as musketeers with the regular cavalry. 'They ought to be taught to give fire on horseback', says Turner, but he emphatically declares, 'Their service is on foot, and is no other than that of musketeers'.

Narratives of the Civil War illustrate these services. Lilburne, who commanded Manchester's Dragoons, says, speaking of the Marston Moor campaign, 'I and my regiment of dragoons were constantly quartered in the van of the whole army; always nigh the enemies garrisons, where constantly in a manner we fought both for horsemeat and man's meat or else with a great deal of vigilance stood upon our guard'. Okey, colonel of the dragoon regiment of the new model, speaking of the period just before the Battle of Naseby, describes himself as 'watching every night with my regiment upon their quarters, having the forlorn guard every night'. The following winter, during the blockade of Exeter, it was Okey's dragoons who had to hold all the most exposed posts between the besieging army and the Royalist army of the west. In short, the bulk of outpost work seems to have fallen to dragoons. One reason was the regular cavalry having no firearms except pistols. Later, when the regular cavalry were provided with carbines or firelocks, they too could perform these duties.

Rates of pay of Cavalry, Infantry & Dragoons

CAVALRY

Colonel *per month*	37	0	8 *Sterling*	444	8	10 *Scots*
Lieutenant Colonel	22	4	5	266	13	4
Major	14	16	3	177	15	6
Rout Master	11	2	2	133	6	8
Lieutenant	5	0	0	60	0	0
Reg Waster	5	0	0	60	0	0
Cornet	4	0	0	48	0	0
Surgeon	3	6	8	40	0	0
Waster	3	6	8	40	0	0
Minister	2	19	3	35	11	1
Corporal	2	13	4	32	0	0
Trumpeter	2	4	5	26	13	4
Trooper	2	6	8	28	0	0

INFANTRY

Colonel	24	13	9 *Sterling*	296	5	9 *Scots*
Lieutenant Colonel	14	16	3	177	15	6
Major	9	17	5	118	9	9
Captain	7	8	1	88	17	9
Lieutenant	3	6	8	40	0	0
Reg Waster	3	6	8	40	0	0
Surgeon	3	6	8	40	0	0
Minister	2	19	3	35	11	1
Ensign	2	13	4	32	0	0
Scrivener	2	4	5	26	13	4
Drum Major	1	6	8	16	0	0
Provost Marshal	1	6	8	16	0	0
Sergeant	1	2	2	13	6	8
Corporal	0	17	9	10	13	4
Drummer	0	17	9	10	13	4
Private	0	13	4	8	0	0

The rates paid on service in England, so far as accounts allow them to be calculated were as follows:

CAVALRY

Colonel	*per month*	81	0	*Sterling*	972 *Scots*
Major		45	0		540
Captain		27	0		324
Lieutenant		18	0		216
Cornet		12	0		144

INFANTRY

Lieutenant Colonel	35	0		432
Major	30	0		360
Captain	18	0		216
Lieutenant	6	0		72
Waster	5	0		60
Scrivener	3	15	(?)	45 (?)

In addition to pay, all ranks received Billet Money:

A schedule of allowance to be made to officers and soldiers, horse and foot, in the Scottish Army, for the entertainment in their march, or as they shall be quartered in England, not exceeding these proportions and rates here under mentioned:

	l	s	d
To a major of horse daily	00	06	00
To a route master or captain of horse daily	00	06	00
To a lieutenant of horse daily	00	04	00
To a cornet	00	02	06
To each corporal, quarter master, and trumpeter	00	01	06
To every trooper for his own diet daily	00	01	00
To every horse officer or trooper for his horse: 5 sheaves of straw or a stone of hay, and 3 gallons (English) of oats	00	00	06
To a lieutenant colonel of foot daily	00	05	00
To a major of foot daily	00	04	00
The captain	00	03	00
The lieutenant	00	02	00
The ensign	00	01	06
The quarter master and sergeant each	00	01	00
The corporal and drummers each	00	08	00
The common soldiers daily	00	00	06

To the carriage men the same as the common foot soldier;

And for the carriage horse 3 penny worth of straw or hay and 2 penny worth of oats The officers of dragoons are to have entertainment at their discretion, not exceeding the rates following:

The lieutenant colonel daily	00	06	00
The major daily	00	05	00
The captain daily	00	04	00
The lieutenant daily	00	03	00
The ensign daily	00	02	06
The sergeant daily	00	01	04
The corporal and drummers each	00	00	10

The dragooner is to have for himself 8*d* a day and for his horse 3 penny worth of straw or hay and a groat's (4*d*) worth of oats.

These rates create a framework within which the quality and value of the dragoon may be set against that of the cavalry and infantry. While some musketeers endeavoured to obtain a nag of any description during his travels to claim dragoon status, there was also a considerable rivalry between some horse and dragoon units – the dragoon sometimes squandering his pay in an attempt to fulfil his aspirations of matching the cavalry trooper's finery.

Ranking somewhere between cavalry and infantry – effectively infantry transported on horseback – dragoon training did not differ fundamentally from that of regular infantry. Their organisation too was similar to infantry. About half of the dragoon troops of the early seventeenth century were armed with short 'firelock' muskets. The rest were mounted pikemen using the typical infantry pike of the period, slightly modified to facilitate carrying on horseback.

Authors of the period, writing on the problems of combat training and deployment, considered the dragoons to be a very useful service. Since these troops rode to the battlefield, they were able to keep pace with the regular cavalry columns. When attacked by enemy cavalrymen, dragoons were able to protect their cavalry with musket fire, especially if charged from the flanks. Forming the centre of a cavalry formation, dragoons could provide a very effective defence, since their long thrusting lances offered cover to musketeer and cavalry detachments and could protect them from a direct charge by enemy cavalry. Dragoons were used for both day and night combat, for assaulting small remote forts, for blowing up the enemy fort gate with a powder charge, or for surprise attacks of enemy encampments.

If dragoons were ordered either to build or wreck some field fortifications, they would be issued with basic sapping tools.

Formation of the Armies, 1643[35]

After the Bishops' Wars, the Scottish Army had been scaled down but not disbanded, and the rebellion in Ireland, requiring the intervention of thousands of Covenanters, ensured the continuation of a professional core of Scots troops. This well-trained and well-organised national army would set the example for Oliver Cromwell's New Model Army in years to come.

At the end of 1642, the Civil War in England had reached stalemate and both sides sought the support of the Scots with their powerful army. Opinion in Scotland was divided, the Privy Council voting that the Scots should not do anything which would prejudice the king's honour. However, in June 1643 the Covenanters in the General Assembly of the Kirk endorsed a plea from English Parliamentarian commissioners to give them military aid, and in August a deal was presented to the English whereby the Scots would attack Royalist positions from the north in exchange for a single Presbyterian Church on the Scottish model which would unify religious practices in the three kingdoms.

The arming of Scotland continued through the summer of 1643, as Colonel David Leslie, a veteran of the Swedish army's campaigns in Germany, returned to his homeland. On 28 July the Convention of Estates decided he would remain in Scotland for the public service from fighting in Ireland. The following month, on 18 August, all fensible men in Scotland were put on 48-hour standby, on the 22nd routmasters were commissioned, on the 25th the foot commanders were commissioned, and 26 August saw the first nomination of colonels, while Leven was made commander-in-chief of the country's forces.

The Act of the Committee of Estates for amalgamating several troops of horse out of the shires into regiments, states that troops not yet formed in regiments, nor have any colonels to command them, are to be divided into seven regiments, each consisting of eight troops, and each troop of sixty troopers (i.e. 480 troopers to a regiment), besides officers. One regiment is to be commanded by the Lord General including two troops brought out of Ireland, viz. the troops of Major Bannantyne and Sir Robert Adair, and 240 horse out of the sheriffdom of Roxburgh, Selkirk, and Peebles, to make up four troops.

One regiment to be commanded by General Leslie, to consist of three troops already levied, the laird of Polmais' troop appointed to come out of the sheriffdom of Stirling, and four troops to be levied, and levy money to be granted.

One to be commanded by the Earl of Eglinton, and to consist of 240 horse, to come out of the sheriffdom of Ayr and Renfrew, which will make up four troops; the 200 appointed to come out of the sheriffdom of Lanark, which will make up three troops, and twenty horse to be levied.

One to be commanded by the Earl of Dalhousie, and to consist of 120 out of the sheriffdom of Berwick, which will make two troops; 120 out of the sheriffdom of Haddington, to make up the other two; 120 from the sheriffdom of Edinburgh, to make up another two; one of the troops out of the sheriffdom of Stirling, of which Sir William Bruce is rout master, and the troop appointed to come out of the sheriffdom of Linlithgow. At Edinburgh, on 18 August 1643 the Scottish parliament published a resolution to put the kingdom speedily into a posture of defence; 'all fensible persons between sixty and sixteen years of age to provide themselves with 40 days provision,[36] ammunition, arms and other warlike provision of all sorts for horse and foot, with tents and other furnishings requisite, and that horsemen be armed with pistols, broad swords, and steel caps; and where these arms cannot be had, that they provide jacks (metal-reinforced or padded leather jerkins), lances and steel bonnets; and that the footmen be armed with musket and sword, or pikes and sword, and where these cannot be had, that they be furnished with halberds, Lochaber axes or Jedburgh staves and swords.'

There was now great preparation raising men and arms. General Leslie sent to Holland, France and Sweden for commanders and officers, who came to him daily, set on going into England. Also a great store of arms, powder and ball was daily furnished and brought from Holland.

Colonels and committees of war were appointed in each shire to muster all fensible persons, and a list made up of fensibles, armed and unarmed, and how many and what sort of arms were needed for every shire.

As many arms had to be furnished as men sent forth with the army; so that the colonels and committees had to send representatives to the committee of estates, with money or surety for providing as many muskets, swords, pikes and pistols as was sent forth in this present expedition, together with 3lb weight of powder, 3lb weight of ball,[37] and 5lb weight of match for every musket.

The colonels, committees and magistrates of burghs were ordered to organise their fensibles into regiments, foot companies, and horse troops.

The regiments and chief officers of Leven's army comprised:

21 territorial regiments of foot	18,000
9 bodies of horse	2,000
1 regiment of dragoons	500–1,000
and an artillery train	

General* – The Earl of Leven,[38] Lieutenant general of the foot – William Baillie of Lethem*
Major general of horse – David Leslie*
General of artillery – Sir Alexander Hamilton*
Treasurer and commissary general – Sir Adam Hepburn of Humbie
Quartermaster general – Ludovick Leslie*

DRAGOONS

COLONELS	LIEUTENANT COLONELS	MAJORS
Hugh Fraser*	William Crawford *	John Monro*

REGIMENTS OF HORSE

Earl of Leven*	James Ballantyne*	Sir Rot. Adair*
Major Gen David Leslie*	Sir John Brown*	Thomas Craig
Earl of Eglinton	Robert Montgomerie*	John M'gomerie*
Lord Kirkcudbright	James Mercer of Aldie	Alexander Crook
Earl of Dalhousie	Innes*	Blair*
Earl of Balcarres	Alexander Strachan	Alexander Home*
Michael Weldon	Alexander Home*	

Lord Gordon's Troop	Ogilvie
Marquis of Argyll's Troop	Hugh Crawford

REGIMENTS OF FOOT

TERRITORIAL UNIT	COLONELS	LIEUTENANT COLONELS	MAJORS
Kyle & Carrick	Earl of Cassillis	John Kennedy	Archibald Houston*
Galloway	William Stewart*	John Gordon	Alexander Agnew*
Fife	Earl of Crawford-Lindsay	Thomas Moffat*	Mungo Murray*
East Lothian	Sir Patrick Hepburn	Wm Home*	Robert Hepburn*
Strathearn	Lord Coupar	John Browne*	George Brown*
Loudon-Glasgow	Earl of Loudon	Robert Home*	John Haldane*
Midlothian	Lord Maitland	Colin Pitscottie*	John Hay*
The Merse	Sir David Home	George Home*	Lumsdale
Stirlingshire	Lord Livingston	Andrew Bruce*	Alexr Livingston*
Tweeddale	Earl of Buccleuch	Walter Scott*	Thomas Moffat*
Edinburgh	James Rae	Andrew Melville*	Thomas Logan*
Fife	Earl of Dunfermline	Robert Halsall*	David Finnie*
Clydesdale	Sir Alexr. Hamilton	Wm Carmichael*	Walter Lindsay*
Perthshire	Ld Murray of Gask	Lachlan Ross*	Duncan Campbell*
Teviotdale	Earl of Lothian	Patrick Leslie*	Sir George Douglas*
Nithsdale & Annandale	Douglas of Kilhead	John Hogg*	Thomas Macburnie
Angus	Viscount Dudhope	Bonar*	William Scrimgeour

Linlithgow & Tweeddale	Master of Yester	Johnston*	William Hamilton*
The Mearns & Aberdeen	Earl Marischal	Sir James Wood*	Andrew Leslie
Ministers' Regt.	Arthur Erskine	James Bryson*	John Leslie*
The Levied or College of Justice Regiment	Ld Sinclair	James Somerville*	Sr James Turner*

We can add to this supplementary information on the composition of Fraser's dragoon regiment, which composition altered over the years from the unit's formation in 1643, through 1646 when the regiment would convert to a regiment of horse, before its disbanding in 1647.

COMPOSITION OF FRASER'S DRAGOONS

Colonel	1643	Hugh Fraser/Hew Frizell.
Lt. Colonel	1643	William Crawford[39]
	1646	John Monro
Major	1643	John Monro
	1647	David Lumsden?
Captain	1644	Alexander Ferguson, David Lumsden, John Forrester, Michael Bruce
	1645	Andrew Monro.
	1646	? Muir.
Q'rmaster	1644	James Acheson, Malcolm Smith, David Simpson, Somerville, Alexander, Fraser
	1645	Thomas Urquhart, William Gillespie.
	1646	Tweedie, David Baillie, Kerr, Richard Beck.
Lieutenant	1644	Alexander Hamilton.
	1646	Andrew Beck.
Cornet	1643	Andrew Kerr
	1644	William Elphinstone, William Borthwick
	1647	Edmund Borthwick
Chaplain	1646	Fergus Alexander.

Scrivener	1644	Thomas Urquhart.
Sergeant	1644	Andrew Stenhous, Robert Stevenson, (?) David Simpsone
	1645	Thomas Fergusone, George Thompson, William Peebles
	1646	William Maxwell
Corporal	1645	Jon Huntar, Jon Veech,
Dragoon	?	Jon Bruntoun
	1644	David Kennedy, James Somervill, Jon Evermor, William Borthwick
	1645	Andro M'Heart, Robert Phillip, Roger Gordoune, Andro Urquhart, Thomas Scott, James Bailzie, Wm. Lindsay (servitour to Lieutant-Colonel Crawford).

In this army, the religious instruction of the soldiers was elaborately provided for. Not only were there to be morning and evening prayers and sermons on Sundays and Fast-days, both in the morning and afternoon, but also a complete system of ecclesiastical jurisdiction was to be established in the army. Church discipline and military discipline were to flourish side by side in it.

On 26 November, the colonels of horse were named, and David Leslie commissioned colonel for a horse regiment of eight troops. By January 1644 the Estates would make him Major-General of Horse for the whole army.

On 29 November a military treaty was signed with the English parliament agreeing that the Scots would enter the fray in England on the side of parliament. In mid December, the Scottish levies marched into the southern lowlands, rendezvoused at Harlaw on 1 January and, in accordance with the treaty, the Army of the Solemn League and Covenant entered England under Leven in January 1644. In June 1644 the military situation would demand an extra force under the Earl of Callendar.

Around this time back in Hugh Fraser's home county, the Covenanters sent the Laird of Lawers and the Lothian Kerr's regiment to garrison Inverness. The town was sconced round with an earth wall, a deep trench, ramparts and palisades, and made up to a considerable strength. In the country Culbokie (Hugh Fraser's eldest brother) made a sconce on the corse of Kingilly ('Fort Field', now on Home Farm of Kingillie)[40] based upon a design draughted by Hugh Fraser to include corners and bastions all of a fensible strength. Later in the war Sir James Fraser of Brea, tutor of Lovat and a staunch Covenanter who managed to persuade the entire clan to support his party, was to get hold of a gun and save the lives of a number of women and children by getting them to safety there. Alexander Fraser of Phioneas and a company of men garrisoned Lovat Castle, and the Castle of Beauly was fortified with a sconce, constructed by John Fraser of Clunavackie (Hugh's elder brother).

2. The Scots Advance on Newcastle and York

In December 1643, the Earl of Lanark had gone to Newcastle where he had some dealing with its governor Sir John Marley, to 'betray the town to General Leslie.' This failed attempt to suborn Marley followed hard upon the ratification of the Solemn League and Covenant entered into between Scotland and the English parliament the previous month. From that moment on, London and parliament eagerly awaited the fall of this Royalist stronghold in the north. The news sheets of January 1644 carried optimistic statements that the Scots had already arrived at Newcastle, and that the town had surrendered. At the same time, news reached London which would strengthen Royalist hopes in the town's ability to sustain a siege:

> Two ships have come to Newcastle from Denmark, one with twenty brass pieces (cannon), ammunition and powder, the other laden with corn.

Other statements on the readiness of the town to withstand a siege specify that while the town had a garrison of only 500 men – all townsmen – and that the 'High Castle' was the only place fortified, within ten weeks the garrison had received 150 barrels of powder, some small guns from Amsterdam, 500 muskets which arrived in two cobbles from Scarborough, and the *Ipswich Sarah* was at the town, laden with coal for Hamburg from where she was to return with arms. There were also five men-of-war at Newcastle and a ten-gun ship, recently run ashore at Coquet Island, her guns taken ashore and secured by Sir Thomas Glemham at Alnwick. Two ships from Holland with arms and ammunition were expected daily. Glemham's forces were estimated at 5,000, although half of these were unarmed.

However in Newcastle, many were well inclined towards the Scots.

The Scots' advance south was hampered by an exceptionally severe winter, and the campaign could not commence without the necessary religious observances. From Friday to Monday there had been a fast throughout Scotland. A week later on Tuesday 18th, the army, well armed with field pieces, swine feathers, and all necessary engines of war, lumbered south from Dunbar, travelling 18 Scots miles (23–24 English miles) on the first day, through bitterly cold weather and atrocious snowstorms. Blizzards were so heavy that even the guides could hardly find their way and troops could barely see the man in front, staggering knee-deep through drifts, although reportedly in cheerful spirits. It was so cold, in fact, that part of the army was able to walk over the frozen Tweed at Kelso, even taking their heavy baggage and the light artillery they carried with them over the ice.

The following day, Wednesday 19th, the Scots were at Adderstone, 6 miles from Alnwick and 28 miles from Newcastle.

The Royalist Colonel Sir Thomas Glemham, Governor of Newcastle, consulted with the Royalist gentlemen of the county to decide what should be done in the face of the Scots' vast numerical superiority, and the likelihood that they may be forced to evacuate as Leven advanced. Some were in favour of laying waste to the country in front of the advancing Scots, while others were not so disposed to consider such an extreme measure. All agreed, however, that it would be hopeless to try and resist the advancing host. The result of the meeting was Glemham calling in his forces, destroying the bridge across the Aln – so that the Scots did not reach Alnwick until Saturday 22nd – and retiring to Newcastle.

A day later Baillie marched from Kelso to Wooler with six regiments of foot and one of horse. By Monday 24th, Leven was at Adderstone waiting for his artillery to catch up. A writer in the Scots' army wrote:

> We are confident our quarters shall be about the town of Newcastle upon Saturday the 27th [29th?], which, if they will not yield up, we have no purpose to stay there, unless to seize the Block-houses on the river, so that the Parliament ships may come in safely.

When the Scots Army arrived at Alnwick, Argyll marched to Coquet Island (east of Amble) and took possession of it after firing only a single shot. He took seventy officers and their men prisoner and captured seven pieces of ordnance with their ammunition, together with a year's worth of provisions. He garrisoned a body of men on the island and continued towards Alnwick.

From Friday 28 January to 1 February, the Scots arrived at Morpeth where they stopped to allow the rearguard to catch up with the main body of the army. Leaving Morpeth on 1 February, Leven had intended to camp within 2 miles of Newcastle the following day. Progress was stalled again, however, at Stannington on the 2nd while the flooded rivers subsided, and so the Marquis of Newcastle was able to throw himself and his forces into the city only a few hours before the arrival of the Scots. Covenanter musketeers immediately and furiously assaulted the city forts, standing in the open fields almost fully in view of the enemy and firing from both the east and west sides, but the town soldiers, answering their musket shots with shots of musket and cannon from the fortifications, 'gave them such an entertainment', until midnight that the Scots Army was obliged to retire a mile from the town to quarter about Northumberland in strong bodies. The Marquis's timely arrival and the resistance he inspired caused considerable disappointment among the Scots.

The next day (3 February), Leven summoned the city to surrender and attacked an outlying fort in Shieldfield:

> Some of our Scots musketeers [possibly out of Fife's regiment] were drawn up to a stone bridge a quarter of a mile from the town, at the entrance into the shield-field, to beat out some men of theirs from a little sconce that lay near it, and did it presently without loss; but they [the Royalists] retired to a sharper work near the windmill [which used to stand on the east bank of the Pandon Burn] where the controversy was more hot, and our arguments not strong enough; the great pieces [Leven's heavy artillery only now being transported by sea from Berwick to Blyth] being not come in regard of the uncertainty of the Sea by which they were to come … In six hours or thereabouts we lost only fourteen men, including Patrick English, captain lieutenant to the Lord Lindsay, and some common soldiers. The enemy having lost about seven or eight, fled to the town, and we possessed the fort, which is within half musket shot of the walls: After that they sent forth eight troops of horse which the General-Major of the Horse [David Leslie] charged with five, though they could not charge above three abreast together in respect of the coal-pits; notwithstanding which the charge was so hard upon the enemy that they presently retired into the town. We took two prisoners, one of whom a lieutenant who cursed and railed for half an hour …

Sir Thomas Glemham, now Governor of Newcastle, replied to Leven's summons to surrender that if he would grant five days respite he should receive a full answer. Leven was quite happy to accept this response, as it would allow more time for his siege guns to catch up to his army, an assault on the town in the meantime being impossible.

The big guns arrived at Blyth Neuk three days later, and were transported to the Scots camp the following day. On their arrival, the Scots extended operations to surround the town and secure the coal-pits on the Gateshead side of the river.

The English meantime sought to lay waste the country from where the Scots were drawing supplies. On the 11th, Sir Thomas Riddell, commanding Tynemouth Castle, sent fifty musketeers to destroy the corn in the Scots quarter. They unfortunately encountered a Scots foraging party of twenty-five of Eglington's troopers under Major John Montgomery, who fell on them, killed some and reportedly took forty-five prisoners which, on being taken to Leslie, were sent to the Marquis of Newcastle as a token. Newcastle only hoped that in the coming days he would be able to repay this gesture with interest.

The huge Scots army had to be quartered across a vast part of the countryside around Newcastle, from Hebburn and Seaton in the east, Morpeth and Ogle in the north, round to Prudhoe and almost as far as Hexham to the west, where Leven's flank was secured by his horse.

Newcastle, urged on by his General of Horse, Sir Marmaduke Langdale, was unwilling to sit penned in the town while Leven had free range all over Northumberland. Both men were experienced in contemporary warfare and decided to send out a force to 'beat up the quarters' of the Scots Army. The plan appears to have been to direct two separate thrusts at the Scottish foot and a third, under Langdale, further afield at the Scots horse stationed just outside Corbridge, 3 miles east of Hexham.

The attacks on the Scots foot failed to materialise, possibly because the Tyne was still in spate, the Scots forces heavily outnumbered Newcastle's, and he could not risk getting what would have been a considerable part of his army trapped on the wrong side of the Tyne.

Langdale's expedition was a wholly different story, however. In the small hours of Monday 19th, thirty-five troops of horse of Marmaduke Langdale's, Colonel Robert Brandling's and Colonel Sir John Fenwick's, plus possibly selected elements of other regiments of Newcastle's mounted arm, mostly locals once described as 'staunchly loyal ... but they are murderers, thieves, embezzlers and quite untrustworthy; they are lawless men ... they were continually at feud with one another', clattered out of Newcastle on the road to Corbridge.

This sort of work must have been very much to their liking, and those from the more remote areas of the countryside may well have been used to it from their local raids and cattle stealing. They were also, without a doubt, glad of the chance to fight the old foe rather than their fellow Englishman.

This raiding party was completed by the inclusion of 300 musketeers, possibly mounted on nags as dragoons, raising the total number of the force to roughly 1,500 men.

Riding along the road via Dilston to avoid detection, Langdale's troops outflanked the Scots and arrived at Hexham. On the opposite side of the river, three Scots regiments under Lord Balgonie[41] had encamped along the old Roman Road between the remains of Corstopitum[42] Roman Fort and the Red House, an area of fairly flat land along the riverbank. Some also encamped in Corbridge itself (a local tradition attests that the old Saxon Church was used as a stable by the Scots, who fastened their horses to the north wall of the nave). These units are believed to have been fifteen troops of horse comprising Lord Kirkcudbright's regiment and the Earl of Leven's Lifeguard, along with three of the four companies of Fraser's dragoons and apparently some elements of the Loudoun-Glasgow and Galloway regiments of foot. Their strength in total perhaps equalled that of their English opponents.

Langdale, Brandling and Fenwick decided on a pincer attack, which would not only catch the Scots by surprise but also trap them between two forces. Colonel Brandling with his ten troops of horse retraced their route through High Dilston to the old ford just east of Corbridge. They were to ford the Tyne, clear any opposition in the town and come round into the Scots rear, down Well Bank. Meanwhile,

Langdale and Fenwick would launch the main attack, supported by the musketeers if anything went wrong.

After waiting for Brandling to reach the ford to Corbridge, Langdale led his force across the bridge at Hexham and towards the Scots encampment from the west. He may have had his musketeers dismount to line the hedges and banks behind his horse. Coming within sight of the Scots camp, he was taken aback to discover that the Scots had already got out of their quarters and were formed up in the open waiting for them. As it was too late to withdraw at this stage, he immediately ordered his men to charge.

It is perhaps worth pointing out at this stage the inequality in the levels of equipment of either side. There can be little doubt that the Royalist horse were woefully under-equipped. Most of their equipment had been gathered from small family armouries dating back to the days of the border reivers; pistols and armour were unusual except for officers, and very often even their mounts would have been cart or plough horses, or of very poor stock (most of the Marquis of Newcastle's funds were spent on equipping the foot, evidenced by the helmet, reputedly that of John Fenwick, preserved in the Border Reivers Museum at Hexham and of a style popular in the Wars of the Roses fought two centuries earlier).

Whether or not this was a deciding factor, the Scots, equal in number to the Royalists, held the assault, and Lieutenant Colonel James Ballantyne counter-charged with the lancers of Leven's Lifeguard, causing Langdale's Cavalry to give way with some loss. The Scots successfully charged again and, having taken a good number of Langdale's troopers prisoner, launched a third charge which drove the Royalists back to their musketeers, Newcastle's white-coats, who in their turn stood firm and stopped the Scots advance with a volley of shot. The Scots, disordered, their lances now of little use in a stand-up fight against the English swords and muskets, were turned and routed, thundering towards Corbridge, their horses, fresher though smaller than those of their English opponents, outrunning their pursuers. This may explain the next step in the skirmish.

Colonel Brandling had brought his ten troops of horse and dragoons across the river below Corbridge, and was now pushing on along the Carelgate to take the main body of Scots horse in the rear, only to find to his horror what appeared to be a Scottish force of three times their number bearing down upon them with little sign of the main body of their comrades. Not surprisingly they halted in confusion but Brandling, undaunted, urged his men onwards and galloped forward to encourage them. His troopers watched as he swerved his horse to discharge a pistol at a Lieutenant Elliot who was leading the Scots rout. The shot missed and, each having exchanged shots, wheeled to draw swords. At this point, Brandling's horse stumbled on the rough ground, pitching him forward. Elliot took the opportunity and pulled him from the saddle. Seeing their commander taken prisoner, and fearful of the Scots' lance points bearing down on them, the men of Brandling's regiment did not wait for the impact, but turned tail and galloped pell-mell through the town marketplace, closely followed by the Scots, who killed some and pursued them so hard that several of the English were drowned as they recrossed the river.

While the remnants of Brandling's regiment escaped to safety across the bridge and ford, Langdale decided to call off further pursuit of the Scottish horse for fear of encountering further Covenanter forces and, rallying his men, he too crossed the river, gathered up the remainder of Brandling's force on the other side, and returned to Newcastle.

Having either killed or captured well in excess of a hundred Scots in the attack, Langdale had done some considerable damage to the pride of Leven's forces, as well as boosting the flagging morale of Newcastle's troops, while only losing some thirty or so of his own men, mostly in the rout of Brandling's force and the Scots' first charge against his own main force. Had the sortie actually gone as planned he may well have devastated a good portion of the Scots horse. As it was, David Leslie was shot through the shoulder, a number of officers were reported killed, amongst whom was a Captain Haddon; Major Alexander Agnew of the Galloway foot unit was most seriously injured and taken prisoner along with Loudoun-Glasgow's Cornet Kerr (grandchild to Lord Roxburgh), and an Archibald Mackie, Quartermaster. Over and above the casualties, the Royalists captured two cavalry colours and one of Fraser's dragoons' colours.

Two grave pits have since been discovered at Corbridge and linked to this battle. The first in 1767 in a limestone quarry found to contain several adult male bodies at a depth of around 18 inches. The second was exhumed in Priory Gardens in 1880, along the line of the Scots retreat. This contained twenty adult male skeletons and that of a child, in all probability trampled in the rout through town. One of the skeletons had a broken lance-head by it, perhaps suggesting that the corpses were English.

Leven had been shown how dangerous his position was, and what a close escape his horse had had:

> I trust it will make us more watchful and confident in God, whose great providence it was that we were not wholly cut off ... that the enemy ... had been so careful in the surprise as to provide ten troops to fall upon our rear, which was miscarried by their Colonel's single forwardness to a single combat.

On the same day a Colonel Dudley, or Douglas, crossed the river at Prudhoe with some horse and dragoons, and attacked one of the Scots quarters with such success – slaying or capturing all, to the tune of fifty-five prisoners – and so alarming the Scots that the Covenanters abandoned four other quarters in the immediate neighbourhood in disarray and with some loss. But with the inadequate forces at his disposal the marquis found it impossible to effectively defend the many river fords between Hexham and Newburn against the inexorable advance of the Scottish host. So in the face of such advance he was obliged to leave them, as he expressed it, to their own wills.

The day's combat shook Leven from his inactivity, and three days later, 22 February, he abandoned the siege, leaving Sir James Lumsden and six regiments – the Mearns and Aberdeen, the Strathearn, the 'Levied' regiment, the Perthshire, the Merse, and the Nithsdale and Annandale – along with some troops of horse, as a covering force, and pushed on across the Tyne into Durham. Strategically, therefore, the small action at Corbridge was not insignificant, and provided the first battle in this campaign.

At the same time a (supposedly jealous) Leven posted Lieutenant Colonel James Somerville of the College of Justice Foot in Morpeth Castle to protect his supply line, Somerville complaining bitterly about his appointment because the place was in ruins. The other five companies of the regiment continued south to the Newcastle area, marching 4 miles up-river to Haddon on the Wall. The army rested in the fields that night almost in the same place where they had quartered the night before crossing the Tyne at Newburn during the Bishops' Wars, since when the Royalists had built fortifications on the river side and above, near the top of the hill. On the 23rd, during a break in the weather, the Royalists appeared on the other side of the river marching towards the Scots but, at about midnight, their regiments of horse marched off, leaving behind their prisoner, Major Agnew,[43] as a safeguard against the Scots doing any damage to the house of Colonel Fenwick, who had used him courteously. A few days later, on Wednesday 28th, the Scots Army crossed the Tyne at three fords – Ovingham, Bydwell and Altringham – the foot having to wade through deep water to quarter that night in villages near the river, just in time as it transpired, as the melting snow swelled the river to an impassable torrent a short time later. They marched to the Derwent Water to find it an impassable flood with no opportunity of crossing other than by a narrow tree-bridge near Ebchester, which half the army crossed in files, while the other half stayed on the near side overnight, the whole army having again to spend the night in the open fields.

On Friday, 1 March, the rest of the army crossed the tree-bridge and marched towards Sunderland, judged to be the best place to collect intelligence and re-supply the army. The day was again cold and during the afternoon they continued through a thick misty drizzle of rain to within a mile of Chester-le-Street. Passing the Wear at the new bridge near Lumley, they spied the enemy amongst the hills 2 miles ahead and quartered on the Saturday in Harrington and the adjacent villages. The Scots rested on the Lord's Day (3 March).

On the 4th the Scots entered Sunderland, spending all day provisioning the army, which was done with considerable difficulty, as for the most part, the country was against parliament and unwilling to part with supplies. So far the Scots advance had been relatively unmolested. The Marquis of Newcastle however, strengthened by twelve troops of horse from Yorkshire under Sir Charles Lucas, which brought the estimate of his forces to a very substantial 14,000 horse and foot, pursued Leven, and on Wednesday 6th at one o'clock crossed the Wear at the new bridge which the Scots had crossed four days before. Soon after he caught sight of his enemy and drew up in battle order. Those of the Scots Army that could be made aware of the presence of the marquis' forces were drawn up within half a mile of the Royalists where they remained standing in the fields and in the snow throughout that night.

The following day, Thursday 7th, in exceptionally snowy conditions, the Scots took up positions on Boldon Hill, Newcastle, drawing up his forces 2 miles from them. However the snow was so heavy that no progress could be made until the middle of the day when the weather cleared a little. The Scots advanced towards Newcastle while he marched northwards, to gain the wind.[44] Both armies remained drawn up in battle order, the marquis having the advantage of ground but there being many impassable ditches and hedges between the two forces. Both armies faced one another until the sun set, at which point Newcastle retired north, leaving the field to the Scots where they remained throughout the cold night. On Friday 8th after some skirmishing between some small parties of horse, the Scots learned from those taken prisoner that many of Newcastle's men had been wounded. Commanded musketeers and horse advanced and took ground formerly held by Newcastle as he withdrew, apparently with a view to retiring altogether, as his forces torched the nearest villages and pulled out under cover of the smoke, south towards Durham.

The Covenanters' commanded men decided to charge their rearguard; however a snowstorm blew up, continuing for over an hour and obliterating all trace of the enemy. Before the Scots could find Newcastle the snow started to fall again, this time continuing all night. Leven's forces claimed that from intelligence received, during the two days that Newcastle's men lay in the fields, they suffered great losses, both of men and horses dying and many running away.

On Tuesday 12th the Scots set out for Durham, leaving two regiments to secure Sunderland. The Scots were by now in dire straits through lack of provisions, the Royalists having wasted and spoiled the surrounding country, and driven away all before them. Five barques sent from Scotland with provisions were lost – three sunk and two driven into the Tyne by storms and captured by the enemy; so that at times the whole army was on the point of starvation, having neither meat nor drink. They 'never had above twenty-four hours provisions for them.' Reports arriving in Aberdeen later that month advised that the army lying at Sunderland and spread across both sides of the Tyne was 'destroyed with great hunger and famine, soldiers dying daily'.

On the 13th, to extend the Scots quarters and to straighten the enemy, the Covenanters drew towards Durham, but after staying as long as the horse provision lasted, the main army, not wishing to risk losing their sea-base of Sunderland, or to give up a place of so great importance to them until it was better fortified, returned and quartered on the north side of the Wear towards Newcastle, during which march they saw no enemy.

On Thursday 14th the Scots at Newcastle and Leven's regiment at Elswick were reported as skirmishing with Royalist forces.

On Friday, the Marquis of Montrose joined Newcastle at Durham, while Covenanter operations against South Shields Fort began. At night, a Scots assault party attacked the fort on the south of the Tyne by Tynemouth Castle but were beaten back, reportedly with little loss. The Scots pondered the assault for a few days, fasted on the 19th and on Wednesday morning another party, not as strong as the first, assaulted the fort, the general going with them in person to encourage the men. Colonel Stewart, Colonel Lyle, Lieutenant Colonel Bruce and Lieutenant Colonel Johnston, with some lesser officers, led the party. The fort was very strong, the graffe (defensive ditch) in front of the defences being estimated as 12ft broad and eleven deep, the works above ground 3yd high with five iron pieces of ordnance in it, some taking nine pound ball and some more; a hundred soldiers, seventy musketeers and thirty pikemen. A local man, Captain Chapman, commanded the fort.

It was a very favourably positioned, defended on one side by the ordnance of Tynemouth Castle and on the other by a Dunkirk Frigate with ten cannon. Despite this, 140 Scots, armed only with swords and carrying bundles of straw and sticks to fill the ditch, set up scaling ladders (some of which did not reach the top of the fort as the ditch was not well enough filled) and fell on with their swords, followed by parties of musket and then of pike, marching up until they entered the ditch, where they disputed the matter for over an hour – during which time the defenders discharged twenty-eight cannon shot of musket balls or cut lead and iron. The Scots scaled the ladders and entered through the gun ports. The defenders behaved gallantly until matters came to exchanging sword strokes, at which point they fled and escaped in the dark to the waterside, where boats were waiting for them. The fort was taken with the reported loss of only nine men on the Scots part, plus wounded, while the defenders lost sixteen men, a lieutenant and five men taken prisoner. With the fort were captured the five pieces of iron ordnance, seven barrels of powder and seventy muskets along with their colours.

Lieutenant Colonel James Ballantyne of Leven's Lifeguard, hearing that the marquis's horse was at Chester-le-Street, charged into the town, managing to capture forty horse and their arms.

On Friday, 22 March, a Scots party and some keelmen and seamen were sent out to draw ships laden with coal and salt over to the Durham side of the Tyne.

The Battle of Boldon Hill

ALTHOUGH THE ROYALISTS HAD not been able to face Leven in the field so far, they had been very successful in their policy of laying waste to all the districts that the Scots depended on for food and fodder, to the extent that the Scots commissariat were now insisting on a change of quarters. It seemed that Leven was considering marching into the south of Durham and Yorkshire where supplies might be more

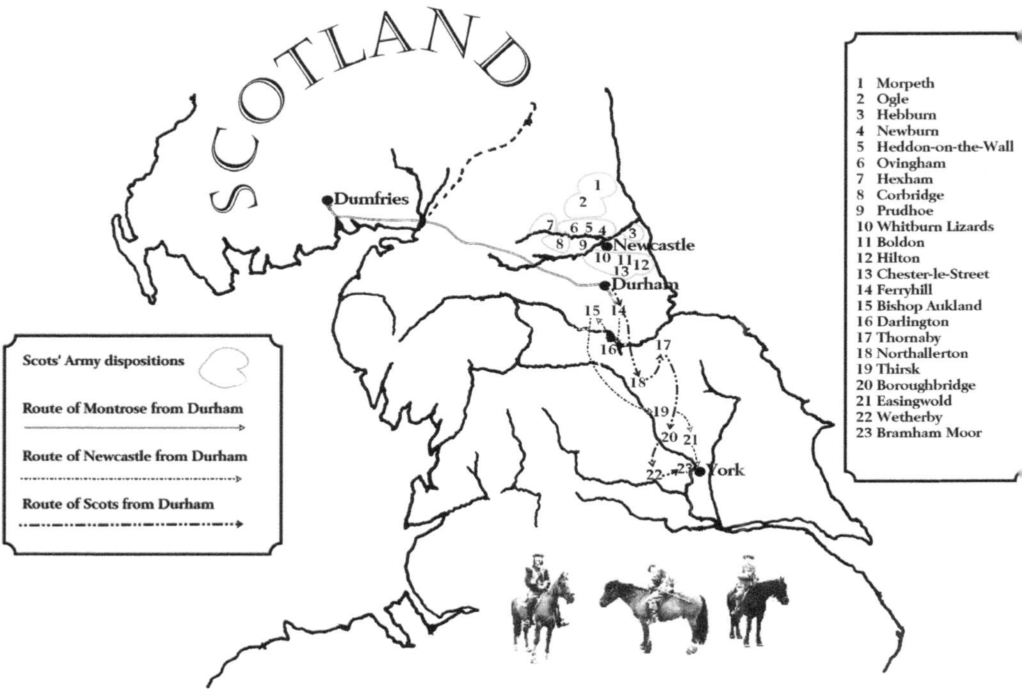

accessible; plus he would be in better contact with the English parliament's commanders. It was essential for the Royalists that any such joining of forces should be prevented; so Newcastle, whom Montrose had joined at Durham on the 15th, decided to risk an engagement.

On Saturday 23rd he drew his forces out of Durham and marched to Chester-le-Street, the next day taking up a position at Hilton, north of the Wear. The Scots positioned themselves at Whitburn Lizards (Cleadon Hill) between Newcastle and the sea to the east. The armies faced each other for most of the day until sometime between 3.00 p.m and 5.00 p.m. A Scot writes:

> On Sunday, March the 24th the enemy marched towards our quarters intending to have set upon us in Sermon time, and being a foggy day to have surprised us; their approach being discovered, a great part of the army was presently drawn together.
>
> The enemy sent down from Boldon Hill where they were drawn up, some commanded musquetiers to line the hedges betwixt them and us, and we did the like, for the armies could not join, the field between us being so full of hedges and ditches; our dragoons began the play, and then the musquetiers in the hedges upon both sides, our bodies of foot advancing at all quarters to the hedges, the enemies cannon discharging upon them an hour and a half with

> very small hurt. This service continued very hot, till after twelve of the clock at night. Many officers, who have been old soldiers, did affirm they had never seen so long and hot a service in the night time; there were divers killed on both sides, but the number of their slain did very far exceed ours as we understood by the dead bodies we found the next day upon their ground, beside the seven wagons' draught of dead and hurt men not able to walk, that the Constable of Boldon affirmed he saw carried away. The enemy quit their ground, where they left much of their powder, match and arms behind them; and retired to the hill where the body of the Army lay.

On Tuesday the 26th Newcastle withdrew to Durham en route to York. Montrose, who had been present at the engagement, set off for Scotland, entering the country in the second week of April, and continuing to Dumfries.

On Sunday, 31 March, the Scots broke camp at Sunderland and followed the Marquis of Newcastle at an unhurried rate, going first to Bruntfield Moorhouses.

On Monday, 1 April, they travelled by forced march to Easington Hill, midway between Hartlepool and Durham where they found reasonable quarters for their horse, and decided to stay until they made the enemy either fight or take flight. They stayed until the 8th and after fasting the day before moving off, the army marched to the Quarrington Hills, a mile or two south of Durham.

In March Sir Thomas Fairfax had been ordered north to join the Scots who were short of horse and not therefore able to make an impression on Newcastle's forces at Durham. Fairfax had 2,000 horse and dragoons. By this time English troops were often in rags, poorly equipped and in arrears of pay after two years of fighting – a practice previously alien to them as peaceable folk. Sir Thomas had proved himself a remarkable leader and a valiant commander of horse – he and his father successfully combating numerically superior Royalist forces in the north under Newcastle.

On his way north he had a notable victory at Selby, which helped shift the balance of morale between the Scots and the Royalist forces opposing them. The effect of the action at Selby was dramatic. As the Royalist Sir Henry Slingsby wrote, 'this proved a fatal blow to us … so it proved of consequence to ye parliament as ye very dawning of that day which brought prosperous success unto them.' Fairfax's assessment of the consequences of this action can be quoted:

> This good success put them into great distraction and fear at York, who speedily sent to the Earle of Newcastle to haste back thither, leaving the Scots who were reduced to great extremity, but now advance without delay after him.

The Scots had really been in a bad way. Slingsby wrote that the Scots might have been forced to retreat had it not been for Sir Thomas Fairfax's assistance in the timely arrival of the news of his beating and routing of the Royalist Yorkshire forces.

Sir Thomas' victory at Selby also immediately raised him to the first rank of generals of parliament in the opinion of Westminster, and the two houses marked the importance of his services by ordering a public thanksgiving for the victory.

This devastating news caused alarm in York, from where message after message was sent to the marquis to come at once to the rescue, as the main strength of their garrison was dispersed and the surrounding country open to the victorious Fairfaxes. When the news reached Durham, both Covenanter and Royalist armies immediately advanced into Yorkshire by forced marches. At midnight on the 10th, the Scots Major Ballantyne[45] with some commanded men, continuing his tactics of harrying the Royalist forces, is reported as having captured another twenty men including a captain, thirty horse, pistols and saddles.

Newcastle and his army raced for Darlington via Ferryhill ('Westward towards Bishops Auckland around which they rested that night') in the greatest anxiety very late on the night of Friday 12th or in the very early hours of Saturday morning, 'leaving his troublesome provision (baggage) behind him', the marquis taking no chances until he was safely within the walls of York.

Leven did not know of the marquis' departure until three in the afternoon and, his forces rejoicing to escape from the starvation and snowstorms of the country palatine, and without even taking the time to ransack the Royalists' deserted quarters, raised his leaguer from Quarrendon Hill, gave chase and, close on the Royalist force's heels, reached Ferryhill that night, by which time Newcastle had reached Darlington.

The next day the Scots marched off before the sun had risen and the advance guard reached Darlington before 7.00 a.m., while Newcastle's force was still in the process of quitting the town. A Scots major[46] and his party killed and wounded forty, captured horses, slew stragglers and took 2,000 merks[47] of silver plate, plus considerable cheese, pork and bread. They opted to stay there till nightfall.

The main army crossed the Wear that night and day, then marched on to Northallerton with Newcastle somewhere ahead of them. On Tuesday morning they marched to Thornaby, acquiring provisions from the towns and villages en-route.

Next day the Scots marched to Boroughbridge, which may suggest that, while the Royalists continued on the direct route to York via Thirsk and Easingwold, the Scots, perhaps sought to link up with the Fairfaxes whose army was in the Selby area and thus branched off westward.

On Thursday morning, the army marched to Wetherby and met up with Fairfax's troopers and dragooners. Lord Fairfax reviewed the army of the Earl of Leven on Bramham Moor.

When Newcastle arrived at York on 19 April, he found chaos and confusion; no governor, a defeated garrison and the townsfolk divided in their allegiances. He brought with him about 6,000 men to guard the walls and man the guns; among them his regiment of white-coats raised in the border lands, nicknamed Newcastle's 'lambs' from their dress. It has been claimed that the marquis, unable to get enough red cloth, took undyed cloth for this regiment, until he could get it dyed. But the men asked to be allowed to keep their coats undyed, promising to dye them in the blood of their enemies. Newcastle was seconded by two very able officers, General King, now Lord Eythin,[48] and Sir Thomas Glemham; but the poet laureate, Sir William Davenant, was a strange choice as general of the ordinance. The marquis himself supposedly cared more for poetry than for gunnery.

On the 20th the Scots rendezvoused at Tadcaster where some of Fairfax's troops joined them. From Sunday to Tuesday the Scots from Tadcaster and the rest of Fairfax's forces from Selby advanced on to York and, numbering some 20,000 men, took up positions around the city. The siege of York had begun.

3. York & Morpeth

At the commencement of the siege, the Scots camped at Middlethorpe and Bishopthorpe and blockaded the section of York, west of the river called Micklegate Ward; meanwhile, the Fairfaxes crossed the Ouse by a bridge of boats, and, quartering[49] their men in the villages of Fulford and Heslington, threatened the walls of York from the Ouse to Walm-gate bar. But their united forces were not sufficient to complete the blockade, so the north side of the city remained open for a fortnight more. By this time the Scots had lost over 4,000 men from their original 21,000 and now numbered 14,000 foot, 2,000 horse and 600 dragoons, many of which were scattered throughout Northumberland, pinned down in garrison and other duties.

On the night of the 22 April, all of Newcastle's horse broke out of York and fled, pursued so closely by Scottish and Fairfax's horse that they had to remove the staffs from the colours and throw them away. Sir Marmaduke Langdale with all his northern horse went to the king at Oxford, determined to return with Prince Rupert to relieve the siege. Captured Royalists told the Scots they got a mutchkin of beans, an ounce of butter, and a penny loaf each per day as Newcastle and General King had ordered the city searched and were rationing food.

Fairfax, accompanied by Lord Lindsay, was dispatched to the Earl of Manchester to ask him to co-operate in the siege of York with his army of the associated counties. He had just taken the city of Lincoln, and immediately agreed to join Leven and Fairfax.

At the beginning of May, Manchester would march via Thorne and Selby to Tadcaster, reaching the leaguer with 6,000 foot, 100 horse and twelve field pieces. He was to cross the Ouse at Poppleton on a bridge of boats that the Scots had built and, encamping about Clifton, complete the blockade of the city. The majority of his horse were to be stationed around Halifax to watch the Royalists in the west, and capture Walton house, with Sir Francis Wortley in it, on the same day Manchester's army arrived before York.

Each flank of the Scots besieging forces on the sector west of York rested on the banks of the River Ouse to the north and south of the city, across which they had built two pontoon bridges so communications could be maintained with Fairfax and Manchester's forces. Manchester's army included a regiment of dragoons which he was to place on his right flank at one of these boat bridges at Poppleton, over the Ouse between himself and the Scots. Most of his dragoons had been raised in Essex late the year before, with the intention that his companies should be filled by volunteers, but these not being forthcoming, the Essex committee had been forced to take pressed men to make up numbers. This background, along with examples of Manchester's dragoons reverting to infantrymen, suggests that their status was not regarded highly. In March 1644, shortly before his arrival at the York camp, only some of his dragoon companies were reasonably strong, while others were short of both men and horse – for example a Captain Miller's company consisted of only twenty men with horses and a further eighteen without. As a result of such deficiencies, a number of companies had been disbanded in April, and the dragoons re-organised into a regiment of five companies under Lieutenant-Colonel John Lilburne.[50]

The Siege of Morpeth

WHILE THESE EVENTS WERE unfolding, some way to the north, Captain James Somerville, who had been left garrison commander in Morpeth, believed that Leven had left him in this position with insufficient ammunition. To support the garrison of 500 men, Leven had left Colonel Michael Weldon's horse and some of Fraser's dragoons in nearby villages; otherwise the place was isolated. For three months Somerville had seen no enemy. Things were about to change. In mid April James Graham, Marquis of Montrose, had received a field command. The marquis, having headed into Scotland after the Battle of Hilton, had tried without success to rally the Royalists in the north and had now returned to Northumberland where Leven's withdrawal offered him the chance to do some useful service for Charles. Montrose marched to Newcastle and, about 10 May, he and Lord Crawford (who was later to be taken prisoner after the fall of Newcastle in October), led an expedition against Morpeth. Montrose had 2,000 English infantry, 500 English cavalry, and 200 mounted Scots nobles and gentry under his command.

The castle, defended by Somerville and a Captain John McCulloch, succeeded in repulsing the first attack.

Montrose sent for six guns from Newcastle, and sat down to besiege the place. He launched a further assault that was repelled with the loss of eight defenders. The siege continued for almost three weeks, during which time the Scottish cavalry under Weldon, aided by Fraser's dragoons, tried without success to relieve the castle, until the morning of 29 May when Somerville, out of stores, food and ammunition, and with his fortress crumbling around him, was obliged to surrender. During the siege the garrison inflicted significant casualties on the Royalists, while they themselves suffered the loss of a major, three captains, three lieutenants, four ensigns, two drummers and 180 soldiers killed or captured. Out of the original 500 strong garrison, '180 soldiers and half our Scottish foot soldiers were overcome about Morpeth where divers by the Banderiss [bandits] stripped out of their clothes and arms, and sent home naked'. They had expended 200 cannon shot during the siege. After the loss of the troops under his command, Somerville promised never to fight against Charles again.

On relinquishing the castle, the remnants of the garrison marched north to Edinburgh. In late June Somerville rejoined Leven's army outside York and was acquitted of any charge by a council of war.

Colonel Michael Weldon, in charge of the cavalry force that had attempted to relieve the garrison, was one of the few foreign colonels in the army. In autumn 1643 the English parliament had sent him to Scotland. There he decided to levy a horse regiment on his own charge. To aid him he selected a Scottish veteran of the continental war, Alexander Home, as his lieutenant colonel. The regiment of seven troops served under Leven as an advance element and later remained in north-east England to protect the Scots' line of supply. On 5 May the committee with the army ordered the regiment to Northumberland to take dragoons from Morpeth (Fraser's), slight Blyth's Neuk and protect the county from the Newcastle garrison. The execution of these orders engaged the regiment in a great deal of activity, from which it suffered notable losses. In mid June the regiment was quartered in Durham shire and probably remained quartered in northern England throughout most of 1645, while Fraser's regiment, after the fall of Morpeth, proceeded to the Scottish camp outside York.

Five months had passed since the coming of the Scots had been reported in London with such confident claims that Newcastle had fallen or would shortly fall to them. Yet the town's capture seemed no nearer. Leven was investing York. With Montrose at large in Northumberland, every day seemed to add to the difficulties that an assault on Newcastle would clearly involve. On the subject of Lord Callendar marching south from Scotland at the head of a supplementary army, Lord Lindsay wrote from York on 24 May to the Committee of Estates at Edinburgh, 'We entreat your lordships to delay no time in sending of those forces into England; for if it had been done in time, a few horsemen, with our foot forces there, and Colonel Weldon's regiment, might have been more than sufficient for the securing both these counties opposing the commission of array, and bringing the town of Newcastle to great straits, which we fear shall now become a work of greater difficulty to a stronger power.' Baillie noticed the same fact, 'The delay of Callendar's incoming so long has given time to the Marquis of Montrose to make havoc of the northern counties, which will make the siege of Newcastle the harder.' In early June both England and Scotland began to turn to the provision of men and money for this task. The Scots had commissioned Lord Callendar on 9 June to raise his army. His commission was supplemented on the 10th with definite instructions; 'You shall by all means endeavour to reduce and secure the town of Newcastle, castle of Tynemouth and all other places possessed by the enemy for the use of the king and parliament of England and make such use of the forces as may conduce most for these ends but with a special regard for the safety of the town of Sunderland.' On 20 June Sir Harry Vane reported from York that Callendar was expected at Blyth's Neuk on the 23rd. It was not however, until the 25th that Callendar began his march. Callendar's army numbered perhaps 8,000 and included the following units:

FOOT	CAVALRY
Earl of Callendar	Sr Frederick Hamilton's regt
Sr Mungo Campbell of Lawers' regt	Earl of Lanark's regt (horse & dragoons)
Master of Cranstoun's regiment	Viscount Montgomery's regt
Earl of Glencairn's regiment	Sr Mungo Campbell of Lawers' troop
Sir John Home of Aytoun's regiment	Lord Sinclair's troop
Viscount Kenmure's regiment	Routmaster Dundas's troop
Earl of Lanark's regiment	Routmaster Naismith's troop
Sir John Ruthven of Freelands' regt	Routmaster Hamilton's troop
Sir John Wauchope of Niddrie's regt	Routmaster Henry Drummond's troop
	Routmaster Elphinstone of Quarrell's troop
	Routmaster Douglas' troop
	College of Justice troop

This breakdown, translates into around 750 men per regiment of foot, 300 per regiment of horse and forty men per troop, compared to target figures of 1000, 400–480 and sixty respectively. This is perhaps an indication that recruitment was now becoming harder, which may also explain the lateness of the army progressing south.

Before attempting Newcastle, Callendar had to strengthen or regain certain positions around Newcastle which Montrose's activity in May had wholly or partially detached from parliament. On his march he re-captured Morpeth, which had fallen to Montrose in May. Crossing the Tyne at Newburn, Callendar passed on to secure the town of Sunderland. A plot for the betrayal of the town had recently been frustrated by the seamen of Sunderland who placed themselves under arms, planted cannon in position and, with the help of Colonel Charles Fairfax, had beaten back Montrose, Musgrave and others into Newcastle. For their 'Affection and Fidelity' the seamen were voted £200. About the same time, Sir John Marley in Newcastle had intrigued with Captain Thomas Rutherford 'of Ranfertlie' for the surrender of the fort at South Shields, which the Scots had held since March. Montrose had successfully assaulted it, but when Montrose retired before Colonel Fairfax into Newcastle, it would appear to have been regained by the Scots, and Rutherford, its commander, having treacherously surrendered it, had early in June been sentenced by a council of war for its betrayal.

Callendar, therefore, without halting before Newcastle, directed his march towards Sunderland. In July, he dispatched a letter from Birlington Leaguer to the Scottish Estates, and three days later wrote to inform them he was marching on to Sunderland. On the 24th he summoned Hartlepool, and after negotiation, Sir Edmund Carey and the garrison marched out at three o'clock the following afternoon. Stockton surrendered on the same date. Major Douglas and six companies of foot were placed as a garrison in Hartlepool while Stockton was left under the charge of a captain and 120 men.

The way was now clear to Newcastle. His forces already weakened by garrisons left in Hartlepool, Stockton, and probably Sunderland and Morpeth, a siege of Newcastle was beyond the capacity of Callendar's command. He could therefore only partially invest Newcastle, and anxiously await the arrival of the main army under Leven from York.

The Siege of York

At this time, York, spanning the river Ouse, is divided into four wards named after its four city gates: Mickle-gate on the west of the river, Bootham, Monk-gate, and Walm-gate on the east; and besides the Minster, contains twenty-one parishes, each with its church. The circumference of the walls is exactly 2 miles 5 furlongs and 76yd (4km), and there are four principal entrances, or 'bars', plus six postern gates. The Ouse flows through the town but forms no part of its defences, while its tributary, the Foss, skirts the city on the east and serves as a broad deep moat.

Coming from Tadcaster by the Great North Road, the city enters through famous old Mickle-gate bar, a stone gateway with high-embattled turrets, and closed by means of a massive iron chain and portcullis and a strong double wooden gate. A broad street leads from there to a bridge over the Ouse, and there are posterns near the river banks, where the wall comes down to them, called North-street Postern at the north end, and Skelder-gate Postern at the south. Although the west side of York contains six churches, a considerable area comprises gardens and open spaces. The Mickle-gate, running from the bar to the bridge, is still at this time a street of tall timber houses with projecting upper stories, and richly carved corners and portals; intersected by a street called Skelder-gate, with lanes leading down to the staiths or wharves on the river; while the Trinity and Friar's gardens occupy all the space near the walls. By the south wall is an ancient artificial mount called the Old Bailey, which remains to this day. South of the Mickle-gate is the parish of Bishop-hill, where the house of Lord Fairfax stands, with gardens and a courtyard, ornamented by a curious Roman carved altar on a pedestal.

The tide came up river as far as York, where the rise and fall averaged 2ft. The old bridge, built in 1566, had five arches, the centre one being 81ft (24.7m) span and

17ft (5.2m) high. There were several buildings on it – a chapel of St William (then used as a merchants' exchange), a council chamber of the city, and a debtors' prison.

The main part of the city – the three wards of Bootham, Monk-gate, and Walm-gate – was east of the river. At the south end, where the Foss meets the Ouse, was the castle, with the ancient fort called Clifford's Tower on its high artificial hill. From there, running parallel to the river, led a street called in its different parts, Castle-gate, Spurrier-gate, Conyng Street, and Lendal, with water lanes leading from it to the staiths or landing wharves. Conyng Street was the principal street of Old York, very narrow, with high wooden houses; and at its north end stood the guild-hall, a spacious room, supported by two rows of massive oak columns, each cut from a single tree. Parallel to Conyng Street, and passing through the centre of the city, was another thoroughfare leading from Bootham bar, the gateway opening on the great north road, across the river Foss, by a stone bridge of three arches to Walm-gate bar, which opened on the road to Hull. This street was called Peter-gate in its northern part, and Foss-gate and Walm-gate in its southern and divided York into two nearly equal parts. The two parallel lines were connected by Stone-gate, with its old timber houses, running from opposite the guild-hall in Conyng Street to the Minster-garth, and crossing Peter-gate; and Ouse-gate leading from the bridge, dividing Spurrier-gate from Castle-gate, opening into a wider space called the Pavement, where stood All-hallows Church with its beautiful lantern tower, and ending at Foss-gate. In the space between these four main lines, the central point of the city, were the open court called Thursday Market, and several small lanes and streets.

Beyond the northern walls, between the river and Bootham bar, were the precincts of the once great and wealthy Abbey of St Mary, the most important institution of its kind north of the Trent. In olden times the monks and citizens had hated each other bitterly, and the abbot had built a wall round the precincts to guard against sudden attacks. This wall, with the church of St Olave, now formed a sort of outwork, which was included in the city defences, though projecting beyond the old walls; and at the north-west angle, beyond Bootham bar, was St Mary's Tower, where all the records and charters of the suppressed monasteries, and other valuable documents, were deposited. The Abbey Church was in ruins, but on the site of the monastic buildings stood the manor house, which was the official residence for the presidents of the north. It was enlarged by James and beautified by Strafford, and had a large garden, a fine bowling green, and an orchard attached to it, under the walls.

The yard or garth surrounding York Minster, at the north-east corner of the city, was nearly three quarters of a mile in circumference, and was formerly separated from the streets by a wall with bars opening on Peter-gate. The old Deanery was on the south-east side of the minster garth. Sir Arthur Ingram's house, where Charles lived during his last visit to York, was to the north, with a large garden extending to the city walls; and that of Sir Henry Jenkins, built round a quadrangle, was

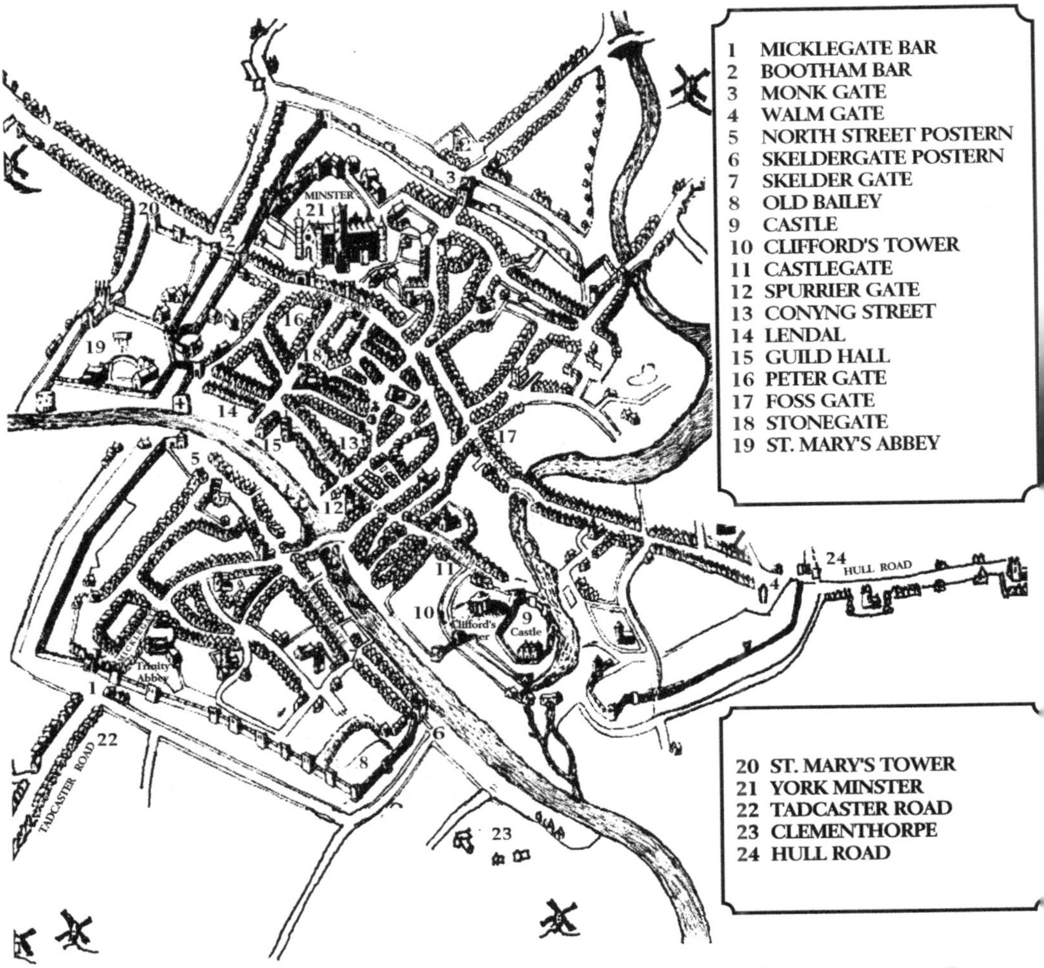
1 MICKLEGATE BAR
2 BOOTHAM BAR
3 MONK GATE
4 WALM GATE
5 NORTH STREET POSTERN
6 SKELDERGATE POSTERN
7 SKELDER GATE
8 OLD BAILEY
9 CASTLE
10 CLIFFORD'S TOWER
11 CASTLEGATE
12 SPURRIER GATE
13 CONYNG STREET
14 LENDAL
15 GUILD HALL
16 PETER GATE
17 FOSS GATE
18 STONEGATE
19 ST. MARY'S ABBEY
20 ST. MARY'S TOWER
21 YORK MINSTER
22 TADCASTER ROAD
23 CLEMENTHORPE
24 HULL ROAD
MINSTER
Castle
HULL ROAD
TADCASTER ROAD

the old college of St William on the east. Here Charles set up his printing press. The glorious old minster, with its three incomparable towers, rose high above the many steeples of the city, and offered a tempting mark to the besiegers.

Before the Civil War the suburbs of York beyond the city walls were considerable and extensive. Outside Mickle-gate, on the Tadcaster road, was a large stone building called St Thomas Hospital, formerly occupied by a religious guild, and beyond that was a street of houses leading to the Mount. Beyond Skelder-gate Postern was the hamlet of Clementhorpe, the property of the Fairfaxes.

Along the Hull road, beyond Walm-gate bar, were a street of houses, St Lawrence's Church, and the church and hospital of St Nicholas. A street led from Monk-gate bar to the other bridge over the Foss, and another street of good houses straggled along the north road from Bootham bar and St Mary's Tower.

Heavy guns were planted round the walls and on the bars; and two outlying forts, one beyond Mickle-gate bar and the other in Bishop's Fields, were garrisoned and armed. Clifford's Tower, in ruins in 1642, had by now been repaired by the Earl of Cumberland, a deep moat dug round it with a drawbridge, and a platform fixed on the top upon which Newcastle planted two demi-culverins and a saker. York had been well stored with salt meat and biscuits, and there was no shortage of beer and other liquor, but the price of all fresh vegetables soared. Each citizen had to support a certain number of soldiers according to his means, either to find them food or money to buy it; from which there was no escape, as the soldier knew the man that was appointed to pay him, whom, if he refused, was roughly laid hands on, along with anything he had.

The Besiegers

The Scottish troops under the Earl of Leven were particularly well officered, as almost all the lieutenant colonels had served on the continent, as had several of the colonels. Their line extended round Mickle-gate ward from the Ouse below Poppleton, to a point on the river above Bishopthorpe, each wing resting on a bridge of boats which was guarded by a regiment of dragoons (this would have had to have been Fraser's), and by which communications were maintained with the rest of the besiegers. The Scots were reported as being very expensive to maintain. One of the villages where they were quartered was Acaster Malbis, where the Scots wasted all the corn, and ate all the sheep, kine and swine, to the value of £2,000, obliging the unfortunate landlord, young Viscount Fairfax of Gilling, to forgive his Acaster tenants a whole year's rent in consequence of the visit.

The Earl of Manchester's troops of the associated counties[51] extended their line from the Ouse, along the manor house wall and St Mary's Tower to Bootham bar, and from there via Monk bar to the Foss.

Lord Manchester's second in command was Oliver Cromwell. His major-general was a Scotsman, named Laurence Crawford, son of Hew Crawford of Jordan Hill in Renfrewshire, who had served for many years under Gustavus Adolphus. He was described as a brave man, but self-sufficient and arrogant, and had already quarrelled bitterly with Cromwell.

The Fairfaxes, with their Yorkshire levies,[52] held the sector east of the city from Fulford in the south to the king's Fishpool on the river Foss in the north, taking in Foulforth and Heslington in a line from the Ouse, by Fisher-gate Postern and Walm-gate bar to the Red Tower, while their horse watched the two bridges over the Foss. Fairfax had about 1,200 horse around Durham and Sunderland.

Sir Thomas Fairfax had little to do during the siege. Newcastle had sent away most of his cavalry, and siege operations were essentially for infantrymen and engineers. Nevertheless, it was lucky for York that Sir Thomas was among the besiegers, his efforts tireless to prevent damage being done to the public buildings. Hildyard goes so far as to claim that Fairfax made it death for any soldier to level a gun against the minster. Any such order was beyond his authority, but there is no doubt that he used all his influence to get strict orders against damaging the minster issued by the other generals.

The three Generals – Leven, Fairfax, and Manchester – held independent commands; though Leven, as the senior and most experienced, usually received precedence by courtesy.

On the 16 May Leven sent 2,000 horse and dragoons to assist Manchester in his sector of the siege, north of the Scottish sector, on the other side of the Ouse.

The following day 160 horse fell in at Northallerton where some dragoons from the Scots' regiments lay. 'A sergeant, with some musketeers, beat them off, kill some, among whom a Lieutenant Colonel (perhaps Gerard Salvin of Colonel Tempest's regiment of foot), and take some.'

On Saturday, 1 June siege operations began. A heavy fire was opened on the besiegers from Clifford's Tower and from the city walls before they could get their guns into position.

On Wednesday, 5 June, Lord Fairfax completed a battery on the hill, by the side of the road to Heslington, where a windmill used to stand, and planted five guns on it, which laid down fire all afternoon on Walm-gate bar. The Scots assaulted and took the forts outside Mickle-gate, and Manchester captured the houses outside Bootham: allowing the besiegers to become firmly established in the suburbs, extending along all the main roads into York.

Having observed this, on the evening of the 6th the garrison sallied out, and set the whole of the suburbs on fire. Great but unsuccessful efforts were made by the besiegers to extinguish the fires, wishing to save the houses for their accommodation, and there was some hot skirmishing during this.

Meanwhile, Prince Rupert, having captured Stockport, Bolton and Liverpool in succession, was sweeping north through Lancashire, joined by Goring and Lucas as he advanced. He was to be at Skipton on 26 June and three days later stayed at Denton Hall, Ferdinando's house, where Thomas Fairfax had been born. A portrait in the house would remind him of the two Fairfaxes who had been killed in the Palatinate twenty-three years before, fighting for his parents, and he gave orders that the house was not to be touched. Next day he would be at Knaresborough.

On 7 June, the Scots attacked three Royalist gun emplacements to the south-west of the city, capturing two of them.

On the 8th, Newcastle, who had news that Prince Rupert was on his way north, tried to gain time by opening negotiations with the three generals. It was agreed that commissioners should be appointed; two by each of the besieging generals and five by the marquis, to treat for surrender. There was to be a ceasefire during the conference, extending to three hours before and after.[53]

A week later the commissioners met in a tent halfway between the city walls and the lines of the besiegers, with a secretary and a guard of musketeers on each side. They were unable to agree to terms, and the besiegers came to the conclusion that the negotiation was just a ploy to gain time, so it was broken off on the following day.

The three generals resumed operations. Lord Fairfax built huts for his men, as all the suburbs outside Walm-gate had been burnt. He planted two field guns in the street, and another on a place called the Dovecote, within a stone's throw of Walm-gate bar, opening a heavy fire (one ball killing a maid in Thursday Market; it also went into the house of Mr Clarke the writing master, cut the string by which some dried fish were hung to a rafter, and came down and knocked old Mrs Clarke under the table); he also commenced mining in two places.

The Scots battered the top of Mickle-gate bar down as low as the gate, and worked hard to mine beneath it, while the besieged countermined, but these operations were stopped by water.

Meanwhile Lord Manchester, to whom Lord Leven had sent 2,000 horse and dragoons the month before, was making progress against the wall round the manor house. He opened approaches towards St Mary's Tower, worked a mine under it, and raised a battery against that part of the wall behind which was the orchard. By Trinity Sunday, 16 June, all was ready; and early in the morning he opened fire and made a breach in the wall, which the besieged endeavoured to repair with sods of earth. At noon, during morning service in the minster, Major-General Crawford sprang the mine under St Mary's Tower and the building tottered and fell. 'The rubble formed an easy breach, and about five hundred assailants rushed the orchard, and then the bowling green; while another party got up the breach in the wall by scaling ladders, and entered the Manor House'. The alarm was immediately given, and the besieged hurried to the spot. Sir Philip Byron, leading a body of Royalists to the breach, was killed the moment he opened the doors into the bowling green; but Newcastle's white-coats, passing out of Lendal Postern and round the ruins of the abbey, occupied the orchard, and cut off the assailants' retreat. They were surrounded, but fought bravely until their powder was spent, then the remaining 200, of whom sixty were wounded, laid down their arms. The orchard, bowling green, and garden were scattered with dead bodies.

Sir Thomas Fairfax writes of General Crawford's conduct with some severity, and Crawford's own countryman, Principal Baillie, speaks of his foolish rashness and vanity. No notice was given to the other generals of the intention to spring the mine, so that there was no concerted attack, and Crawford brought the whole strength of the garrison upon himself. His ungenerous attempt to monopolise all the honour in the event of success was the immediate cause of the disaster. After this memorable assault the Royalist sentries, who seem to have conversed routinely from the walls with those of the parliament, had a joke which they were never tired of repeating: 'Who tried to steal the king's apples in the orchard, but was caught in the manor?'

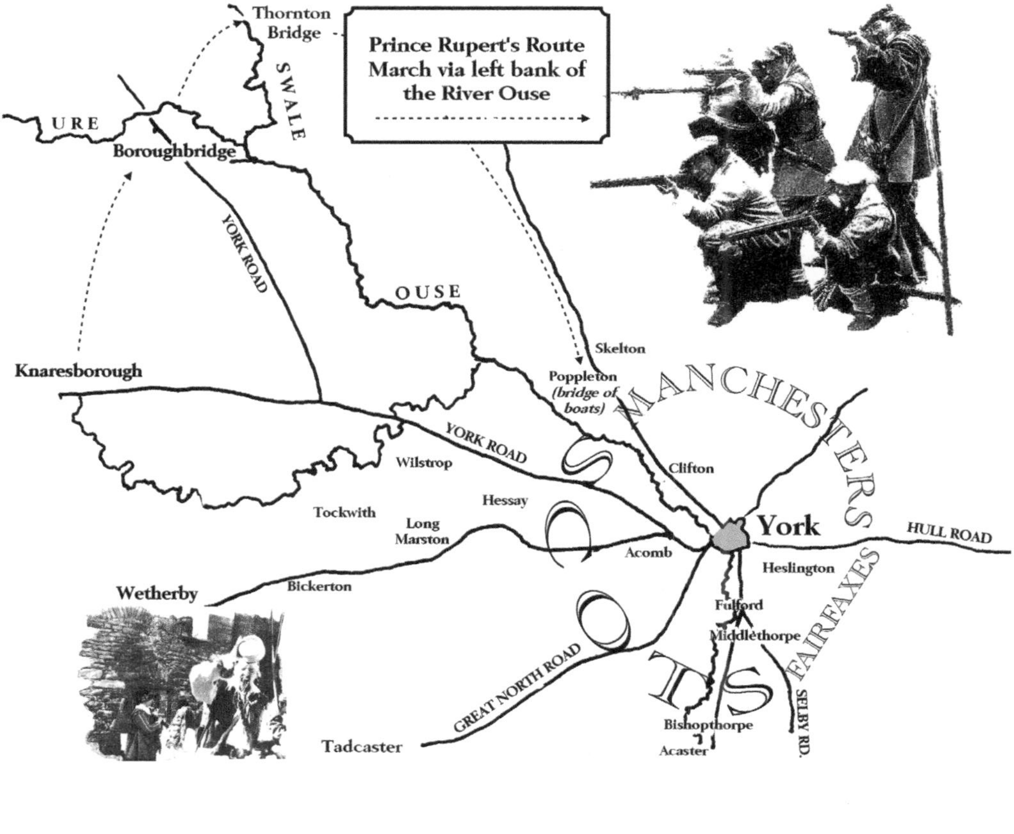

There were no more sallies or assaults until more than a week later when, on the 24th, a party of 600 Royalists rushed out of Monk bar at four o'clock in the morning, and attacked Manchester's lines at Bowdon bar, but were forced to retreat after some sharp fighting. 'Twenty Royalists are reported killed; along with two or three Manchesters hurt and killed.'

On 26 June 1644, Prince Rupert of the Rhine, marching to raise the siege with 20,000 men, including the horse under Sir Charles Lucas which had originally escaped from York, reached Skipton – a major battle now looked inevitable. He stayed there for three days preparing his men before setting out for York.

It was Sunday 30 June, when news arrived at the Allied camp that Prince Rupert was approaching and already at Boroughbridge, only 12 miles from York. The besieging generals decided to draw off their troops.

By the morning of 1 July Manchester and Fairfax had recrossed the Ouse by bridges of boats at Poppleton, and at Acomb above Bishopthorpe, and the whole army of the parliament was formed on the moor, in the Ainsty, 7 miles west of York, ready to dispute the advance of Rupert.

The blockade had been so well kept that no news of the besiegers' departure filtered beyond the city walls, but during Sunday night the Royalist sentries were surprised to find that their enemies had stopped talking to them, and did not answer any of their sparkling jokes. So at early dawn, Sir James Dudley, the commander at Walm-gate bar, sent out some troopers, who found that the besiegers' huts were abandoned. A party of Royalist horse then went out of Fisher-gate Postern, and rode down the Selby road to Fulford where half a troop of parliaments horse were guarding the passage by which Fairfax had just crossed the Ouse. And so the siege of York was raised.

4. Marston Moor, 2 July 1644, The Marshalling of the Armies

THE ALLIED ARMY, HAVING raised their siege of York, drew up across the high road from York to Boroughbridge and prepared to dispute the passage of Prince Rupert. They formed on Marston Moor; 7 miles from York, facing Skip Bridge over the Nidd, which the Royalists would have to cross if, as anticipated, they were to advance to raise the siege by the high road.

Early on 1 July, some Royalist cavalry advanced from Knaresborough and appeared on the moor, and the allies prepared for battle. However, Rupert had, instead of advancing down the high road over Skip Bridge to York, made a 22 mile (35 km) flanking march to the north-east with his main body, crossing the River Ure at Boroughbridge and the River Swale at Thornton Bridge. These two rivers merge to form the River Ouse, which Rupert had successfully put between himself and the Allied armies, avoiding an encounter. When the Earl of Manchester raised the siege he left behind the regiment of dragoons under Lieutenant Colonel John Lilburne to guard the bridge of boats over the Ouse in the Clifton/Poppleton area a few miles north of York. This regiment of five companies was not included in a muster of the rest of Manchester's army in the summer of 1644, but in January 1645 the regiment, which had probably been made up to around 100 men per company by the forced introduction of pressed men at its re-organisation in April, was by that point so reduced that it listed only 263 men. Disease and desertion may have taken their toll, but the task given to them and subsequent failure at the Poppleton bridge of boats to repulse Rupert, who was to make use of the bridge to transport his army across to Marston Moor; the regiment's further participation in the battle the following day, and Lilburne's own account of his men's service – 'I and my regiment of dragoons were constantly quartered in the van of the whole army; always nigh the enemies garrisons, where constantly in a manner we fought both for horsemeat and man's meat or else with a great deal of vigilance stood upon our guard' – may suggest a higher casualty rate amongst them than amongst the cavalry or infantry within the Eastern Association Army.[54]

At this river crossing the existence of some sort of defence work, at least on the south-west Poppleton/Holgate side, is implied by the York Corporation Housebook, which records that in May 1645 orders were given to demolish 'the work at the brick kilns in or near Holgate fields'. Brick Kiln Bridge is the name of the bridge that carries the modern Salisbury Road over Holgate Beck near Acomb Landing.

On the analogy of seventeenth-century military practice in general, and of the Newark defences in particular, there is a strong argument that in this western sector of the original city outworks the various sconces, batteries, emplacements etc. were connected by a series of trenches or similar defensive works. There are hints of these in sources from around that time. Defoe's 'the lines and bastions and demolished fortifications' and 'old additional works' may refer to these, while the Housebook entry – 'the work in Holgate and the breastwork in Bishopfields' – implies more than just a redoubt to Holgate Hill.

Later that day, having defeated Lilburne's dragoons, Rupert posted camp for the night in Caltres forest 3 miles north-west of York. His fast, flanking march on 1 July remains arguably one of the boldest, best-executed manoeuvres in the history of warfare.[55] By that evening, he stood in a position to relieve York, join its defenders and then offer battle to the shocked Allies lying 5 miles away at Marston. Rupert's cavalry cleared the road into York and established pickets across the eastern edge of the moor to maintain reconnaissance. Sending Goring into the city with orders for Newcastle to march to the moor early next morning, Rupert spent the night in his army camp.

The pontoon at Poppleton had been the only crossing available to the Allies above another bridge of boats, upon which the Scots besiegers had their right wing, at Acaster Malbis, 5 miles (8 km) south of York, and its capture prevented the Allies crossing the Ouse to engage Rupert.

While the relief was opportune, the arrival of the prince was not particularly welcome to the Marquis of Newcastle, who had up to that point exercised vice-regal powers in the region, with authority to create knights and to coin money. The marquis was fifty, and his pride must have revolted at becoming second in command to a young German prince-adventurer who was not yet twenty-five. Newcastle's advice was not to give battle to the Allies, but to let them retreat or at least to wait for the arrival of Colonel Clavering, who was marching from Northumberland with 2,000 reinforcements. But Rupert declared that he had positive orders from the king to fight at all hazards, and that fight he would. He said that he had a letter to this effect, but did not show it, and the letter does not support his claim. It urges him to relieve York at all hazards, even if he has to fight a battle, but does not order him to fight if he can relieve York without that risk. Newcastle, however, moodily expressed his readiness to obey the prince; and so the night passed, and the morning of Tuesday dawned.

The Allies waited on the moor all Monday, observed the party of Royalist horse which crossed Skip Bridge, and reconnoitred them for a short time; but it soon became clear that the main body had avoided an encounter and was on the opposite side of the Ouse. Towards night the Allied army marched to the village of Long Marston, where it made its headquarters, very few men being able to find either food or lodging. The horse camped all night on Hessay Moor. They all knew that a battle was coming. But the minds of some ordinary Yorkshire countrymen were on other things. An officer on reconnaissance duty nearby encountered a labourer and asked him whether he was for king or parliament. 'Be them two fallen out then?' was the reply. Within twenty-four hours even this yokel would have been aware that there had been a difference of opinion.

The following morning a party of Royalist cavalry appeared briefly, then wheeled out of sight again, creating the suspicion that Rupert was marching to Tadcaster to cut off the Allies' route of withdrawal. A council of war was held. The English commanders wanted to commit to battle; while the Scots were for withdrawing south towards Cawood and Tadcaster to gain time and a more advantageous position; the opinion of the veteran Earl of Leven prevailed. The foot and artillery marched towards Tadcaster, by Wighill and Healaugh, while the horse of the three armies, under Sir Thomas Fairfax, David Leslie – including Fraser's dragoons – and Oliver Cromwell remained on the rising ground between Tockwith and Marston, to bring up the rear.

Soon, however, parties of the enemy were observed arriving on the moor in increasing numbers as the morning progressed, and before long there was no doubt that, having left the regiments of Bellasis, Glemham and Slingsby in York, the prince, with the whole Royalist army, was in full march to the moor, in pursuit of the Allies. It seems that some of his forces had crossed the Ouse at the bridge of boats at Poppleton overnight. At noon Sir Thomas sent an urgent dispatch to Lord Leven, reporting that the enemy was in strength on the moor, but that he hoped, having the advantage of the ground, to hold his own with the cavalry until the foot and artillery could return. The Scots were already nearly at Tadcaster, 5 miles south of Long Marston, and Manchester's foot between Bilton and Healaugh.

The whole army was ordered back at all speed but, the Scots Army, having made such good time on the march to Tadcaster, were not present when the Parliamentarians reformed on the moor for the second time. This wasn't the disaster it might have been, as it had taken some time for the Royalist commanders to remove the looters from the earthworks around York, where a wealth of Parliamentarian baggage (reputedly including 4,000 shoes) had been left behind when the siege of York was raised. Once the garrison was formed up, they refused to march to the moor until they got their long-awaited pay sorted out. So it was two o'clock on that summer's day that the Allied army was posted between Tockwith and Marston, and the entire north moor occupied by the king's forces.

These were the two largest forces that had faced one another on English soil since the Wars of the Roses. Rupert with his army of 8,000 foot and 6,500 horse, supplemented by 4,500 foot and 300 horse of the York garrison, making a total of 19,300, less the regiments of Bellasis, Glemham and Slingsby's left in the city;

against the larger forces of the Allies – the Scots and Yorkshires making 16,000 foot and 4,000 horse, Manchester's another 6,000 foot and 100 horse – a total of over 26,000 men at arms. This battle arguably decided the fate of the war, so requires a detailed study.

Most of the western half of the land between Wetherby and York was moorland, overgrown in places with gorse, its various areas called Monkton, Hessay, Tockwith, and Marston Moor. The Netherby road, after passing through Acomb and Rufforth villages, crossed Long Marston and continued west, by Bilton and Bickerton, to Wetherby. Long Marston was a village of brick and thatch cottages, built along the road which crossed the high road to Wetherby, and extended for a mile and a half, with gardens and small enclosures behind the cottages. It was a mile and a half from its west end to the hamlet of Tockwith – the road running along a gentle slope rising to the south. Going west to Tockwith, the hill to the left was unenclosed arable land under crops of wheat and rye. The highest part, where there was a clump of trees, was a mile south of the road. This hill behind Long Marston formed the watershed of the Ainsty, the drainage to the south finding its way, by Catterton Beck, to the Wharfe, and the streams flowing north across the moor – such as the Foss and White Syke Beck – emptying into the Nidd and Ouse. To Wilstrop Wood, on the other side of Marston Moor, the slope was a foot in 35yd or a 1/95 gradient – a very easy incline, but such as it was, favouring the Allies. Just west of Long Marston, Atterwith Lane branched right to the village of Hessay. A quarter of a mile further on was another lane called Moor Lane, crossing the moor to the Boroughbridge road. For the first three quarters of a mile it had ditches and hedges on either side, but then came out on to open heath; the space between these two lanes covered with gorse. Where the hedges stopped was the convergence of four lanes – crossing Moor Lane to the right and left, one going to Hessay, and one to a square enclosure in the middle of the moor, with a ditch round it, called White Syke Close – to be the centre of the battlefield. A quarter of a mile north was an extensive plantation called Wilstrop Wood, forming the northern edge of the Royalist position. The moor was quite open, except at White Syke Close, and the area of the battle extended a mile and a half west from Long Marston to Tockwith, and three quarters of a mile north from the ditch to Wilstrop Wood. A quarter of a mile before reaching Tockwith a lane turned left to Bilton, and at the angle this created there was a large field called Bilton Bream, with a rabbit warren on the other side of the lane. Bilton Bream bordered the cornfields of Marston Hill. There were small gardens and enclosures behind the cottages at Tockwith. Syke Beck, a little stream or drain, flowed down to them from Bilton on its way to the Nidd, receiving a ditch extending between Tockwith and Marston, which divided the arable land on the hill from the unenclosed moor. This deep, wide ditch, with a hedge along its southern side,[56] formed an important feature in the battle. On that warm July day the corn was ripening, and the hedges were well adapted for concealing and providing shelter for musketeers.

As soon as the Allied army had returned to Marston fields, the Earl of Leven, to whom the place of honour was conceded by the other generals, proceeded to marshal the troops for the battle. Alexander Leslie, Lord Leven, was immensely experienced in the art of war, with a European reputation – he had fought since 1605 for Charles IX and the King of Sweden, Gustavus Adolphus, against Wallenstein and the Imperialists all over Europe. Gustavus had a very high opinion of his military capacity; but he appears to have been a man of no originality, and does not seem to have adopted any of the innovations even of his own master Gustavus. The architect of many victories, this little 'crooked' and surprisingly modest man, at sixty-two, was the oldest of the commanders on either side.

Leven had with him nine Scottish foot regiments of twenty companies each, about 9,000 men in all; and he selected four of these to form his centre or 'battle', the rest serving as a reserve. He drew them up in solid squares or tertias, the pikemen in the centre and the musketeers on either flank, rather than the more modern system of a reduced number of ranks which would provide a greater and more effective frontage to the enemy, but his reason may have been the limited space at his disposal along which to form his line of battle. On the right was the Fife regiment, commanded by Lord Lindsay, a staunch and uncompromising Covenanter. Next came the regiment of Mid Lothian, under Lord Maitland, then a tall red-haired young man of twenty-eight, with a tongue too big for his mouth, who afterwards, as Duke of Lauderdale, achieved infamous notoriety. The third regiment was formed of men of Kyle and Carrick, led by John Kennedy, Earl of Cassillis, 'the grave and solemn earl,' as he was called, a zealous Presbyterian, and a virtuous God-fearing man. The fourth regiment, on the left, was recruited in Annandale, and commanded by William Douglas of Kelhead, a grandson of the Earl of Queensbury. This brigade of four regiments forming the 'battle' was under the command of Lieutenant-General David Baillie, a brave old officer who had served in the Low Countries. Three regiments of Scots foot were formed up in the rear as a reserve, commanded by General Lumsden, another experienced officer who had seen service overseas. They consisted of the men of Glasgow, under the Earl of Loudoun, those of Strathearn under James Elphinston and another Fife regiment under the Earl of Dunfermline.

Manchester's army of the associated counties was stationed on the left. His foot consisted of a brigade commanded by Major-General Laurence Crawford, 'a headlong audacious fighter of loose loud tongues as Mr Carlyle calls him', who had been responsible for the precipitate blowing up of St Mary's Tower, and the subsequent great and useless bloodshed in the manor house orchard. The brigade, numbering 3,000 men, consisted of three regiments, led by Colonels Russell, Montague, and Pickering.

The Yorkshire men of Lord Fairfax, also about 3,000 men, formed the right centre. Sir William Fairfax of Steeton commanded the brigade, with three colonels under him: John Bright of Badsworth, Needham, who fought at Selby, and Forbes, hero of Leeds Bridge. To the rear were stationed the two remaining Scots regiments in reserve, being the force recruited in the city of Edinburgh, and led by Colonel Rae; and the men of Tweeddale, under the Earl of Buccleuch, then only 18 years old. The whole of the Scots foot regiments had experienced lieutenant colonels and majors who had served in Germany or the Low Countries, except that of Lord Cassillis, though none of the lords who commanded them had seen service out of Scotland.

The cavalry was, according to the established rule of the day, formed on the wings. The left wing consisted of Manchester's horse of thirty-eight troops (about 2,280 men), under Lieutenant-General Oliver Cromwell, three regiments of Scots horse, containing twenty-four troops (1,440 men), led by Major-General David Leslie, and the Scots dragoons on the extreme left under Colonel Frizell (Fraser), with William Crawford of Nether Skeldon as his lieutenant-colonel. The dragoons numbered about 400 men, in eight troops. Consequently the whole cavalry of the left wing consisted of 4,200 men, in seventy troops. David Leslie (no relation of Leven and whom Fairfax calls 'Major-General Lashley'), who, with Cromwell, commanded the left wing, was a son of Patrick Leslie, Commendator of Lindores and grandson of the Earl of Rothes. He had served overseas, had risen to be a colonel of horse under Gustavus Adolphus, and was an able and dashing cavalry officer. Sir Thomas Fairfax commanded the right wing of horse. It consisted of his own faithful old regiment of 500 men in five troops; of some regiments composed predominantly of raw Lancashire recruits under Colonel John Lambert, who commanded Fairfax's second line consisting of 2,200 sabres in fifty-three troops; and of three Scots cavalry regiments: the Lancers of Ayrshire, under the 53-year-old Earl of Eglinton, nicknamed 'Grey Steel' from his intrepid courage; the second under William Lord Ramsey of Dalhousie; and the third led by Lord Balgonie, Leven's eldest son.[57] The three Scots regiments numbered about 1,320 men in twenty-two troops; so that the whole right wing consisted of about 4,220 horse.

Leven found the whole moor occupied by the enemy up to the ditch, so was obliged to form his line of battle in the fields some quarter of a mile south of it,[58] where the height of the corn, with some showers of rain, caused some inconvenience to the forming up of the regiments. Fairfax's right wing was opposite the gorse-covered part of the moor between Atterwith and Moor Lanes, with his extreme right resting on the houses of Long Marston; while the Yorkshire foot brigade was just facing the end of Moor Lane. The left wing was formed on Bilton Bream and the rabbit warren, with the Scots dragoons on its extreme left, almost in Tockwith Street. The artillery, commanded by Sir Alexander Hamilton, was brought to the front while the army was forming its order of battle. The whole Allied force therefore numbered over 23,000 men; 15,000 foot and almost 9,000 horse, as well as gunners. The baggage was placed under a guard round the clump on the hilltop.

The Royalists, meanwhile, were just as late in getting into position on the moor itself; not only was part of Rupert's foot on the other side of the Ouse, and had to be brought across at Poppleton, but there was great trouble in persuading some of the regiments of Newcastle's garrison to come out of York at all. Old Fuller's excuse for them is that 'soldiers newly relieved from a nine weeks' siege will a little indulge themselves,' but it appears, from Mr Trevor's account, that they were in a raging mutiny for their pay, and that both Rupert and Newcastle were 'playing the orators' to them all morning to induce them to join their comrades, which at last they reluctantly agreed to do. Another disadvantage under which the Royalists laboured was that their nominal commander was an 'incapable self-sufficient boy'; that they had no experienced officer to form their line of battle, and that the commanders of the different divisions were forced to draw up their units without any general plan to work to, or any one head to arrange and organise the whole.

Lieutenant-General King, the Marquis of Newcastle's right-hand man, appears to have commanded in the Royalist centre, but was very late in arriving on the field from York with about three quarters of Newcastle's foot (possibly as late as five o'clock). He drew up his brigade under Major-General Porter to face the four regiments of Scots forming the 'battle' of the Allied army. Rupert's regiment of foot, wearing blue coats and commanded by Colonel O'Neil, fronted Manchester's brigade of infantry; and Newcastle's white-coats, when they arrived, formed up in the second rank behind the centre of the Royalist lines across Moor Lane and faced Sir William Fairfax's brigade. Rupert, upon seeing the white-coats eventually arrive, noticed that they were 'all drunk'.[59] Some reserves, consisting of Irish foot under Major-General Tilliers and Lord Bellasis and wearing green coats, plus a body of men called the 'Blue Regiment,' were in the rear, near Wilstrop Wood.

The Royalist right wing of horse was commanded by Prince Rupert in person, three brigades consisting of 5,000 men of Rupert's own Lifeguards, led by Sir Richard Crane, a Norfolk man who had served with the prince since his first skirmish at Worcester in 1642; the Newark and Irish horse under 'that most unlucky and imprudent officer', Lord Byron; and a body of cavalry led by young Lord Grandison.

The left wing of horse, facing Sir Thomas Fairfax, also numbered about 5,000 men, and was commanded by 'that daring worthless villain' Goring, with Sir Charles Lucas in charge of his second line and Sir Marmaduke Langdale among his officers. In drawing a comparison between Wilmot and Goring, Lord Clarendon says that both drank to excess, but while Wilmot kept sober in action, Goring put no restraint upon himself at any time. So it is fair to suppose that Goring was half drunk, and, while ready to lead a wild charge, not necessarily capable of drawing up his troops or of performing the duties of a general. Amongst his command, the northern horse were battle-hardened and experienced but had a bad reputation amongst the godly, for 'they carried along with them many strumpets ... those they made use of in places where they lay; in a very uncivil and unbecoming way'.[60] Amongst their officers was the terrifying female Captain Frances Dalyell, the illegitimate daughter of an earl, who rode under the ominous standard of a hanged man.[61] Goring's second in command was Sir William Urry, a Scotsman and mercenary soldier of fortune, but an excellent cavalry officer who had a good deal of experience abroad. At the beginning of the Civil War he had joined parliament and did important service on that side at Edgehill. But, believing that the Houses of Parliament did not value him at the rate he set on himself – no easy matter, Clarendon asserts – he went over to the king at Oxford, betrayed all their plans, and was knighted for his villainy. In the autumn after Marston Moor he tired of the king's service, deserted to parliament again, and told Lord Manchester all Charles's plans. Finally he changed sides a third time, joining forces with Montrose in 1649, and was hanged at last. He was 'a licentious unprincipled scoundrel', but a very able and intelligent officer in the field. The horse of the Marquis of Newcastle was also in the Royalist left wing under Goring, and was commanded by Sir Charles Lucas.

Sir William Urry had served under Gustavus Adolphus and, among the generals of either side, he alone adopted one of the favourite innovations of that great master of the art of war, with very notable success. The king of Sweden had devised the technique of placing musketeers in the intervals between the troops of horse and on their flanks, especially when acting against lancers, with the object of checking a hostile charge and doing execution among the ranks of soldiers whose cuirasses were proof against pistol but not against musket-balls. Urry formed the left wing of the Royalist army on this principle, receiving some commanded bodies of infantry from Porter's brigade for the purpose. But the English soldiers of these days hated all new foreign fashions. One of the regiments under Urry's command was 'the king's old horse,' and the troopers declared they had always charged together as a whole regiment, and understood no other system. There were even whispers of treachery and foul play, and hints that there must be some evil design in this breaking the horse up into small bodies, which, in soldiers who knew Urry's history and had probably never heard of Gustavus Adolphus, was not altogether unnatural.

There were nearly 50,000 men waiting for the signal to join battle, and a soldier could not easily distinguish a Parliamentarian from a Royalist officer (at Naseby Prince Rupert had been mistaken at one point for Sir Thomas Fairfax), so it was necessary to have some means of identification. The Allies had chosen to wear a white handkerchief or piece of paper in their hats, and the Royalist sign was the absence of bands or feathers. The password of the Royalists was 'God and the King'; that of the Allies, 'God with us'.

Sir Thomas Glemham remained in command at York with his own regiment, that of Lord Bellasis, and the city bands, of which Slingsby was colonel; but both Lord Bellasis and Sir Henry Slingsby, like the true and brave knights they were, went out themselves to the moor to do battle for their cause.

The Royalist foot had possession of the line of the great ditch before Leven could bring his men to the front, and they not only lined it with musketeers, but planted several cannon along its edge; so that, as Cromwell's scout-master remarks, 'their foot was close to our noses'. The brave Colonel John Russell commanded this 'forlorn hope' of Royalist musketeers. Rupert had twenty-five pieces of ordinance, and those weapons not used at the ditch were placed in a battery thrown up on the Royalist extreme right.

Imagine these two great armies drawn up in battle array; a great field of rye running down to the road and a few hundred paces north, a deep ditch all that separated the lines of horsemen, their breastplates glittering in the sun; the mass of pikes, and the hundreds of fluttering pennons of all shapes and colours, including the standard of Prince Rupert, with its red cross, and nearly 5yd long.

Marston Moor – The Battle

WHILE THE GENERALS WERE still marshalling their armies, a little while after two o'clock, Sir Alexander Hamilton gave fire with his artillery pieces, which was returned by the Royalist drakes and demi-culverins along the ditch. Munitions varied from 15lb ball to wooden boxes filled with nails, and musket balls which exploded upon impact, one hitting a Catholic Royalist gentleman, Thomas Danby, so he was 'cut off by the midst of his body'.[62] One cannon shot struck Cromwell's nephew on the leg, and killed his horse.

The prince found it was so late when he reached the moor, after his oratorical labours at York, that he determined not to fight that night, and the line of the ditch was strengthened with guns to defend his foot from attack until morning.

Then an observant Royalist commander spotted a most important post unoccupied, which both flanked the ditch and would give the advantage of sun and wind. It seems to have been a rising ground behind the cottages at Tockwith, just where the ditch joined Syke Beck, flowing from Bilton. A regiment of Royalist red-coated musketeers and a party of horse took ground to the Royalist right, in an effort to occupy this position, called by some the 'rye-hill,' which would have allowed them to pour in a flanking fire when the Allies attempted to storm the ditch. But Leven spotted this move and ordered Colonel Fraser, with his regiment of dragoons, to beat off the Royalist detachment, and occupy the vantage point themselves, which they duly did and deployed to the left of the Allied line (in a position perpendicular to the line) in the cross-ditch at Syke Beck.

Then, at about five in the afternoon, there was a silence – no movement on either side; a fearful ominous pause, while rain showers swept over the ground. The tension of such silence, at such a moment, was more than the men could endure, and Sir Henry Slingsby describes how before the battle commenced the roundheads in Marston cornfield fell to singing psalms. Rupert 'that bloody plunderer', in order 'to seem religious', had a sermon preached before him and his army. His chaplain took the text out of Joshua xxii, 22: 'The Lord God of gods, He knoweth, and Israel shall know; if it be in rebellion or if in transgression against the Lord, save us not this day'.

It was round about this time that William Cavendish, Marquis of Newcastle, with his brother Charles Cavendish, 'a man of the noblest and largest mind, though the least and most inconvenient body that lived,' came out to the moor late in the afternoon in a coach-and-six, in an exceptionally bad humour. He found Prince Rupert behind their lines where the officers' coaches were drawn up and asked the prince if he still intended to take on the Parliamentarian army, as the numbers were stacked against them and they had now lost the element of surprise. The prince in answer showed Newcastle his drafted order of battle which elicited the disapproval of the experienced General King, who was also present, and his exclamation that it was all very well on paper but there was no such thing in the field. King considered the Royalist army too close to the enemy and in a disadvantageous location, and warned Rupert not to be impetuous, declaring, 'Sir, your forwardness lost us the day in Germany, where you yourself were taken prisoner.'[63] Yet the warning of the siege-weary officer against the plan made no difference to the prince who stated, 'We will charge them tomorrow morning'.[64] But such matters were not in Rupert's control, and the leaders of the opposing army were resolute that, 'with the help of God, there should be a battle that night.'

After this exchange, the prince was soon 'set upon the earth at meat, a pretty distance from his troops and many of the horsemen dismounted and laid on the ground, with their horses in their hands.'[65] Newcastle, therefore, returned to his coach and was heard to call for a pipe and tobacco.[66]

***

Leven had hoped that the Royalists would advance to attack him, as the greatest risk would be on the army that attempted to take the ditch, disrupting and confusing its line. But there was no indication that the enemy intended to do this; there are even rumours that a Scottish officer from the Parliamentarian army had slipped in among Prince Rupert's horse and returned with the intelligence that the Royalists intended to wait until morning to attack. So Leven resolved, by the help of God, to charge them. It was seven o'clock when the order for a general advance was sounded, but a 'summer's evening is as long as a winter's day,' and he considered there was time yet to join battle before night fell, and even then a harvest moon would give enough light for them to complete their work.

The Allied line came down through the corn in the bravest order, the solid squares of foot and masses of cavalry looking like so many thick clouds. They joined battle along the ditch and the previous silence was now replaced by the deafening noise of shouts, fire and steel. The Royalists were forced back at all points. Manchester's foot, led on by General Crawford, drove the enemy out of the part of the ditch in their front with some slaughter, capturing four drakes. While the armies were still marshalling their forces, some of Prince Rupert's cavalry advanced and tried to gain the ground south-east of Tockwith. On the right of Prince Rupert's position was the line of Syke Beck – the cross ditch where he had attempted to post a body of musketeers. 'Opposite to them on the parliamentary left there were Colonel Hugh Fraser's dragoons – said to be one of the best regiments in the Scottish army.' When the battle had begun, the dragoons had prepared the way for the advance of Cromwell's horse by driving these musketeers out of the cross ditch and, 'By the good management of Col. Frizell, they acted their part so well that at the first assault they beat the enemy from the ditch, and shortly after killed a great many'. Afterwards the dragoons drove them back in the direction of York, securing the location for the Allies' left wing body of horse, and as the battle commenced in earnest, the dragoons cleared the ditch in front of Cromwell's horse, which permitted the parliament horse to charge and rout the Royalist horse. This enabled the main battle of Scots foot to pass the barrier with little opposition. Sir William Fairfax also, on the right centre, with his Yorkshire foot, beat the enemy from the hedge to his front, capturing a demi-culverin and two drakes, and began to lead his men up Moor Lane.

The Allies had now carried the ditch and gained a position on the moor along the whole line. The Royalist musketeers in the ditch having fallen back, battle continued on a new line, nearly as far north as White Syke Close, and Fraser's regiment was able to rest briefly before further engagement.

Both wings had delivered their charges: on the parliament left David Leslie and Cromwell's horse fell on the Newark horse under Lord Byron close along the ditch, and, after some sharp fighting, routed and dispersed them. But as Byron's horse opened to right and left, the main body of the Royalist wing, consisting of Rupert's Lifeguards and Grandison's regiment, appeared in the gap, ready to charge, a few hundred yards across the moor. At this point it is reported that a problem of some sort occurred in the ranks of the parliament horse. Manchester's horse under Cromwell, until now in the vanguard and making good ground, encountered mounting resistance from Byron's horse and their advance stalled. 'They stood at sword's point a pretty while, hacking one another.' Major-General Laurence Crawford, leading Manchester's brigade of foot on Cromwell's right, stated that he came up to the cavalry in a great passion, reviled them for poltroons and cowards, and asked them if they would stand still and see the day lost. Cromwell, as Crawford alleges, came forward and answered that he was wounded and unable to charge, so Crawford had him led off the field to Tockwith to recover and have his wound dressed, and took command himself. William Crawford of Skeldon (no relation, but Hugh Fraser's second in command) who was on Cromwell's left with the dragoons, declared on oath after the battle that Cromwell got a little wound in the back of the neck, which made him absent himself from the battle, and that his troopers were led on by David Leslie. Sir Adam Hepburn, Lord of Humbee, the Commissary-General of the Scottish Army, also asserted that Cromwell and his troopers were so humbled that he would have fled if David Leslie had not supported him.

The variations in these three accounts would suggest that they are not derived from one source, but all agree in essence that some problem befell Cromwell and his troopers. Against these allegations is the absence of any reference to such a misfortune in the account written by Cromwell's scout-master, which is perhaps only to be expected. Cromwell himself, in a letter to his brother-in-law, takes full credit for the defeat of the Royalist right (at the expense of truth and of honour), declaring: 'The left wing which I commanded, being our own horse, saving a few Scots in our rear, beat all the Prince's horse. God made them as stubble to our swords.' The 'few Scots' consisted of 1,920 men out of 4,200, and every eyewitness who mentions them contradicts Cromwell's contention that they were in the rear. Principal Baillie, who received a long account of the battle from his namesake (amongst other sources of information now lost), says that David Leslie, in all places that day, was Cromwell's leader. Somerville too, said that, 'Cromwell disdained not to take order from David Leslie.'

Taking on balance the various accounts, it is reasonable to accept that Cromwell and his men did hesitate at a critical moment, when David Leslie dashed on to the charge (Rushworth says that Leslie's regiments behaved very well), and met Rupert's horse in full career, giving the troopers of Manchester's brigade time to recover themselves and support him. A desperate conflict ensued.

For some time the two bodies of horse stood at swords' point, hacking one another. Ludlow recounts a story he heard that, having discharged their pistols, they flung them at each other's heads, and fell to with their swords. Young Lord Grandison received up to ten wounds. At last the Royalists wavered, broke, and fled in irretrievable rout, riding over and dispersing their own reserves of foot, (while it must not be forgotten that up until this point they had bravely disputed every inch of ground for nearly an hour). They fled along Wilstrop Wood side as fast as they could, hotly pursued by the victorious Allies, who chased them down the York road for 3 miles, committing dreadful slaughter, to which the bullets found long after in the heart-wood of Wilstrop trees bore silent testimony. Rupert himself might have been taken prisoner if he had not hidden in some 'bean-lands'. He played the 'creephedge,' as John Vicars spitefully puts it. The brigade of Manchester's foot, under Laurence Crawford, advanced by the side of the horse, dispersing the enemy's infantry as fast as they charged, and utterly routing Rupert's foot regiments, under O'Neil, which formed the right of the Royalist line.

After the rout of his cavalry on the Royalists' right wing, Newcastle proceeded to make his way across the battlefield, riding through the noise and mayhem of battle, towards his white-coats, accompanied by his brother, Sir Charles Cavendish, Captain Mazine, a major and a page, this small band being joined by some volunteer

6 PR= Prince Rupert's horse, right wing: *Rupert's Lifeguard; Byron; Grandison; Trevor; Vaughan; Molyneaux; Tyldesley; Leveson*
7 PR= Prince Rupert's foot, right wing: *O'neil*
8 MGP= Maj. Gen. Porter: Ld. *Byron; Warren; Emeley; Gibson; Tyldesley; Chisenall; Cheator; Frescheville; Eyre; Millward*
8 JK= James King, Lord Eythin: *Newcastle's Whitecoats; Hutton; Girlington; Phil. Byron; Conyer; Eythin; Hilton; Kirkbride; Lambton; Lamplugh; Mansefield; Metham; Basset; Strickland; Towneley; Widdrington*
8 RES= reserve: *Tillier; Blue regiment*
9 NWC= Newcastle's Whitecoats
10 GG= George Goring's horse: *Dacre; Blakiston; Widdrington; Tuke; Carnaby; Porter; Metham*
10 CL= Charles Lucas' horse: *Lucas; Newcastle; Langdale; Urry*

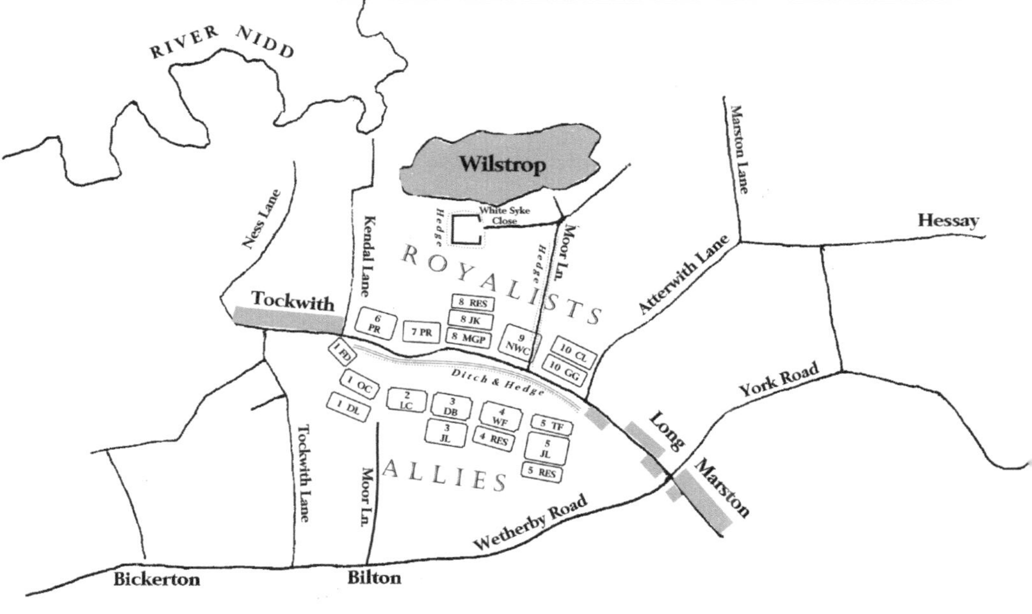

1 FD= Fraser's Dragoones *William Crawford 6 companies*
1 OC= Oliver Cromwell; *Manchester's horse: Whalley 14 troops; Sydney 11;* Vermuyden 5; Fleetwood 6; Lilburne's dragoones
1 DL= David Leslie; *Scots horse: Leslie 8 troops; Balcarres 8; Kirkcudbright 8*
2 LC= Laurence Crawford; *Manchester's brigade: Manchester 18 coy; Pickering 10; Montagu 10; Russell 10; Hobart 9; Crawford 8*
3 DB= David Baillie; *Battle: Fifeshire; Midlothian; Kyle & Carrick; Nithsdale & Annandale (plus possibly Stirlingshire; Clydesdale; Linlithgow)*
3 JL= James Lumsden; *Reserve: Glasgow; Strathearn; Dunfermline's Fifeshire regt. (plus possibly Angus; Ministers; Levied)*
4 WF= William Fairfax; *Yorkshire foot: Fairfax; Forbes; Needham; Bright; Constable; Lascelle; Overton; Ashton; Doddington; Rigby*
4 RES= *Fairfax's brigade reserve: Edinburgh; Tweedale*
5 TF= Thomas Fairfax; *Lord Fairfax's horse 5 troops*
5 JL= James Lambert; *Brigade: Thomas Fairfax's horse; Charles Fairfax; Bethell; Lambert; Copley; Boynton; Norcliff; Dodding 53 troops*
5 RES= Reserve; *Scots horse: Leven 8 troops; Dalhousie 7; Eglinton 7*

cavalrymen who recognised Newcastle. Managing to lose his sword, he took his page's weapon and succeeded in slaying three Scots before he was blocked by a pikeman, who was cut down by some of his party.

All this time the Scots brigade, forming the centre, was bearing the brunt of the action, and repulsing the assaults of Porter's division, led by Lieutenant-General King; while the Fairfaxes were suffering disaster on the right.

Sir William Fairfax, after crossing the ditch, courageously led his men up Moor Lane through a terrific crossfire. But, as they emerged onto the moor in column, they were met by murderous musket volleys from Newcastle's white-coats, so that there was more slaughter here than on any other part of the field. They started to waver just as considerable numbers of their own retreating cavalry, routed by Sir William Urry, galloped straight over them in wild disorder. This threw them into confusion, and, with the two regiments of Scots reserves, they broke and fled towards Tadcaster.

While the foot were advancing up Moor Lane, an engagement had commenced between the horse of Fairfax and Goring on the extreme right. Sir Thomas had drawn the most difficult ground on the whole battlefield. As well as numerous ditches, there was dense undergrowth of furze – a type of particularly spiny broom – in that part of the moor, which threw his 2,000 cavalry – many of them raw and inexperienced – into some disorder before they even reached the enemy. He was also adjacent to hedges already occupied by the enemy but, regardless of these inconveniences, he saw his right wing properly formed and, placing himself at the head of his regiment of 400 troopers, charged the enemy in most gallant style. He was faced by Sir William Urry's alternate bodies of horse and musketeers, whose fire was devastating and caused Fairfax heavy casualties. They were a long time hotly engaged at swords' point, suffering terribly from the galling fire of the muskets; but at last he routed this part of the Royalist wing, and his regiment chased the fugitives some distance along the road towards York. This was the most desperate fight in the whole battle, and many of the officers and men were killed and wounded. Sir Thomas himself received a deep sabre cut across the cheek, the mark of which remained with him until the grave. Rushworth says that he carried himself with great bravery, but that he was unhorsed, flung to the ground, and wounded on the head and face, but rescued and carried off by a party of his own regiment. His major was not so lucky, having at least thirty wounds, of which he later died at York. The captain of his troop was shot in an arm; his cornet had both hands severely cut, maiming him for life; and Captain Micklethwait, another of his officers, 'an honest stout gentleman,' was killed.

Young Charles Fairfax, with Colonel Lambert, charged in another place, and, deserted by his men, was mortally wounded. Here there was a panic amongst the newly levied regiments, and it was they who rode over Lord Fairfax's infantry in their retreat, causing the rout of the right wing. Urry and Lucas, pressing hotly forward, then attacked the Scots horse; and Lord Eglinton's lancers alone stood their ground. They behaved most gallantly, and both the lieutenant colonel and young Robert Montgomery were severely wounded. But at last they too were broken; so that the whole right wing except Sir Thomas's regiment was utterly defeated.

Fairfax, as soon as the success of his own regiment was assured, left the chase to look after the other troops of his wing. But they had been hopelessly routed, and he found himself encircled by bodies of Royalist horse. So he took the white handkerchief which was the recognition sign for the day out of his hat, and rode, with his troopers, through the enemy ranks without being recognised – joining Manchester's horse on the left wing, with whom he acted, at the head of his victorious regiment, for the rest of the day. The account in 'A Full Relation of the late Victory' says that: 'Sir Thomas Fairfax, Colonel Lambert ... with five or six troops charged through the enemy and went to the left wing of horse, the two squadrons of Balgones regiment being divided by the enemy ... one of them being lancers charged a regiment of the enemies foot, and put them wholly to the rout, and after joined with the left wing of horse, the other by another way went also to the left wing. The Earl of Eglinton's regiment maintained their ground ...'

Old Lord Fairfax left the battlefield along with the fugitives of his brigade and of the Scots reserve, as far as Tadcaster. But he returned later the same night, and sent by messenger his account of the victory to the Mayor of Hull, which was the first that reached London, and the first written.

A 'Mr Trevor' describes meeting the fugitives of the battle as he was coming to York. Horse and foot were mingled together – speechless, breathless, and full of fear: shoals of the Scots crying out, 'WAE'S US! WE ARE ALL UNDONE;' ragged troops, consisting of four men and a cornet; foot officers without hat or sword, or indeed anything but feet and just enough tongue to ask the way to the next garrison. 'It was a sad sight to behold many thousands posting away amazed with panic fears,' observed a Mr Ash, who took the fugitives severely to task, in a later sermon.

The left wing of the Royalists was, at this point, completely victorious. Part of the troops galloped up the hill, and began plundering the Allies' baggage located round the clump of trees. The rest, consisting of Newcastle's white-coats, and the cavalry led by Lucas and Urry, made a furious attack on the right flank of the Allied centre, which was already committed to a hot engagement with Porter's division in its front. The fate of the entire battle now hinged on the bravery and steadiness of this brigade of four regiments of Scots foot under General Baillie, and its reserves under Lumsden. 'They had,' says Principal Baillie, 'the greatest burden of the conduct of all.' If they could hold their own until the Allies' left wing could come to the rescue, the day was won; if not, utter ruin was inevitable.

Both sides saw this, and the struggle became desperate. An eyewitness claimed that there was such a noise and clamour of shot and shouts that it was deafening; the smoke of the powder so thick that no light could be seen except that which issued from the mouths of the guns. Twice the Royalist cavalry charged furiously, and twice they were repulsed, the Scots regiments in alternate Tertias of pike and musket maintaining their ground for nearly an hour. Under a third charge they wavered, and some reserves broke and fled, a dangerous sign of the finality of their position. But Lumsden and Lord Lindsay rallied two or three regiments, and at that moment David Leslie and Manchester's foot appeared on the scene, and the day was won. The Royalist Sir Charles Lucas's horse was killed beneath him, and he himself taken prisoner when he charged the final time.

When the reserves of the centre broke, the old Earl of Leven urged them to stand their ground. 'If you fly from the enemy,' he exclaimed, 'at least stand by your General.' But it was all in vain. They were panic-stricken, and fled; and he, thinking, like Lord Fairfax, that all was lost, fled with them. The time of this flight can be identified from the direction he took. Instead of following Lord Fairfax to Tadcaster, he turned sharp right, because Marston Fields were already overrun by the victorious left wing of the Royalists, and rode away to Wetherby, or, as some say, as far as Leeds. Both Scots and English, friends and enemies, seem to have taken special pleasure in detailing their various versions of the poor old veteran's mishap, while forgetting how ably he formed the line of battle, and how hard he strove to rally the fugitives.

The left wing of the Allies had been made aware of the reverses on the right from Sir Thomas Fairfax when he joined them with his regiment as they were chasing the Royalists along Wilstrop Wood side. He and David Leslie, with Crawford and Cromwell, then rode back under the light of the harvest moon leading their troops across the moor, to the support of their centre now so sorely pressed in both front and flank. When the plundering Royalists saw them approach, they hurried down from Marston Fields and for a short while there was a sharp renewed conflict, but the Royalist cavalry were demoralised by success and soon routed by Manchester's horse; while David Leslie and Fraser's dragoons charged the Royalist foot that still held their ground.

Newcastle's heroic white-coats resolved to die in a last stand rather than submit, and retreated into White Syke Close, where it is related that they showed extraordinary valour and beat off all attacks of Cromwell's and Leslie's horse who found themselves unable to break through the hedge of Royalist pikes. At last Fraser's dragoons were brought up and by their shot forced a gap in the Royalist line, made a way for the horse to enter and put the white-coats to the sword – so that, their ammunition exhausted, they were killed as they stood, in rank and file. Fairfax hated this massacre of brave men. He is reported to have called out, 'Spare the poor deluded countrymen … who are misled and know not what they do.'[67] But his words fell on deaf ears. Captain Camby, who came up with some of Manchester's horse in support of Leslie, and was one of the first to enter the close, describes it as 'a small parcel of ground ditched in.' For a whole hour, after the day was utterly lost, did these brave border men continue to fight, repulsing the charges of the cavalry, and of Colonel Fraser's dragoons, at near push of pike. They would take no quarter and when the Allied horse did enter the close, there were not thirty white-coats alive. Captain Camby protested that 'he never, in all the fights he was ever in, saw such resolute brave fellows, and that he saved two or three against their wills.' It was now round about 11.00 p.m. William Cavendish, Marquis of Newcastle, accompanied by his brother and one or two of his servants, was, according to the duchess, the last to ride off the field to return to York, taking with him about thirty white-coat survivors, but leaving his coach-and-six behind him.[68] It was taken with all his correspondence, some of which, revealed as being with the treacherous Hotham family would later be used to incriminate Sir John Hotham.[69]

***

Long before this, the battle had already been won. The horse of Manchester and Leslie charged every party remaining in the field until all were routed and put to flight. Vicars relates how during the fight: in the rout of the (Royalist) enemy, and in their flying and scattering about, many of them ran most affrightedly and amazedly to the place where some of the regiments of horse of the parliament side were standing on their guard, and all or most of the riders were religiously singing psalms, to whom as the aforesaid runaways of the enemy came near and by their singing of psalms perceiving who they were, they all most fiercely fled back again, and cried out 'God damn them, they had like to have been taken by the Parliament Roundheads'. For they only knew them to be the parliament soldiers by their singing of psalms. 'A blessed badge of cognisance indeed'. Lord Saye mentions the, 'psalm of praise sung to God after the victory'. By nine o'clock that night the field was cleared of all but prisoners and the dead. There would have been many more slain in the heat of the pursuit had not Sir Thomas Fairfax galloped up and down, calling to the soldiers to spare their enemies. The whole Royalist army fled in utter rout to York, Lieutenant-General King covering the flight to some extent with a small body of horse. At Mickle-gate bar was the harrowing sight of a street thronged up to the gates with wounded and exhausted men, crying out pitifully for help or some relief to their sufferings.

Back on the battlefield the scene was yet more shocking; the field strewn with wounded, and over 4,000 bodies, later to be buried by the country people, either in White Syke Close or along Wilstrop Wood side. Prince Rupert's favourite dog 'Boy' had also been killed and his sumpter horse captured along with all his possessions.[70] Prisoners taken included Sir Charles Lucas, Generals Goring, Porter, and Tilliers, about 100 other officers, and 1,500 soldiers. Sir Henry Slingsby lost his nephew, Colonel Fenwick, and his kinsman Sir Charles. Sir William Wentworth, Sir Thomas Metham, and young Lionel Carey, the Earl of Monmouth's eldest son,

had also been killed. Sir Charles Lucas was taken to view the bodies, but would not identify those whom he knew. There was one cavalier, however, with a bracelet of hair round his wrist, whom Sir Charles recognised. He desired the bracelet to be taken off, saying that he knew an honourable lady who would give thanks for it. The Allies captured twenty-five pieces of ordinance, 130 barrels of powder, many thousand stand of arms, and about 100 colours, some of which were sent to the parliament in the charge of a Captain Stewart.
One eyewitness wrote that they took colours enough to have made surplices for all the cathedrals in England, had they been white.

After the battle was over, the Earl of Manchester, who was the senior general in the absence of Leven, rode amongst the soldiers and gave thanks for their exceeding good service. Manchester told his men that although he could not possibly make provision for them that night as they deserved and needed, he would certainly do so the following morning. 'The soldiers unanimously gave God the glory of their great deliverance and victory, and told his Lordship cheerfully that although they had fasted long and were faint, yet they would willingly want three days longer, rather than give off the service, or leave his Lordship'. They certainly did have to tolerate cruel hardships in addition to the conflict itself. Few ate as much as the quantity of a penny loaf from the Tuesday of the battle until Saturday morning; there was no beer to be had; the wells were drained to the mud, and men had to drink water out of ditches, or out of places puddled with the horses' feet.

Many too had to mourn the loss of friends and relations. Fairfax and Cromwell, both wounded, were too spent to move and for two days stayed amidst the wreckage of the battlefield, while their men collected pikes and muskets and buried the dead.

The battle over, the victors immediately began to take liberties with the truth in their accounts of the victory. Two of the parliamentary leaders, Leven and Ferdinando, who had run away believing that all was lost, were brought back somewhat shamefacedly with Manchester, who had also at one stage sought safety in flight but had got back earlier, to compose a suitable dispatch describing how they had together won the day. Cromwell, ever the propagandist, claimed, inaccurately, that 'we never charged but we routed the enemy'. He dismissed Leslie's troopers, who had played such a decisive role in his wing, as 'a few Scots in our rear', and, as master of the memorable phrase, said of the enemy – not for the last time – that 'God made them as stubble to our swords'.

Honours of the day were due to Sir Thomas Fairfax, Cromwell, and David Leslie; while Generals Baillie and Lumsden deserved considerable credit for their staunch, dauntless conduct in command of the centre. If they had yielded beneath the onslaught of the Royalist charges on them before the left wing was able to come to their support, the battle's outcome would have been very different. As it was, victory was complete and decisive.

Fraser's men too played an instrumental part in the Allied victory, providing the regiment with an impressive reputation. Their success in clearing the ditch on the left flank in front of Cromwell's horse as battle commenced, routing their opponents, which permitted Cromwell to charge the Royalist horse; their support of David Leslie in recovering control of the centre ground of the battle, and later, when only Newcastle's white-coats still offered active opposition to the Allied force, ensconced as they were in White Syke Close repelling the charges of Cromwell's and Leslie's troopers, it was Fraser's men who breached the Royalist pikemen's defences and allowed the Allied horse to break through and slaughter the white-coats.

The Surrender of York

The victory at Marston Moor was so comprehensive that Royalist commanders abandoned any idea of trying to salvage the affairs of their unfortunate master. Newcastle, seeing all the fruits of his hard work smashed in one day, 'and being utterly destitute of that noble perseverance which shone forth so brightly in his opponents when their fortunes were at their lowest ebb', decided to leave Britain.

Rupert, having ruined his uncle's affairs in the north,[71] left York to its fate, marched away through Monk bar to Middleham, and into Lancashire. So, only twenty-four hours after the battle, Sir Thomas Glemham, having been deserted by both Rupert and Newcastle, prepared to defend the town with about a thousand half-mutinous troops; having, in order to persuade the garrison to stand fast, made up false reports that Rupert had returned, attacked the Allied army and routed it. Even so, great numbers of soldiers deserted, justifiably reluctant to endure the hardships of another siege.

The Allies rested in the villages near the moor the day after the battle, and took up their original positions around York on Thursday, 4 July. The approaches were pushed forward with great vigour. The Scots threw up a battery in Bishop-fields left of Mickle-gate bar, while the Fairfaxes prepared another between Walm-gate bar and Layre-thorp Postern. On the advice of Sir Thomas Fairfax it was decided that a general assault should be delivered at the Layre-thorp Postern, where the wall ended and the only obstacle was the River Foss. A bridge was assembled to throw across it, and a large supply of hurdles collected, when Sir Thomas Glemham offered to capitulate, and commissioners were appointed to arrange articles of surrender – namely Sir Adam Hepburn on the part of the Scots, Sir William Constable for the Fairfaxes, and Colonel Montague for Lord Manchester.

Glemham (as deserved) obtained honourable terms. He was to deliver up the city, forts, Clifford's Tower, and all munitions of war, on the 15th; he and his garrison were to march out with all honours of war, and be safely conveyed to the nearest

Royalist garrison; no officer or soldier to be stopped or plundered on the march; the citizens were to enjoy all the privileges, and no soldiers were to be quartered within the walls.

On Tuesday, 16 July, Sir Thomas Glemham, with Sir Henry Slingsby, and about 1,000 men, marched out of York, most of the soldiers being half-drunk. The besiegers were drawn up in line on each side of the road for a mile beyond Mickle-gate bar. As soon as the Royalists were clear of the town, the three Allied generals went to the minster, where a psalm was sung, and thanksgiving offered up by Lord Leven's chaplain.[72]

The work of the Allies in Yorkshire having been completed, the armies marched off in different directions, where they might be of more service to the cause. The Scots went north to reduce Newcastle, Manchester led the army of the associated counties south to reinforce Lord Essex and Sir William Brereton, and Sir John Meldrum, who had arrived just too late to take part in the battle, with the Cheshire forces, immediately set off to shadow the movements of Prince Rupert.

Lord Fairfax was appointed Governor of York, and the only work that remained for him to do was the reduction of the castles still held by Royalist garrisons. Lord Manchester performed some of this work during his march south.

5. The Siege of Newcastle

The Scots' next and formidable task was to be the taking of Newcastle. On the 17 July Leven's army had arrived at Doncaster, from where he moved to Leeds to establish camp there.

Ten days later, on Saturday 27th, without awaiting the arrival of Leven's forces, Callendar took possession of Gateshead, and the following day, a further struggle took place for the possession of the bridge connecting Newcastle and Gateshead. Lithgow describes it:

> The next day he [Callendar] begun to dispute for the enjoying of the bridge, with the fiery service of Cannon and Musket, which [bridge] indeed was manfully invaded, and as courageously defended. [At length] he gained the better half of the bridge, and with much ado fortified the same with earthen Ramparts and artillery, which still so defensively continued, until the town was taken in by storm. This being regardfully done, he caused to erect five batteries, along the Bankhead, and just opposite to the town, from whence the cannon did continually extreme good service, not only against the walls and batteries, but also against particular places, and particular persons: Besides the frequent shooting of Pot-pieces [mortars], and other fireworks of great importance, which daily annoyed the inhabitants within the town.

Capturing Gateshead and blocking up Newcastle on the south, Callendar had done everything possible until the main army under Leven arrived. Ten ships of the parliament's fleet had already reached the mouth of the Tyne to block up the town from that side.

On 1 August 1644 Leven sent forward Lieutenant-General Leslie with Fraser's dragoons plus three regiments of horse from Doncaster to aid Callendar, who dispatched Armyne and Robert Barwis to meet and concert measures with him at Leeds. Callendar was actually far from satisfied with the measures being taken for his support. Writing to Loudon on 4 August, from Usworth, to inform him that David Leslie was expected with the horse at Durham the next day, he adds, 'I wish your lordship's commands has been as positive for the speedy advancing of the foot here, as it was for the horse; for this work being of great difficulty, a river dividing the army without a bridge, the enemies being masters of all boats and keills, the uncertain approach of an enemy, and certainty of the winter requires their present marching forward … If this siege shall continue, greater store of powder, ball, and match, both for cannon and musket, must be had.' On the 7th Leven broke camp at Leeds to arrive at Bishop Auckland in three days time. Callendar rode out to meet him a day later.

On the 12th the army advanced to Gateshead and remained there while Leven paid visits of inspection to Sunderland and Hartlepool on the 13th. On Wednesday the 14th, the Scots crossed the Tyne at Newburn (6 miles west of Gateshead) and halted. The next day they established a siege camp at Elswick and immediately commenced siege operations against the town. Leven had brought the artillery with him, and it was to play its part decisively in the assault. Six batteries were set up, named after various officers. The most powerful was the general of artillery's which contained 24 and 18 pounders. Cassillis', Gask's and Sinclair's had a mix of 24, 12 and 3 pounders. Lieutenant-General Baillie's had 24 and 3 pounders while Loudoun's had a brace of 18 pounders.

Newcastle's medieval walls were fronted by a ditch 22yd wide, and 6 to 8ft deep. The wall was 25ft high to the walkway and 10ft thick. Critically, no berm[73] was in place below and beyond the wall and while this assisted the defence by making the positioning of assault ladders against the wall more difficult, the berm served to stabilise the base of a wall from subsiding and its omission was a weakness which the Scots immediately moved to capitalise on. Mines were started and artillery worked forward to within battering range.

Temporary outworks and trenches had also been created to strengthen the defences. The most notable and severely contested of these outworks was to be the Shieldfield Fort. Of the main gates on the town walls, Newgate and Westgate were considered the most important, the latter described as 'A mightye strong thinge'.

An account of the measures taken by the besieged for their defence reads: 'The streets to which the gates gave entrance, and several passages were cast up with defensive breastworks and posted with demi-culverins of iron: and above all other works the town castle itself was seriously enlarged, with diverse curious fortifications, besides breastworks, redoubts, and terreniat demi-Lunes;[74] and withal these distinctive horn-works, two of which were strongly pallisaded outside, and of great bounds [dimensions].' The capstone of the battlements around the town was under-propped with stakes ready to fall on the besiegers should they attempt to scale the wall. The gaps in the battlements were filled with lime and stone, leaving only narrow slits. All the gates were closed and barricaded, egress being allowed only by the small postern gates. The trench outside the walls had been deepened, and the outward surface of the walls themselves had been steeply lined with a clay mix to prevent the besiegers from climbing up. Certain structural alterations appear also to have been made in the walls, since in August 1644, the company of Barber Surgeons ordered an inspection to be made of Ralph Cock's house with a view to their occupation of it, the hall over Pandon gate having been taken down before the siege commenced.

On his arrival, Leven summoned the town to surrender. The following day the town returned an answer, refusing to treat. Following this refusal the siege was actively pushed forward. Leven and Callendar were already in possession of the houses and suburbs outside Sandgate, Closegate, Pilgrim Street gate and Newgate, and an attempt on the part of the besieged to shake the Scots from their position on the bridge had been recently frustrated. The apparent imminence of a close investment was not without its effect on those inside the town who were half-hearted in the cause and apprehensive of the consequence of a siege. Leven also enlisted the help of 3,000 colliers, keel men and others to help in the mining operations. On Saturday 20th, these mining operations were far enough advanced around Closegate to tempt the besieged to make a sortie. 'They fell on at three in the afternoon, near Closegate where Lindsay and Maitland were guarding the works; the soldiers fled, Lieutenant Colonel Sir James Maxwell, Major to E. Clydesdale's regiment, an ensign and 9 or 10 common soldiers were taken and 2 or 3 killed; the officers were not there that day.'

Shortly after this, Callendar and the chief officers of his command complained to the Committee of Estates that his 'part of the army since the coming up of the Lord General's army, they being on the other side of the river, has not much been taken notice of by them, and, further, that while a sum of £4,000 was being distributed amongst Leven's army, Callendar and his forces were in great straits'. An equally urgent appeal reached the estates in a dispatch from Crawford and Lindsay, dated Elswick, 19 August, a few days after Leven's army had joined Callendar, in which he requested that 'ten thousand weight of powder, with the like weight of lead, and double weight of match, may be provided there and sent to Sunderland.' Also 'considerable quantities of meal … for without it we have but small hopes of any maintenance from those who are obliged to it.'

The preliminary steps taken by the Scots towards the investing of the town are described in a dispatch from Callendar on 21 August, in which he states that Leven 'quarters himself at Elswick upon the west end of the town of Newcastle at the waterside; and that the east end thereof is assigned to me for my quarters, by and attour [around] Gateshead, and the most part of the bridge, whereof I am in possession already'. He continues:

> Upon Thursday the 15th of this instant I crossed the water likewise a little beneath the town at the glass works, taking with me the Lord Sinclair's and the Earl Marischal's regiments, with some commanded men, whom I lodged that night [notwithstanding of many cannon shot from the town and Shieldfield[75] fort, and musket shot upon both sides] in the Sandgate, where I am now busied about the making of approaches towards the town, and I have recovered many keels and boats, as has made a bridge over the water a little beneath the glass houses.[76] … The besieging of the town is much hindered for lack of materials, such as spades,

> shooles [shovels], mattocks etc. And as the beleaguering of it will be hard work [sic], so the soldiers are put to extraordinary duty. And we cannot get so much money as will be half months means to every officer, four merks to every trouper, and a shilling to each soldier, for the commissary here has it not. Wherefore seeing their pains and labour is great, your lordships would be pleased to send up money here for their further encouragement, and give a special command and order to the treasurer of the army or his deputies, that their forces may get some satisfaction, and not to be distinguished in that only from Leven's army; for it seems they are by pay and proviant, though nothing short and inferior in duty. The last oatmeal which was sent here was directed to Hartlepool, which is now returned back to Sunderland for the use of this army, in respect of our necessity and of the evilness of the victual which was here; yet seeing that is a place very fit to be a magazine, your lordships would take it to your consideration, and send victuals there. This day [21 August] some pieces of battery are sent over to the other side of the river.[77]

It would seem that within a week of Leven's arrival, Callendar had made the extended position assigned to him – Sandgate and the east side of the town in addition to Gateshead – effective. A bridge of boats below Ouseburn connected the two portions of his command, and a battery was in position, probably on the high ground on which St Ann's church stands, between Ouseburn and Pandon. Mining operations had also been commenced at or near the Sandgate. The fire from his Gateshead batteries must have been very galling to the besieged, evidenced by Whitlock's statement that 'most of the inhabitants of the lower town fled to the high town for shelter.'

Leven also built a bridge of boats by his headquarters at Elswick, out of sight of the besieged and beyond cannon shot, in the bend of the river above the Redheugh. Leven enclosed the west and north-west parts of the town, enclosing that part of town as far as Lord Sinclair's regiment, leaving only the Shieldfield Fort, which belonged to the town, separating them. The Scots soldiers were accommodated in huts made of turf, clay and wattles, their officers in 'circulating' pavilions, 'more ready to receive the blustering winds than the sinking rain'. In regard to Callendar's bridge of boats, he adds that it was 'a pretty way below the glass house', and was guarded by Lord Kenmore's regiment at both ends, and also by 'three watery guards of keill boats, tied with cable ropes,' and that it was used by country people to bring in provisions for the army.

On Thursday 22 August Leven sent a dispatch to the Committee of Estates, which indicates that lack of money and provisions were not the greatest of the difficulties that confronted the Scots. He reminded them of the need of 'sending to the army all such as have run away from their colours and are come home; and also all such as had not appeared out of the numbers that were appointed at the turn of the year to come out of the several shires of the kingdom'. On the same day, the

Scottish chancellor, Lord Loudon, arrived from Scotland to review the progress the siege had made. Leven, accompanied by Douglas, rode out to meet him 'beyond the 3 mile bridge coming from Morpeth.' Siege operations were in active progress at the time of his arrival. 'The enemy from the castle doth mightily annoy us with their great artillery; but the Scots are casting up with incessant labour what works they can both by day and night to defend themselves. In the meanwhile our pioneers are as busy at works under ground as our cannons are playing above it. The endeavours on both sides are indefatigable, and in the thick clouds of smoke the thunder of the cannon perpetually disputing.' On the following Saturday, the 24th, Loudon had an opportunity to witness a sortie of the besieged at Newgate on the north-west of the town. That fortification, together with the line of the western wall as far as Herber Tower or Westgate, appears to have been under the particular charge of Lieutenant-General Baillie. His battery was probably placed on the Leazes, and in the course of the siege it did considerable damage to the wall and to St Andrew's Church immediately fronting it. (In the final assault on 19 October, Newgate would be breached by artillery and not by mines, but at this period of the siege the Scots appear to have been mining the wall here as at Closegate and Sandgate). The mines at Newgate were 'within a stonecast of the wall,' and Baillie, after entertaining Douglas at dinner, went with him in the afternoon of the 24th to view the works. 'A little after I came from the works,' writes Douglas, 'the enemy fell on, horse and foot, upon the works kept by Cassillis' and Killhead's regiments; the soldiers ran away. The reason was no officers were attending; the Royalists were beaten in again, some two killed, as many wounded, as many taken, both the days of outfall.' The lack of officers, to which Douglas had also impliedly attributed the reverse at Closegate on the 20th, presented a serious difficulty. Sinclair writes to the Committee of Estates on 18 September, 'We find so great want of officers, that we have resolved to fill the places of all such as have violated and transgressed their forlosses.'

***

On September 3rd, an entry in the Whickham register of burials speaks to the vigilance of the Scots sentries: 'A man that was shot by the Scottish sentries in the meadows, as he was coming up the water in a boat.' On the same date the besieging force was weakened by the departure to Scotland of Callendar and Lindsay, with three regiments of foot and one of horse. At around the same time, the cavalry units under Leslie, including Fraser's dragoons, had also departed the Scots encampments around the town. Montrose's progress called them away. After the Covenanter's defeat at Kilsyth, the Committee of Estates had fled Scotland to Berwick, and Montrose had entered Glasgow and issued a proclamation to summon a new parliament in the king's name. However, Callendar returned to the lines around Newcastle a short while later.

On 7 September, Leven summoned the town once again, this summons being rejected by Marley and the town. Renewed attacks followed: in one particularly short but effective retaliatory bombardment following sniping at the Scots, Baillie opened fire from his batteries on the Leazes and succeeded, after three hours assault, in 'brashing' down part of the wall near St Andrew's Church to 'within half a yard of the root,' making an opening wide enough for ten men abreast to enter. They did not breach the wall however and the defenders, suffering dreadfully while manfully trying to block this up and prevent an immediate escalade by the besiegers, succeeded in repairing it with rubbish and timber behind a canvas screen.

Leven, uncertain of resupply, preserved his shot wherever possible and placed his greatest hopes on his mines, which were dug under Sandgate, White Friars and several other locations. Leven was not above reasonable persuasion and in a conflict in which all forces – in the early stages anyway – claimed they were fighting for the king or his best interests in one way or another, the use of propaganda pamphlets flung over the walls signed by 'A well wisher' may seem more ironic today than it would have then. Bear in mind that a proportion of Newcastle's population was already disaffected and potentially well-disposed towards the Scots.

So far the besieged had been giving an excellent account of themselves. The dispatches sent from the Scots headquarters at Elswick, though making no reference to the many repulses experienced by the army, speak of other difficulties with which the Scots had to contend. On 18 September, Sinclair writes to the Committee of Estates, 'The Thesaurer of this army has returned, but without either provisions or money as yet; and when we have distributed the shoes amongst our soldiers, any spare shall be sent to you [sic].' Callendar also writes to the same authority on the 24th, to beg them for more oatmeal and, clearly chafing at the slowness of their progress, adds that in his opinion they will best serve the interests of the kingdom by accelerating the business against Newcastle.

The besieged were in little better plight, being so hard-pressed, but were soon to be encouraged by the discovery and drowning of three Scots mines.

Alas the Scots' Allies – the English parliament – were endeavouring to play down the efficiency of the Army of the Covenant – probably to allow them to stop making the agreed payments to the Scots for their service, which the bankrupt English parliament could no longer afford to make.

The argument was nonsense. The Covenanters had single-handedly cleared the north of England, had made a major contribution to the destruction of the largest English Royalist field army and would in due course take Newcastle – a town never before taken by siege. Newark by contrast suffered a years-long series of sieges that various seasoned Parliamentarian forces could not bring to a satisfactory conclusion.

London – staunchly Parliamentarian – relied on Newcastle coal, and as winter threatened, the Scots were easy targets for malicious slander and were criticised for being deemed to be moving the siege forward too slowly.

The Royalists on the other hand claimed 'All Scots are truly evil', and propaganda pamphlets proliferated full of fictitious stories of attacks beaten back with Scots casualties of biblical proportions.

On Saturday, 21 September, and again on the following Monday, the besieged appear to have made successful sorties, after which a Royalist wrote: 'The hungry Scots have been so beaten by [that famous garrison] that the number before the town looks so small as if none were there but honest Scots. Their horse are all gone off into Scotland to secure their ample Patrimonies at home … The Scots before Newcastle are neither numerous nor courageous, being bravely tamed by that excellent blow which the Garrison bestowed upon them on Monday was seven night and the Saturday before, at which two times the brave men of Newcastle slew and took above 500 Scots, killed a principal Commander (we remember not his Scottish name) and took three pieces of ordnance; since when the Scots are withdrawn to Tynemouth Castle, which 'till then they blocked up.'

Ignoring such political manoeuvring, the Scots progressed their mining preparations. Leven, his magazines replenished by stores dispatched from London in September, was determined to throw everything into one last assault. On Monday 14 October, he summoned the town for the third and last time. Marley and his colleagues delayed negotiations until Friday 18th when, in the afternoon, Leven manoeuvred his batteries and supporting Scottish regiments into positions concentrating on the south-east and south-west corners of the town and upon rising ground near a burn at Barras Bridge, all awaiting the order to launch a general assault. More letters were sent between besieged and besiegers in an effort to agree terms, without success, the last letter sent via a drummer to the Scots stating that the Royalists believed Leven was dead, to which Leven responded that he 'hoped to do him some service yet before he died.'

Knowing the end was near, the defenders quit the remaining outworks not in Scots hands – notably the Shieldfield Fort – and early on 19 October the Scots prepared for the final attack. The assault commenced.

The town stood mainly on a hill face sloping steeply down to the bordering river, where one narrow street ran from Sandgate to Closegate. Its defensive walls were high and strong, of dressed stone inside and out, fenced with dungeon towers, turrets and a large defensive battlement with eight assorted ports. While the walls were described as stronger than York's, the town's natural position was unfavourable to the defenders. Except on the north, it offered on all sides excellent positions for an enemy well supplied with artillery. On the east, the valley, through which Pandon Burn ran into the Tyne, rose to a considerable elevation about half a mile from Sandgate and Carpenter Tower. The town's wall climbed along the west side of Pandon Dene, till it reached its north-east corner at Carliol Tower. This stretch of wall was inaccessible and virtually impregnable to direct assault, and seems to have suffered little from the Scottish attack. Its position was also strengthened by the

Shieldfield Fort, which the besieged evacuated on the 18th. The fort stood a quarter of a mile north-east of Carliol Tower, built on a moderate height as a quadrangle of earth and wattles with four-cornered bastions at every angle, the north-east side of one bulwark pallisaded,[78] while along the top of the works, defenders had laid the masts of ships to roll down onto attackers. At its entrance was a wooden drawbridge and inside two courts du guard. The graffe outside was dry and of little defensive importance, except for that repugnancy [the sewage] of the defendants within, around 300 men. West of the fort, on the east side of the Pandon Dene, stood a windmill. While Leven relied largely on his artillery and mining train, it was along the two lines of the wall on the west from Nevil Tower or Westgate to Closegate that he relied upon them almost exclusively. The mines that were exploded were all in these two quarters.

The Scots had four batteries. They only managed to make three breaches in the wall; at Closegate, Newgate (Black Bessie's Tower), and near Carliol Tower. From this information the following positions may be taken as the sites of the attacking batteries:

The south-western battery may have been placed on rising ground, positioned to cover the walls from Westgate to Closegate, and the mining operations at Westgate and White Friar Tower.

The Newgate or north-western batteries had been in position on the high ground on the Leazes since the beginning of the siege, from which they had 'brashed' the wall near St Andrew's on 7 September 7.

The Pilgrim Street or north-east battery would have been placed beyond the burn at Barras Bridge, from which it could command Pilgrim Street gate and Carliol Tower at a distance of a third of a mile (500m), and cover Shieldfield Fort to the south-east of it at a distance of half a mile (750m). The placing of this battery would seem to have caused the evacuation of Shieldfield Fort on the 18th.

There were two Sandgate or south-eastern batteries, the second to protect the mining operations which seem to have been more extensive here than at any other point of the town's defences. These had done considerable damage to the Sally Port or Carpenter Tower, and had received fire from the Shieldfield Fort. A position that satisfies both these criteria is on the high ground separating Pandon Dene and the Ouseburn. The name 'Battle Field' subsequently found near Pottery Bank, on the city road, may mark the position of Callendar's battery at this quarter. Sandgate would lie half a mile west, and the Sally Port and Shieldfield Fort at a slightly lesser distance. Finally, Callendar's batteries at Gateshead commanded the castle and the southern frontage of the town.

The strength of Leven's artillery is not known. On entering England in January 1644, his forces were 'well armed with field pieces, swine feathers, and all engines of war necessary.'[79] He had 120 great guns, the heavier of them reaching Blyth by sea on 6 February. These included a new type of twelve pounder invented by Sir Alexander Hamilton, 'never before discovered, which were made purposely for this design, above ¾ of a yard long, or some a yard, that will carry a 12 pound bullet, to do great execution at a distance, and yet so framed that a horse may carry one of them.' A warrant issued for 200 rounds of 24lb, 12lb and 9lb shot, may imply that 24 pounders were the largest cannon which the Scots had at Newcastle. The extreme effective range of the heaviest Scottish artillery is unlikely to have exceeded 1,000yd, while the point blank range of their heaviest guns – the 24 pounders – would not have exceeded 400yd. The positions assigned above to the Scottish batteries, at about 700–800yd, falls conveniently within the effective ranges of this type of cannon.

The position of the mines laid by the Scots about the walls can also be determined with some certainty. Four breached the wall prior to the assault – two at three o'clock on the 19th at White Friar Tower, (one possibly in the wall below the tower itself), a third at five o'clock at Westgate, (this may have exploded between the Durham and Herber Towers), and the fourth, which Lithgow states to have miscarried, was the second of two mines which Hepburn placed at Sandgate.

The breaching accomplished by the artillery pieces was not so effective; they broke open the wall slightly north of Closegate, between Andrew Tower and

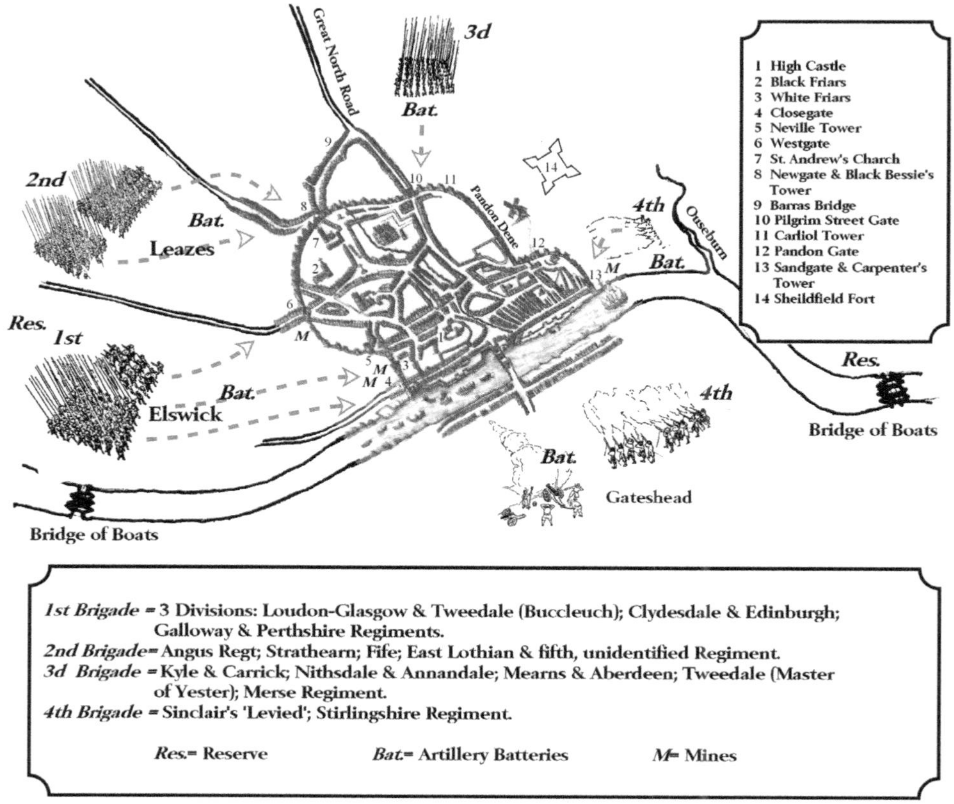

Newgate, between Pilgrim Street gate and Carliol Tower, and possibly at Sandgate. With six separate breaches in the walls, the way was open for the troops to deliver the final assault late in the afternoon.

Four brigades of infantry were already in position, drawn up, standing to arms, their officers having settled their positions in the assault by throwing dice on drum-heads to determine the honour of who should lead which section of the attack, the most coveted positions going to those who threw the fewest 'blacks.'

The first brigade was drawn up in three divisions behind the Scottish batteries, from Westgate to the river at Closegate. Its first division included the Loudon-Glasgow and Tweeddale regiments, under their colonels, Lords Loudon and Buccleuch. It entered the town at Closegate through a breach made by the artillery. Its second division was formed from the Clydesdale and Edinburgh regiments, under their colonels, Sir Alexander Hamilton, general of the artillery, and James Rae. It was placed in position to force the breach made by the mine below the White Friar Tower. The third division of this brigade consisted of the Galloway and Perthshire regiments, under their colonels, William Stewart and Lord Gask, and had the fortifications of Westgate opposed to it. The second brigade was concentrated behind the works that the Scots had thrown up against the more formidable Newgate. It consisted of the Angus regiment under Lieutenant-General Baillie, who apparently commanded the brigade, the Strathearn regiment under Lord Coupar, the Fife regiment under Lord Dunfermline, the East-Lothian regiment under Sir Patrick Hepburn, laird of Wauchton, and a fifth, unidentified, regiment. This brigade was the most powerful of the four, an indication of the strength of the fortification to which it was opposed.

The third brigade, awaiting the result of the artillery engagement on the Pilgrim Street gate and Carliol Tower, was formed of the Kyle and Carrick regiment under Lord Cassillis, the Nithsdale and Annandale regiment, under Douglas of Kilhead, the Mearns and Aberdeen regiment under the Earl Marshall, the Linlithgow and Tweeddale regiment under the Master of Yester, and the Merse regiment under Sir David Home, Laird of Wedderburn.

The fourth brigade, under Callendar's command at Sandgate, consisted of Lord Sinclair's 'Levied' regiment and the Stirlingshire regiment, under Lord Livingstone, both of which had been transferred to Callendar from Leven's command. The total attack force may have numbered 10,500 – 12,600 men plus the reserve, which probably included the Midlothian regiment under their colonel, Lord Maitland; the Teviotdale regiment, colonel the Earl of Lothian; and the Ministers' regiment, all drawn up on the west side of the town and entering at Westgate upon the town being carried by assault.

Callendar's contingent – some 6,000 on entering England in July – had suffered considerable shrinkage from the garrisons required at Hartlepool, Stockton and elsewhere, plus three regiments withdrawn to Scotland on 3 September, and now numbered about 3,000. These men may have been reserved for the support of the Gateshead batteries, for the guard of the bridge of boats under Lord Kenmuir, or for a general reserve force on the east at Sandgate.

Against these forces the defenders could only muster a handful of men. Lithgow states that 'they were but 800 of the Trained Band, and 900 volunteers, pressed-men, colliers, keel-men and poor trades men; with some few experimented [experienced] Officers to overtop them.' Information on their disposition is patchy: Cuthbert Carr was in command at Newgate, Captain George Errington, Lieutenant William Robson, Ensign Thomas Swan, and 180 men held Pilgrim Street gate, where they lost not a single man killed or wounded, though they made frequent sallies from it, and held it after the other gates had fallen to the Scots, refusing to surrender it or to believe that the town had been taken, and shooting at their friends who called to them to surrender. Carr at Newgate also fought until surrounded by overwhelming numbers.

'Winter was drawing on; the Scots soldiers were earnest to have some end to the business.' Those within the town continued obstinately to hold out. 'Early in the morning, the cannon began to play upon the walls from [the Scots'] several batteries, [until] eight o'clock, by which time the hostages should have been released [sic], otherwise the royalists were to expect the extremities of war; but since none came, the service continued from all the batteries.' 'After our batteries began to play, [the defenders] jeered our men from the town, bidding them, "Come on you cowardly rogues, if you dare", who before night were glad to sing another song, and crave quarter for their lives.'

The mines were blown at Whitefriars, which part of the town's defences was assaulted by, amongst others the Clydesdale foot and Edinburgh foot regiments; simultaneously at Sandgate, and assaulted by the 4th Brigade comprising in part Niddrie's, Stirlingshire, Master of Cranstoun's and (Sinclairs) College of Justice's foot regiments. Breaches were blown in the defences by battering ordnance at the Pilgrim Street gate and assaulted by the 3rd Brigade including the Kyle & Carrick, Merse, Linlithgow & Tweeddale, and Mearns & Aberdeen foot and the Nithsdale & Annandale foot regiments; Closegate was breached and assaulted by the 1st Brigade comprising the Earl of Loudoun's and Tweeddale foot regiments; and at Westgate – the last and possibly most significant breach – assaulted amongst others by the Galloway, and (possibly) the Perthshire-Freelands foot regiments.

The regiments advanced all at once in a general assault; 'but they met with a tremendous opposition, nothing being left undone by the enemy to repel the fury of the assault: They played very hotly and desperately from the Castle on the breaches, and from the flanking towers of the walls with scattered shot; yet the regiments advanced without shrinking, though the cannon played from many places upon their full open bodies, so that the difficult access to the breaches, and the mighty advantages of their walls and works inside the town caused considerable loss of soldiers and officers of good quality; yet ... after two hours very hot dispute upon the breaches, they broke through, at the mine sprung on the west side of the town near Closegate; and after their entry, were furiously charged three times by the horse of the Town, the charges gallantly sustained and the bridge-head maintained, until the attackers' reserves arrived to reinforce the assault: after which [sic] they marched for the relief of the rest of the breaches...'

At the breach near Carliol Tower, Lieutenant Colonel Henderson, Major Moffat and others were killed; at a second near 'Black Bessie's' Tower [Newgate], Major Hepburn, Captain Corbett, Captain John Home and Lieutenant Colonel Home were killed; at Westgate breach, Captain John Hamilton, Captain Thomas Hamilton and others of the Clydesdale regiment were killed. At Sandgate, Captain Sinclair and others were killed.

As soon as the dust cleared the Scots assault troops advanced into the breeches and beyond, while others scaled the walls with ladders at various parts of the defence, notably at Newgate by the Angus, Strathearn, Fife and East Lothian foot regiments.

Clambering up the breaches was the most deadly work, as the besieged repelled the Scots with hand grenades, while entrance was easier at the points where the mines had been sprung.

The Royalist defenders were quickly swept off the walls near the breaches, the survivors falling back in street to street fighting and some holed up in towers and gate structures sniping at the assault troops. One such sharpshooter killed a certain Colonel Home who was lamented as a courageous officer:

Woe to that breach beside Black Bessie's Towre,
Woe to itself that bloudy butchering bower!
Where valiant Home, that stern Bellona`s blade,
And brave commander fell: For there he stay`d,
Arraigned by death.

Callendar – the first to lay down camp before the town, and the first that entered it – entered at Sandgate and marched along the quay at Sandhill 'with flying colours and roaring drums'. Upon his entrance he dispatched the Stirlingshire and Nithsdale and Annandale regiments, under Lord Livingstone and Douglas of Kilhead, to clear the walls on the eastern side, while the western and northern brigades were engaged in driving the enemy 'to the choking marketplace' where 'between Scylla and Charibdis' they begged for quarter.

The Scottish soldiers entered the breaches with much valour, while others got over the walls with scaling ladders, at the sight of which, those inside threw down their arms, the principals among them fleeing to the castle and offering to surrender upon quarter, which Leven refused to grant unless they submitted to his mercy.

In the town the surviving defenders maintained a short but spirited defence, but were bloodily overwhelmed, with the town secured in Scots hands in less than 2 hours after the springing of the mines. The diary of one Scots soldier called Lithgow records the bloodshed as the Scots swept the Royalist defenders back to the Bigg Market area where the survivors' final capitulation is likely to have taken place:

> The thousand of musket balls flying from our faces like to the droving haylestones from septentrian blast; the clangour and carving of naked unsheathed swords; the pushing of broughing pikes crying for blood … the carcasses of foemen lying like dead dogs upon the groaning street.

All resistance crushed, the Scots reported that upon the town being taken, 'The principal houses of the town were preserved from plundering by the officers.' However, alternative versions included the town being given over to a sacking for twenty-four hours. Some of the Scots soldiers entered one house in which a baptism feast was being held, as the thirty guests assembled were in the act of drinking to the confusion of the Scots. The soldiers rifled the house and stripped its inmates even of their clothes.

That night the town was carefully secured, guards appointed at the breaches and at the waterside to stop the escape of any within the town. The Scots infantry were posted in the town while the horse kept guard outside the walls. The next day, Sunday the 20th, Leven, Callendar, Baillie, and other chief officers of the army, entered the town and proceeded to St Nicholas's Church to give thanks to God. A proclamation was made that no officer or soldier should trouble or plunder the house of any, under pain of death. It was further ordered that no officer or soldier should stay in the town without special order, but should return to the leaguer and his former quarters; only a proper garrison would be allowed to stay in the town. The fulfilment of this order was prevented, however, by a great storm which swept away the two bridges of boats and compelled the army to come into the town for shelter from Sunday 20th until the following Wednesday.

In the interval, on Tuesday 22nd, Marley, who had previously threatened to use Scots prisoners as human shields only to promptly quit the defence and scuttle to the castle for refuge upon the mines being blown, was taken prisoner when the castle capitulated unconditionally to the Covenanters. Why this creature was not put to the sword as custom permitted following an unnecessary storming is unknown, but instead he was committed to his house with a strong guard to defend him from the fury of the incensed people, being hated and abhorred as having brought ruin to so many. On being taken to the house, he was severely handled by the mob. On the following day he was transferred to a dungeon within the castle from where, on 29 October, he was placed into the custody of Master Weldon, Sheriff of Northumberland, who 'had much ado to keep him from being torn in pieces by the inhabitants of the town, and by those common sort of people whom he had forced to take up arms.'

Regimental returns report modest casualties in most regiments. The Galloway foot appear to have taken more casualties than other regiments, perhaps suggesting that the Westgate to Bigg Market route ultimately saw the heaviest fighting in the drive to clear the town of Royalists. They were, however, still at 569 men strength in November without an opportunity for recruiting, suggesting a small loss at Newcastle, not the apocalyptic losses claimed by the Royalists.[80] Royalist casualties are unrecorded during the siege or in the sacking that followed. The garrison is however unheard of again after the assault.

The fall of Newcastle was followed within a few days by the surrender of Tynemouth Castle, besieged by the Scots concurrently with Newcastle, and its garrison latterly decimated by the plague. The capture of this castle merely served to infect the Scots Army with typhus.

The fall of Tynemouth Castle on 27 October virtually concluded the Civil War in the north and, with the capture of Newcastle, gave the Scots a hold upon Northumberland and Durham, which they retained until February 1647.

The relief in London as coal supplies resumed was such that a day of public thanksgiving was proclaimed on 5 November. Sooner than that however, the Scots Army's attentions were drawn north following a string of reverses to Scots Government forces from Royalists in Scotland itself.

Ultimately several Scots regiments and substantial elements of the Scots horse would head back to Scotland to deal with Montrose and his Royalist coalition after his demolition of a series of Scots militia forces. The main army remained in the north of England while Leven nurtured his supply line from Scotland – and kept control of the 'tap' that controlled London's coal.

6. The Siege of Carlisle

Before the successful conclusion to the siege of Newcastle, and from 1 September to 7 October, Fraser's dragoons accompanied Leslie with seven regiments of horse on an exploratory campaign in Cumbria. The regiment then returned to Newcastle, where it remained until sometime in December, while Leslie, retaining two regiments of horse, remained in Cumbria. Following the reduction of forces in the area in October, Leslie with Richard Barwis, a Parliamentarian burgess of Carlisle, led 800 horse against Carlisle. Leslie ordered Colonel Sir Wilfred Lawson and Colonel Chomley to raise Cumbria for the parliament. He then returned to Newcastle, where he remained for a month before returning with three regiments of horse (including his own), one of dragoons and one of foot. Fraser crossed the Pennines for a third time as part of this Scottish force. Leslie then commenced building siege works at Newtown to the west of Carlisle.

In October 1641 the garrison of Carlisle had been disbanded in accordance with a treaty with Scotland, but the arms and munitions of war were carefully stowed away in the Fratry, the keys of which appear to have been in the custody of the Mayor of Carlisle.

When the Great Civil War broke out, for a long time events remained distant from Carlisle, and many people of distinction sought refuge there from the ravages of war.

An attempt had been made in 1643 to seize Carlisle for parliament. The prime movers were Sir Wilfred Lawson and some of the Barwises of Langrigg. However the gentry of the county, their tenants and neighbours, and the militia defeated them and their followers, and drove them to Abbey-holme, but there released them on their promise of keeping quiet.

After York had surrendered in July, its governor and commander-in-chief in the north for the king, Sir Thomas Glemham, took refuge in Cumberland, with some broken troops.

Michael Studholme, one of those involved in the attempt on Carlisle in 1643, still cherished designs upon Carlisle and through Richard Barwise, the Roundhead M.P. for Carlisle, tried to persuade General David Leslie to march with his cavalry into Cumberland. Consequently, Leslie with 800 horse marched into the county from Newcastle. He expected to meet with no opposition, but when he got to Salkeld and was about to ford the Eden, he found he was opposed by horse and foot regiments raised by the local gentlemen, with Sir Philip Musgrave, Sir Henry Bellingham, and Sir Henry Fletcher at their head. Leslie was on the point of retiring to Newcastle, when Barwise (not the M.P., but Barwise of Ilekirk, known as the great Barwise), rode into the river, whereon Leslie and the horse followed, and the whole of the opposing force promptly ran off as fast as they could to Carlisle, with Leslie chasing them. He drew up his horse in full view of the city on St Nicholas Hill, near the gallows, and some skirmishing took place between them and the garrison on the east side of Carlisle. The next day Leslie went off to Newcastle, though it was claimed that, had he stayed, he might have reduced Carlisle in a very short time, as it was not yet provisioned to withstand a siege. The scandal of the day was that he did this on purpose to give the Royalists time to provision the town, in order that the siege would be more protracted and he and his men might draw pay for a longer period. Leslie had served under Gustavus Adolphus, and was said to have a good deal of the Dugald Dalgetty about him.

Steps had been taken by Sir Thomas Glemham to put Carlisle in readiness to stand a siege: the Cumberland troops had been disbanded, there being some doubt about their fidelity to the Royal cause after their exploits at Salkeld. Vast quantities of provisions were acquired and stowed in the Fratry, and in the Citadels: the arms were refurbished, and drums, drumheads, and drumsticks purchased.[81]

After Newcastle had surrendered and Leslie, with his 4,000 horse and foot, returned to lay siege to Carlisle, he established his headquarters at Dalston Hall, and raised four works to block the roads: one near the village of Newtown, a second at Stanwix under Lord Kirkcudbright, a third, under Colonel Chomley near the Gallows on Harraby Hill, and a fourth under Colonel Lawson near Botcherby. What these works were is not possible to tell, probably palisadings or earthworks, designed to hold parties of sixty to 100 horse: these to be relieved every twenty-four hours by fresh parties of their comrades, quartered in the surrounding villages. The work at Stanwix was in the churchyard and mounted three small guns: it does not appear that the other works had guns. However, they were of strategic importance – the work in Stanwix churchyard closed all access to and from Carlisle on the north; the work at Newton and the headquarters at Dalston Hall closed the western roads; that on Gallows Hill blocked the road to the south, while the work at Botcherby blocked the eastern roads. The Eden was fordable by waths at Rickerby and Etterby; thus communication could be kept up between Leslie's works at Botcherby and Stanwix, and Stanwix and Newton. The other rivers, the Caldew and Petteril, were fordable in several places.

These works left a great deal of grazing ground accessible to the garrison and inhabitants, but Leslie seems to have been in no hurry over the siege: he did not assault the walls, content to bide his time until the besieged should finish their store of provisions. One consequence of the scarcity of engineers in the British armies of this period was that, when it was impossible to make an immediate breach and assault, besiegers generally resorted to blockade. The Scots and the northern Parliamentarians at the siege of Carlisle followed this plan. Siege operations mainly consisted of efforts by the Scots to surprise the cattle and horses of the Royalist garrison when grazing outside the city, while the garrison made efforts to protect them, and to launch sallies out into the country to destroy the various works by which Leslie gradually contracted the grazing ground. At this period the country far and wide around Carlisle was open common and moorland, the country between Penrith and Carlisle still described a century later as 'mostly an open country, full of commons.' To the north, the country was an almost impenetrable morass, traversable by paths known only to moss-troopers, smugglers, and peddlers, while Greymoor Hill and Blackford deserved their names, as did Blackhill or Bleckell Moor, to the south. West of Carlisle, Cummersdale Moor began at Clemson's gate about the end of Shaddongate, and continued to Dalston. The road to Wigton was nearly all through open moor and eastwards, Crosby and Warwick Moors covered vast areas. Cavalry could therefore move about with considerable ease.

The garrison of Carlisle comprised 700 men, including townsmen in arms, and, according to Tullie, 200 reformadoes, or officers whom Cromwell and Lord Fairfax had discharged when they remodelled the army: some of them men of 'great prudence and proneness in arms.' As soon as Leslie had taken up quarters at Dalston Hall a party of these reformadoes sallied out to surprise him there, but all being officers they could not agree on who should be their leader, and were routed with several being killed.

On 8 December 1644 General Leslie, having travelled once again to Newcastle, returned victorious from there to Edinburgh, where he remained until January 1645, taking up [enlisting] men for the defence of the town. About 14,000 men and some of the troopers at Carlisle were sent there. However, around this date the pest [plague][82] came in to Borrowstounness; so Leslie with his wife and family returned to Newcastle.

On 9–10 March, Leven's army was at Tadcaster, Wetherby and Ferrybridge. Leslie, promoted by the estates the day before to the rank of lieutenant-general of horse, marched with 2,000 commanded foot and three regiments of horse to Cheshire, to rendezvous with Sir William Brereton. This force reached Whitchurch on the 29th, returned to Sandbach and on 1 April arrived at Knutsford from where it then returned to Leven's army.

In April 1645 Baillie is told 'that by no means ministers will come to the Army'; and that 'in two and twenty regiments [there was] not one minister'. 'You cannot be answerable to God,' he wrote to one of his brethren; 'if you do not your best quickly to send up an able minister to every regiment, and at least one half dozen of the most gracious, wise, and courageous ministers of the Kingdom.' For not only was the want of religious teaching one of the causes of the disorders which began to spread in the Scottish Army, but it favoured the growth of heresy in the ranks.

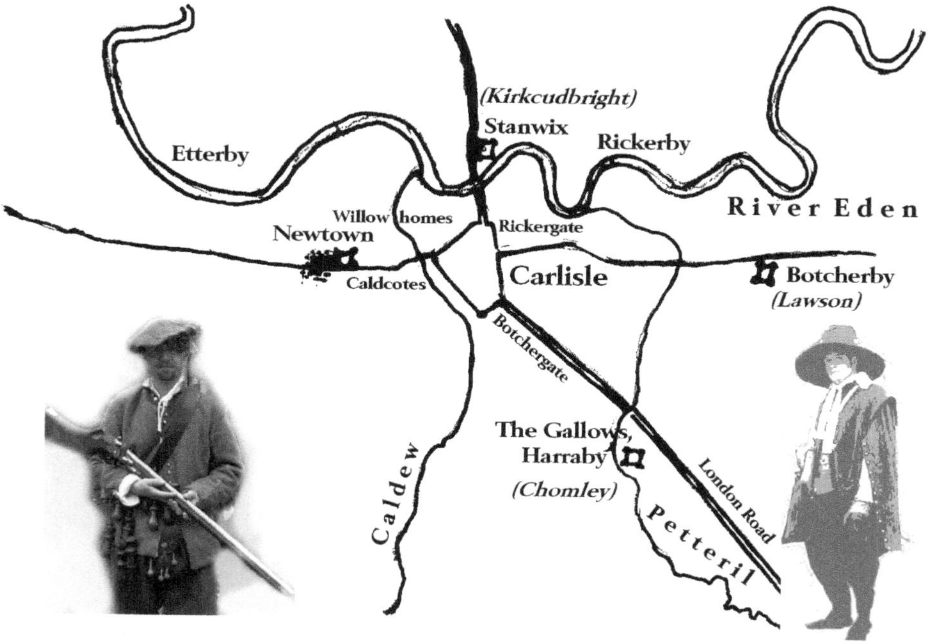

One duty the chaplains performed during the Civil War was to draw up narratives of the proceedings of the armies to which they were attached for publication in the press – effectively the first war correspondents.

The siege went on at a leisurely pace, with no great expenditure of life. An abundance of beer was consumed, drunkenness was widespread, there was a report of the apparition of a Captain Forrester's ghost at the head of a ghostly army of horse and foot; and two spies were tortured on the rack. In April Leslie felt the time had come for him to contract his lines round the city: so he established a work at Etterby, which commanded the wath there over the Eden, by which the garrison had succeeded in carrying off in a sally a large number of cattle from Cargoholmes: a feat the new work would prevent them from repeating. Another new work was made on the top of Caldcotes Bank, which commanded the Willowholme, rendering it useless to the garrison as a grazing ground. The cattle were then grazed south of the citadels, but Leslie put a stop to this by raising a fort at Fusehill. The Swifts were then resorted to. On the 28 or 29 April the besiegers made a determined attempt to capture cattle being grazed there: at a signal from Stanwix, 800 Scots horse from Stanwix, Rickerby, Botcherby, and St Nicholas galloped down on the cattle as hard as they could. Luckily for the besieged, Glemham had spotted some sign of their preparations at Stanwix, and had ordered the cattle guard to move their charge closer to the town, so that they succeeded in bringing them in, with the loss of only six cows and fifteen horses, a couple of men killed and some others wounded.

May was similarly occupied with sallies and skirmishes. Leslie continued the inexorable contraction of his lines around the doomed city. In addition to his four original works and the ones at Etterby, Caldcotes, and Fusehill, he raised new ones at Murrell Hill, on the Swifts, and one opposite the Sally Port, He also cut the dam-courses to stop the mills. This last work Glemham demolished after a tremendous fight: then he erected one himself, restoring the dam-courses.

During the siege Kirkcudbright commanded the Stanwix siege work. On 16 May at 9.00 a.m. he advanced from Stanwix with 300 horse to attack musketeers of the garrison, who were protecting their cattle. The fire of the Royalists forced them to retreat, then the Royalist horse chased Kirkcudbright's men from the field. In late May/early June 1645, Kirkcudbright became the centre of a dispute, which showed the fragile nature of the Covenanter-Parliamentarian alliance. Kirkcudbright ordered Lieutenant Colonel Beecher, of Sir Wilfred Lawson's foot, to remove his men from Botcherby Mount near Carlisle, where they had quartered all winter. When the English did not move, Kirkcudbright appeared with 300 commanded men out of Newcastle to take possession of Beecher's sconces. Then Beecher persuaded Kirkcudbright to wait until Lawson was notified. The colonel said Beecher should stay put. The next day, a Sunday, Kirkcudbright ordered Beecher out again, claiming he was commander-in-chief of the besieging forces. Beecher replied that Lawson commanded the English in Cumberland and demanded to see a commission. Kirkcudbright said Beecher was saucy and promised to capture the works. Beecher tried to dissuade him by saying that bloodshed might ensue, but Kirkcudbright said he would welcome that. An order then arrived from Lawson telling Beecher to stay. Kirkcudbright subsequently surrounded the works with 300 foot and three troops of horse. This situation continued until 9.00 a.m. on Monday morning, when Lawson appeared and Kirkcudbright withdrew. Lawson ordered Beecher to Appleby to meet Leven, who received him well. The Lord General promised he would act favourably. Colonel William Stewart (Galloway Foot) then entertained Beecher and told him that Leven was angry with Kirkcudbright. The next day Leven held a conference with Kirkcudbright, Lawson, Beecher and Richard Barwis, one of the Parliamentarian commissioners. Kirkcudbright now saw that things were running against him, so he charged Beecher with being anti-Covenanter. However, the lieutenant colonel retorted by saying that he had taken the Covenant twice. In the end Kirkcudbright failed to gain control of the English positions.

The siege lasted from November 1644 to June 1645, and the garrison held out until they had eaten their horses. Elsewhere during the Civil War, besieged garrisons were reduced to far worse straits, a Royalist at Colchester some years later recounting that 'horseflesh was ... grown so delicious a food amongst the soldiers that we could scarcely secure our horses in the stables, for every morning one stable or another was robbed, and our horses knocked on the head and sold in the shambles by the pound; nor was there in a short time a dog left, for it was customary for each soldier to reserve half his ammunition loaf, and in the morning walk the streets, and if he discovered a dog, to drop a piece of bread, and so decoy him on till within reach and then with the butt end of his musket, knock his brains out, and march away with him to his quarters.'

Buoyed up by false hopes of relief, the garrison managed to hold out amid terrible suffering to the wretched inhabitants, until 25 June, when the garrison surrendered upon honourable terms to Leslie personally. Fraser's served until the town fell. Three days later the Scots foot entered the town.

To the east, on the 7 June, Leven's army had marched to Wakefield, on the 18th was at Mansfield, then marched through Nottingham and south Derbyshire, reaching Staffordshire and Warwickshire on 2 July. On the 3rd the main army was at Birmingham with a screening party at Lichfield. On the 8th the army was at Alcester, continued to Bromsgrove and on the 17th had moved to Droitwich where it divided – the artillery moving to Pershore then crossing the Severn before reaching Ledbury, while the main army marched to Bewdley, reaching Tenbury on the 19th, from where it continued to reach Bishop Frome on the 20th, a detachment storming Canon Frome (garrisoned with 120 foot and twenty horse) on the 22nd. The following day the army was quartered throughout the Bromyard-Frome-Hope area, setting up its headquarters at Ledbury on the 24th. The foot rendezvoused at Newant and the wounded and sick were taken into Gloucester. It was here that Leslie, with his cavalry from Carlisle, joined Leven's army on the march to Hereford, which was besieged on 30 July. The lieutenant-general remained only a short time at this siege. Due to rumours of the king bringing an army to relieve the city, Leslie led 4,500–5,000 cavalry east to intercept him on 12 August. On the 14th this force was at Stourbridge, on the 15th Uttoxeter, and the next day it rendezvoused with 1,600 horse under Sir John Gell at Ollerton. Five days later Leslie was at Rotherham after rendezvousing with Poyntz's, Rossiter's and Thornhaugh's horse on Doncaster Moor. Meanwhile, at the siege of Hereford, Leven, who was accustomed to issuing promissory notes for his army's food, or having to resort to free-quartering his forces upon the locality when necessary, was facing dire straits on the food front. For ten days in August, his army was almost entirely without bread and had to subsist on beans, green corn and fruit. On the 27th Leven lifted his siege, the army crossing the Severn at Gloucester the following day and moving north via Cheltenham and Warwick.

The Civil War in Hereford[83]

HEREFORDSHIRE IN THE SEVENTEENTH century was a backward and inhospitable county, with very few roads and little communication with the rest of England. There was little industry, any living being made mainly from the soil.

The inhabitants were very poor even by seventeenth-century standards – when being assessed for ship-money in 1636, the Sheriff, Roger Vaughn had pleaded 'for so small a circuit of ground as this shire contains, there are not a greater number of poor people [anywhere else] in this kingdom'.

Roads, as few as there were, were very basic and an opening where two carriages could pass rarely occurred. In fact, journeys were often made in ditches or narrow forest lanes. Bridges too were scarce; only two crossed the Wye in the whole county, so crossings and communication were made by ferries or fords. These fords, of which there were at least twenty between Hereford and Monmouth, were also very hazardous because of the rapid rise and fall of the river. The Scottish Army marching to besiege Hereford complained that they 'found the waies on this side of the Severn exceedingly strait and hard to passe'.

Because of this isolation, poverty and lack of education, the inhabitants were afraid of and often hostile to either strangers or change, even for the better.

As for the city, there is no mention of the state of the castle in military operations of the period. Although, during the reign of Henry VIII, Leland noted the castle to 'have been one of the fairest, largest and strongest castles in England', unfortunately, there are no remains left today.

The condition of the city walls is however, well documented and appears to have been in a sound state. Clarendon wrote of Hereford as 'a town very well affected, and reasonably well fortified, having a strong wall about it', and Nehemiah Wharton said that the 'town was environed with a strong wall … with five gates'. Sir Henry Slingsby described it, 'This city of Hereford is cituate'd not much unlike to Yorke, and in some parts resembles it very much; for it hath a round tower mount'd upon a hill, like to Clifford's tower, and ye mills near it, with some little works about, having ye river Wye running close by, but ye walls tho' they be high yet are not mount'd upon a rampeir as Yorke walls are'.

The county was overwhelmingly in favour of the king, of which the Scudamores, Sir William Croft, Sir Walter Pye, the Coningsbys, Wallop Brabazon and Henry Lingen were the major characters. Many others came out in favour of the king, so the balance of power and wealth was altogether for the Royalist cause.

There were exceptions, in the form of Sir Richard Hopton, Sir John Kyrle and Sir Edward Powell. These men, however, were getting old and took little part in the conflict. It is perhaps noteworthy that there was a division within Hopton's family, his eldest son being a colonel for the king, while another son was a major for parliament. Sir Robert Harley was the leading light for parliament's cause in Herefordshire. A very keen MP who worked hard to defend Puritanism, he was intelligent and very religious, but he also had a keen eye for the arts.[84]

September 1642 had seen the first real events of the Civil War in Herefordshire, when the Earl of Essex ordered the Earl of Stamford to march on Hereford with about 1,000 men.[85] Colonel Robert Kyrle (a relative of Sir John Kyrle), Edward Massey and Sir Robert Harley with his eldest son were among them. They were met en-route by Sir Richard Hopton who, it would appear, was more anxious about preserving his property at Canon Frome than joining in the dispute.

On 30 September 1642 Stamford took the city with little or no resistance, and it seems the army's arrival had been expected, as Brabazon, Coningsby, Croft, Lingen and other active Royalists were conspicuous by their absence upon his arrival. It must be said in Croft's defence that he was with the king the following month at Edgehill.

Although no force was needed to take the city, their presence was treated with some hostility. In a letter to parliament, Stamford wrote: 'The county, as well as this vile city are so base and malignant that although the rougish army of the Welsh papists and other vagabonds that were beaten in the first battle in Warwickshire do plunder, kill, murder and destroy men and women, take away all their goods and cattle, yet such is their hatred to our condition that they would rather be so used than be rescued by us'. Nehemiah Wharton wrote that the people of Hereford to be 'totally ignorant in the waies of God, and much addicted to drunkenness and other vices, principally unto swearing, so that the children that have scarce learned to speake doe universally sweare stoutlye'.

The resentment of the people of Hereford would also have been provoked by the conduct of Stamford's soldiers; they plundered remorselessly and threatened that they would keep them so short 'that they would eat the very flesh from their arms'. They did however leave the cathedral intact. Not only did Stamford have trouble with the people of Hereford, but Lord Herbert was very active in Wales and the west. In Herbert's ranks was a colonel called Sir Richard Lawdey who wrote with an offer to Constance Ferrar, a sergeant major in Stamford's army. It reads:

> Sir,
>
> My good opinion of you makes me believe that your necessity rather than your will, hath made you one in this rebellion. My affection to you finds a way to bring you out of both: which may thus be done: The Royalists shall suddenly approach Hereford with such forces as will (God willing) soon reduce the rebels in it to the kings mercy. If you, in the meantime, will contrive now to advantage us in this design, his Excellency hath commanded me to offer you five hundred pounds in money, and to assure both yourself and your assistants not only of your pardons, but that you shall be preferred to better charges (rank) in his Majesties Army than you have. Sir, bethink yourself betimes, and return your answer by bearer, that I may confidently stile myself, Sir, your most hearty friend to serve you,
>
> *R. LAWDY.*

The state of Stamford's army by this time was poor; they were underfed and the hostility towards them by the locals must have been demoralising, but the reply to Lawdey's letter by Ferrar on 1 December 1642 was one of scorn:

> Sir,
> I received a letter that bears your name, inviting me to such an act of baseness as (these must tell you), I hold in highest disdain; for never yet did my necessity (or ever shall) put me one tittle off my fidelity, or enforce me to violate my honour, which, notwithstanding the offer you make from his Excellency, I shall still endeavour (as hitherto I have done) entirely to preserve. As for his Majesty's pardon, I conceive not myself to stand in need of it, my service and employment being only for the preservation of the true Protestant religion, the safety of his Majesty's person, the defence of the laws of the land, the liberty of the subject, and privilege of Parliament, whereunto, I am persuaded, all true Englishmen are conscientiously obliged. For your undoubted power to reduce the rebels in Hereford (as you term them), doubt not Sir, when you come, you shall receive the entertainment of a soldier.
>
> *CONSTANCE FERRAR.*

Just two days after the date on the letter, on 3 December 1642, Stamford withdrew from Hereford. His situation there had become intolerable, and any movement west to Pembroke was impossible, as Herbert's army lay between the two towns. Worcester had already been evacuated, so Gloucester was the only option left open to him.

Lawdey's detachment of Herbert's army entered almost immediately, with the usual reprisals and pillaging. Sir Richard Cave was left in charge, and the former authorities returned to seek revenge. Sir Richard Hopton's home at Canon Frome was ransacked then garrisoned. William Price, the mayor, was imprisoned and threatened with hanging.

The city stayed in the hands of the Royalists until April 1643, when Sir William Waller approached from Gloucester with Massey, and between 2,500 and 3,000 troops. Feint attacks were made on two gates, but the main assault was on Widemarsh gate. Massey himself is reported to have discharged the first shot which killed an officer and several citizens. Shortly after this action a parley was called. Cave at first rejected Waller's demands with the reply 'He who held this town, held it by commission from the king. If Sir William Waller could produce a better commission from the king, it should be delivered to him; otherwise he who had it by authority from the king would preserve it for the king'. The parley lasted the whole day, but the city had little choice but to give in to Waller's demands. Hereford at that time was still not equipped to withstand the far superior numbers of Waller's army, or capable of surviving a long siege.

From a muster roll of around 800 soldiers, very few were taken prisoner, as most had made their escape during the parley. Several distinguished persons were taken, however; among them Cave, Lord Scudamore, his son James, Coningsby (the sheriff) and Colonel Herbert Price, the governor. Sir Richard Cave was court-martialled later in Oxford, one of the charges being, that he gave up the city dishonourably. He was however acquitted of this and other charges brought against him.

Waller, like Stamford before him, encountered local resentment, and like Stamford, found no reason to stay long. So on 18 May, after less than a month in the city, he and his army left for Gloucester. It took only two days for the Royalists to take complete control again.

The Clubmen Uprising

Barnabas Scudamore became the Governor of Hereford in September 1644, and then sheriff of the county in December of the same year, in effect taking complete control. Many citizens in Hereford, as in other parts of the country, were becoming more and more resentful of the military control they were under, whether Parliamentarian or Royalist. In the spring of 1645, when Scudamore attempted to raise levies and seize fodder, the Clubmen, as these country folk became known, openly resisted – some 16,000 appearing before the city on 19 March, reinforced by others from Worcester and Radnor and many it seems well-armed and well-horsed.

Massey tried to seize this opportunity and enlist the Clubmen for himself, so he set off at the head of 500 soldiers and 150 foot to Ledbury. On meeting some of their leaders he was told that, though they had no grievance with him, they could not join him as they believed that they were 'able to keep the forces of both parties from exacting contribution and quarter in their county'.

Scudamore became concerned about Massey's intervention, and so conceded to some of the Clubmen's demands. Massey retired, but not all of the Clubmen were pacified with Scudamore's concessions and 2,000 were still gathered at Ledbury when Prince Rupert appeared on 29 March and detached his horse and 1,000 men against them. Most of the Clubmen fled, around 200 remained, some firing on Rupert's men, but soon disarmed and arrested. At least three of the leaders were hanged, and Scudamore's promises of concessions went unfulfilled. One account alleged that Rupert's troops (Scudamore was with him at this time) 'plundered everie parish and howse poor as well as others leavinge neyther clothes or provision'.

During Barnabas Scudamore's time in control he strengthened the city, well enough to withstand a siege, something that had previously been lacking, as Stamford and Waller easily found out. The suburbs were cleared, even trees and hedges uprooted; anything in fact, which might give cover to an enemy. One local woman, Joyce Jefferies, was forced to sell three houses and some timber; she received £17 15*s* 0*d* for her trouble. Sir Henry Slingsby, who had been in Hereford earlier in the war, returned with the Royalist army that raised the siege, and sought out his previous lodgings. On finding them, he wrote that he 'found it pull'd down & ye gentlewoman yit had liv'd in it dead upon grief to see ye ruins of her house'. As well as houses, two churches were destroyed; St Owens and St Martins.

On 18 June 1645, shortly after his defeat at Naseby, the king arrived in Hereford. His object was to raise troops, but he had very little success, and so on 1 July he left for South Wales. Close on his heels was the Scottish Army under the Earl of Leven. On 22 July Canon Frome was taken by the Scots, with most of the garrison being put to the sword. About seventy were slain, including the Governor, Colonel John Barnold, who was buried on the 25th at Ashperton. Sir Robert Barley's son, Edward, was left in charge of the new garrison.

The Siege of Hereford

A GARRISON OF 1,500 soldiers defended Hereford by 31 July 1645, when the Scottish Army, 14,000 strong, appeared before the city.

'The Scots marched with a very sorry equipage; every soldier carried a week's provision of oatmeal, and they had a drove of cattel with them for their food.'

A Scot writes:

> The Scottish army hath a very able traine of artillerie, and many pretty engines for war, and devices for killing Cavaliers and Papists … never was a better disciplined

> Army in the Christian world than ours. We have no dangerous mutinies ... but a universal cheerfulness in our whole body ... never did [an] Army make less spoil, commit less violence, fewer plunderings ... Our Army is very hardy too, and can endure all heats and colds, and a small victailing will serve the turn; a little paste well kneaded in the palme of their hands is there usuall dyet, and they are not so tender as your English Cavaliers, who love ease, and eating, and carousing ...

Different sources, however, declare:

> I myself was a great Proselite [supporter] of theirs, till I had experienced their oppression, self seeking and cruelty at the siege before Hereford; where, though they were sufficiently provided for ... yet the great spoil and havoc they made, almost to the impoverishing and ruining of many poore families in that country ... divers houses rifled, doors, chests and trunks broken open, several families undone; most of all their cattle, horses, and goods taken from them, much money, plate, jewels and all kind of rich houshold-stuff, rings, and other rich commodities, as wearing apparel, linen, books, ...
>
> Highlanders. These are not as civilised as we could wish, but they are good soldiers and hardy men, and are usually clad in a light plaid or speckled stuff, and in this attire they usually march, never using any armes [armour] upon their bodies. They have darts, and bows and arrows, and dirks or great knives; and which is a wonder (for they are none of them very religious) yet they all hate bishops, papists, and cavaliers, and they threaten to pull them all to pieces, one limb from another.

Most contemporary descriptions omit an important part of most large armies, namely the hundreds of women and even children who travelled with the baggage train. These women nursed injured soldiers, cooked and washed for their men folk and if the soldiers weren't paid, their families would go hungry too. Committees were set up in areas the army had to pass through to feed and supply the army, but the Earl of Leven complained to parliament that his soldiers were not sufficiently provided for in Herefordshire. He also commented on the terrible state of the roads: 'the Army is not able to march above eight miles a day, though they begin to march at the Sun rising, and continue till ten at night ... the county is unwilling to afford us anything, and the committees give us no assistance.'

Almost immediately the Scots began to 'dig in'. A section of their earthworks, known locally as 'Scotch Row Ditch' is still visible.

Conditions for the Scots were hampered by the departure of David Leslie with the cavalry. This not only weakened their army, it also made getting provisions much more difficult. Leven writes:

> My lord, I should give your Lordship an accompt of the valour of our common Souldiers and Townesmen, that would hazard themselves at the making up of breaches (to the astonishment of the Enemy), till their cannon played between their leggs, and even the Women (such was their gallantry) ventured where the Musquet bullets did so. They were also dealt a cruel blow when Major-General Crawford was shot and killed by a musket ball. Crawford, a professional soldier who had distinguished himself in Germany and Marston Moor, met his end, so tradition has it, at the hands of a baker's boy. Enraged by this they battered the city severely and made a breach in the wall. The defenders though, rebuilt it by breaking down an arch of the bridge and using the stone to effect repairs. There is still evidence of this to this day as the bridge has dis-similar arches.

Several times the Scots attempted mines but Scudamore was able to foil them. On one occasion, under the protection of musket fire, small boys ran out with faggots and torches and managed to suffocate some Scottish miners. On another occasion a mine was sabotaged by the opening of the town ditch which flooded it. The defenders were not only courageous; they were also imaginative in their use of defensive tactics. In a letter to Lord Digby, Scudamore wrote, 'The recreation we had in the midst of our besieging was to turn loose upon the enemies works by night dogs, cats, and outworn horses, having lighted matches tied about them; whereby we put the enemy in such distraction that sometimes they charged one another'. He also mentions that the women and children played a vital and heroic role in the defence of the town.

One legend has it that a bull was covered in a hurdle of twigs, wood and pitch, which was put on fire. This creature was then let loose out of one of the city gates to disrupt the besiegers' lines.

The siege lasted a month, and on the day of a final and probable successful assault, news that the king was approaching reached the Scots. Even though they had considerably more numbers than the king, they had no cavalry, and Leven thought it unwise for his infantry alone to await a strong body of horse. That night the Scottish army withdrew from Hereford. In Scudamore's words the king 'drawing a little nearer to us, like the sunne to the meridian, this Scottish mist beganne to disperse, and the next morning vanished out of sight'.

Charles, to the great rejoicing of the people of Hereford, entered the town on 4 September. Scudamore was knighted and the towns coat of arms given a motto *Invictae Fidelitatis Praemium* – the reward of invincible loyalty. According to Scudamore, the defenders lost only twenty-one, while the Scots lost 2,000 men; the Scots, on the other hand, said they lost only 600. The relief of Hereford was to be the last success Charles was to have in the war.

7. Montrose's Successes North of the Border

One year earlier, in July 1644, shortly after Callendar had re-captured Morpeth from Montrose's Royalists, Alexander [Alasdair] Macdonald, son of Colla Ciotach[86] (Kolkitto, by which name he was also sometimes referred), had landed on the west coast of Scotland at the head of a body of 1,500 troops sent by the Earl of Antrim, with which he advanced through the highlands intent on joining Montrose, who was at the time wandering through the hills of Tullibardine, near the Tay. Montrose, on hearing of the giant 21-year-old adventurer's arrival, had sent him instructions to march into Atholl; but in passing through Badenoch the Irish leader was threatened with an attack by the Earls of Sutherland and Seaforth and some of their followers, along with the clansmen of Frasers, Grants, Rosses, and Munros, who had assembled at the top of Strathspey; however he cautiously avoided them and hurried into Atholl. Here he was coldly received by the natives, until, late in August, he was joined by Montrose, who had slipped into Perth with a couple of companions, disguised as Covenanter troopers. Now at the head of more than 2,000 men, Montrose was to commence his 'Year of Miracles', using the devastating new highland charge to gain victory at the Battle of Tippermuir and the capture of Perth, followed on 13 September 1644 by the Battle of Justice Mills and the sacking of Aberdeen.

The Battle of Justice Mills, sometimes referred to as 'The Fecht of Aberdeen', was fought between the attacking forces of Montrose and the defending Covenanter forces of Lord Burleigh and the burgh council of Aberdeen. From start to finish, the battle took only two hours.

On the Royalist side, Montrose led 1,500 troops, including Alasdair MacColla's Irish veterans and an admittedly meagre fifty cavalry. His army was somewhat reduced after his assault on Perth, but it had won the day there and morale was high.

The Covenanters were led by Lord Burleigh, as well as by a bewildering array of civic authorities and other interested parties. Comprising 2,500 men including a respectable detachment of cavalry and the Fife Regiment, the Covenanter forces had the advantage of numbers, but were hampered by a scrambled chain of command. In addition, a regiment of 3,000 Gordons had been turned away from the Covenanter army through personal squabbles amongst the commanding officers.

Choosing the ground, the defenders elected to fight in the open rather than retreat within the un-fortified streets of Aberdeen, blocking Montrose's approach to the burgh from the most commanding position available on that road – the hill at Justice Mills. At that time the hill offered an army the opportunity to strike at any foe on the low ground on the western approach of the Hardgate.

Finding an army drawn up against him, Montrose sent a letter advising the townsfolk of his terms: Aberdeen was to be given up to him entire, or all who resist were to receive no quarter. As set forth in Chapter 20 of Deuteronomy, peace was to be offered and, if forsaken, all men of that city were to be put to the sword.

His terms were given to the people of Aberdeen in the company of some gentlemen and a drummer. The council drafted a reply, but it was not to reach Montrose under a flag of truce, for the drummer was shot dead whilst returning to his lines, ostensibly by a Covenanter horseman. Montrose was incensed and, giving the townsfolk no time to withdraw, ordered the attack.

The hastily assembled militias of Aberdeen and Fife were no match for the Irish and the battle was soon over. A spirited charge at the press of the militia soon broke the defenders' spirits and the Covenanters withdrew shortly after noon. The retreat to the imagined safety of Aberdeen turned into a rout, and the triumphant Royalists killed 160 as they overtook the fleeing Covenanters. Indignant, Montrose agreed to let his troops plunder Aberdeen, and the council registers tell a terrible tale: 'the enemie entring the toune immediatelie, did kill all, old and young, whome they fand on streittes.' Three days of terrible violence followed, and throughout the war no other burgh would suffer as Aberdeen had until the sack of Dundee in 1651.

On 4 September the Marquis of Argyll, who had been pursuing the Irish under Macdonald, arrived with his men at Stirling, where he was joined by the Earl of Lothian at the head of his regiment, and on the 10th marched to Perth, where he received a considerable addition to his force, now consisting of some 3,000 foot, two regular country regiments, and ten troops of horse. Argyll left Perth for the north on 14 September 1644 and on his route was joined by the Earl Marshal, Lord Fraser of Muchal, and other Covenanters. He arrived at Aberdeen on the 19th, within half a day's journey of his enemy. After spending three days in inglorious inactivity, Argyll moved in the direction of Kintore. Montrose, hearing of his approach, attempted to cross the Spey, but was prevented by a large armed force from the country north of the river, and he instead marched to the forest of Abernethy. On the 24th, Argyll mustered his followers – which now numbered 4,000 men – at the Bog of Gight, but although the army under Montrose was perhaps only a third of that number and less than 20 miles distant, Argyll did not attempt to attack them. Soon after, he instead moved to Forres to attend the Committee of Covenanters gathered to plan operations in the north, at which the Earl of Sutherland; Sir James Fraser of Brea, the Tutor of Lovat; and the Sheriff of Moray, were present. These northern chiefs brought about 1,000 additional men to Argyll's army.

Throughout, however, Argyll showed his utter unfitness for the post he held in the Covenanting army. He followed Montrose over a long and circuitous route, most of which bore recent traces of his passing, and instead of displaying any urge to overtake his retreating foe, seemed happier to keep a distance from him, perhaps 'willing to wound yet afraid to strike.' It would be difficult to imagine a more remarkable example of pusillanimity than that shown by Argyll during this campaign; and it seems surprising that after incurring disgrace among his friends and the contempt of his enemies, he should still have been allowed to keep a command for which he was so utterly unfit.

In the beginning of November, after giving orders to the highlanders to return home, he went to Edinburgh, where he received little thanks for his service against the marquis. In the end of January 1645, Montrose left Argyll and Lorne ravaged, and marched through Glencoe and Lochaber towards Inverness, intending to seize the town. However, he learned that Seaforth was advancing to meet him with an army of 5,000 horse and foot, including the veteran garrison of Inverness and the Frasers Clansmen. But when told that Argyll, with a force of 3,000 men, had entered Lochaber and was laying waste the country to his rear, he turned back and defeated them with great slaughter at the Battle of Inverlochy, on the 2nd February 1645.

During the disasters of this period, the chief of the clan Fraser, Lord Lovat, worn out with physical and mental infirmities, often reproved his brother Sir James, Tutor of Lovat, for the political path he was pursuing. His own natural inclinations led him to the king's service, but through a misunderstanding between Huntly and Montrose, who were commissioned by the king, he could not join either of them. His heart was set on the king's interest, to which he wished success and prosperity; nothing could persuade him to give the least countenance to those he thought the king's enemies. But the Marquis of Argyll, having won over Sir James, the Earl of Leven, who was the young master of Lovat's grandfather and commander-in-chief of the forces in Scotland against the king, took care to keep a watchful eye over Lord Lovat, in case his appearance on the king's side might affect the estate and embarrass the succession of his young grandson. So the Frasers remained loyal to the Covenant.

With Montrose continuing to be more than a thorn in the side of the Scottish Government forces, the Covenanters felt that there was a real risk of them losing the Civil War in Scotland. Regiments were therefore detached from the Covenanter army in England, under Generals Hurry and Baillie, to strengthen the government troops in Scotland and set the task of crushing the Royalists once and for all. It was to lead to one of the bloodiest encounters of the war at the village of Auldearn.

For several months a desultory war in the north was carried on. Having sacked Dundee, Montrose successfully eluded the larger Covenanter forces of Baillie and Hurry, despite Baillie offering a reward of 20,000 crowns to anyone who should bring him Montrose's head. Montrose secured his forces within the fastness of the

Grampians, allowing them to refresh themselves after the strenuous efforts they had made in escaping their pursuers. Whilst his men were enjoying this necessary relaxation from the fatigues of the field, Montrose received intelligence that a division of the Covenanting army under Hurry was in full march to Aberdeen, with the intention of continuing into Moray. Believing Hurry would launch an attack on the possessions of the Gordons, Montrose dispatched Lord Gordon with his horse to the north to assist his friends in case of attack. He himself with only 500 foot and fifty horse then marched to Dunkeld and from there to Crieff, about 17 miles from Perth, where Baillie lay with his forces.

Aware of the weakness of Montrose's forces, Baillie left Perth during the night of 7 April with 2,000 foot and 500 horse, intending to fall upon Montrose by break of day. Hearing of Baillie's approach, and having ascertained the enemy's strength of numbers, Montrose ordered his foot to withdraw with all speed up Strathearn and to retire into the adjoining passes. Covering his retreat with his small body of horse, Montrose took control of the pass of Strathearn and Baillie, and thinking it useless to pursue him, retired once more to Perth. Montrose was joined at the ford of Cardross by the Viscount Aboyne, the Master of Napier, Hay of Dalgetty, and Stirling of Keir, who, along with the Earl of Nithsdale, Lord Herries and others, had escaped from Carlisle. They proceeded north without opposition and had advanced as far as Loch Katrine when they heard that General Hurry was in the Enzie with a considerable force, preparing to attack Lord Gordon, who had not sufficient forces to oppose him.

Resolving to defeat Hurry before Baillie became aware of his movements, Montrose rapidly marched alongside Loch Tay, through Athole and Angus and across the Grampian hills down the Strath of Glenmuck. During this march the Athole-men and other highlanders joined him before Lord Gordon met him at the head of 1,000 foot and 200 horse. Montrose crossed the Dee on 1 of May, at the Mill of Crathie – having obtained ammunition from a ship in Aberdeen harbour – continued his march towards the Spey, and before Hurry was even aware his enemy had crossed the Grampians, was within 6 miles of his camp. Faced with the sudden appearance of Montrose with such a superior force – Hurry had only 1,000 foot and 200 horse – the Covenanters raised camp and crossed the Spey in great haste, intending to march to Inverness where they could be joined by the troops of the garrison and receive substantial reinforcements from the neighbouring counties.

To oppose Hurry as soon as possible, Montrose followed his army towards Inverness to a distance of 14 miles beyond Forres, when, favoured by the darkness of the night, Hurry escaped and arrived at Inverness.

Thinking that Montrose and his forces were intending to besiege the garrison at Inverness, the entire north rose in fear, detachments from Caithness, Sutherland, and Ross gathering at Inverness to join with elements of Rosses, Monroes, Mackenzies and Frasers. This accession of force increased Hurry's army to 3,500 foot and 400 horse. He immediately resolved to act on the offensive, by taking the battle to Montrose.

At this time a Major Fraser, having been in Ireland suppressing the rebellion there, and now returned a colonel, offered his service to Lord Lovat, his chief, as being fittest to have the conduct of the Frasers contingent of these forces, now on their march. But Sir James Fraser would not hear of this, which he would later have cause to regret.

The morning after his pursuit, Montrose took up position at the village of Auldearn, 2 miles south-east of Nairn. During the day, Hurry advanced with his forces and those of the Inverness garrison towards Nairn and, on approaching Auldearn, formed his army in order of battle. Montrose's force, greatly weakened by the departure of the Athol-men and other highlanders to defend their county from the depredations of Baillie's army, now amounted to around 1,500 foot and 250 horse. It was with some reluctance that he considered giving battle to an enemy more than double the size of his own force and consisting in great part of veteran troops. However, pressed by Hurry and in danger of attack from the rear by Baillie, he had no choice but to risk a general engagement.

A few weeks before, towards the end of April 1645, Colonel Hugh Fraser, who had recently travelled back up to Inverness from where his regiment was campaigning, married Christian Baillie.[87] The day before the battle of Auldearn, Hugh Fraser left Inverness, with his new wife, to travel to London in Captain George Scot's ship – 'a ship of prodigious bigness for bulk and burden – none such ever seen in our north seas'. The day after leaving Inverness, the ship anchored in the mouth of the River Narden [at Nairn] to take on fresh water, when the Battle of Auldearn was supposedly fought in full view of the passengers.[88]

Auldearn, 9 May 1645

Montrose arranged his forces in order of battle on what was to be the battlefield. Having formed them into two divisions, he posted the right wing on the north of the village, where the ground was enclosed by a considerable number of dykes and ditches. This body of 400 men – chiefly Irish – under the command of MacDonald was instructed by Montrose not to leave their positions on any account, as they would be well protected by the walls around them from both cavalry and foot and furthermore could, without much danger to themselves, keep up a galling and destructive fire upon their assailants. In addition, to attract the enemy to this difficult spot, Montrose gave MacDonald the royal standard, intending, when Hurry's forces were entangled amongst the bushes and dykes all over this right wing, to attack them himself with his left wing; and to enable him to do this more effectively, he placed the whole of his horse and the remainder of his foot on the left wing to the south of the village. He committed the cavalry to the charge of Lord Gordon while he himself took command of the foot. Having placed a few chosen foot with some cannon in front of the village under cover of some dykes, Montrose awaited the attack of the enemy.

Hurry divided his foot and horse each into two divisions. On the right wing of the main body of foot, commanded by Campbell of Lawers, Hurry positioned his regular cavalry, which he had brought from the south, and on the left the horse of Moray and the north, under the charge of Captain Drummond. The other division of foot was placed behind as his reserve, commanded by Hurry himself.

When Hurry observed the disposition of Montrose's forces, he could not guess his enemy's design, but, knowing his opponent's character, was satisfied that the arrangements were the result of a well-laid plan. What did surprise him, however, was the sight of the large yellow royal standard in the midst of a small body of foot stationed among hedges and dykes and stones, almost isolated from the horse and the main body of foot. To attack this party, at the head of which he naturally supposed Montrose was, was his first object. Montrose's snare proved successful. Aiming to swiftly overwhelm this position, Hurry launched his best horse and his entire veteran troops in a furious assault upon MacDonald's party, the latter defending themselves bravely behind the dykes and bushes. The contest continued for some time and Hurry, who had men to spare, could periodically relieve those who were engaged in the conflict with fresh troops.

Montrose kept a steady eye on the movements of his enemy, looking for the best point to strike with his left wing. Just as he was about to do so, MacDonald, 'a brave enough man, but a better soldier than a general, extremely violent, and daring even to rashness,' was so provoked by the taunts and insults of his opponents, that despite the express orders of Montrose not to leave his position, recklessly advanced beyond it to attack the enemy, and though he was repulsed several times, pressed forward to the charge. He was inevitably borne down by the sheer force of numbers of the enemy's horse and foot, consisting as they did of veteran troops, and forced to retire in disorder into an adjoining enclosure. However, the manner of his retreat and the courage he displayed while leading off his men was admirable. Defending his body with a large target [shield], he single-handedly resisted the assaults of the enemy and was the last to leave the field. So close was he to Hurry's spearmen, that several fixed their spears in his target, which he cut off by threes or fours at a time with his broadsword. However, there is also a tradition that the life of Alasdair Macdonald was saved by a stroke that excites compassionate interest on behalf of its victim. Macdonald 'was engaged hand to hand with Hay of Kinnudie, a tall and powerful man; and perceiving himself about to be overpowered, called out to Hay, 'I'll not deceive you, my men are coming behind you.' Having by this means induced Hay to turn around, he saved his own life by stabbing his adversary.'

Montrose, receiving news of the flight of his right wing, kept his usual presence of mind and, to encourage his men, addressed Lord Gordon, loud enough to be heard by his troops: 'What are we doing, my Lord? Our friend MacDonald has routed the enemy on the right and is carrying all before him. Shall we look on and let him carry off the whole honour of the day?' Scarcely were the words out of Montrose's mouth when he ordered his men to charge. At this point in the battle, when Montrose's men were advancing to the charge, that Captain Drummond, commanding Hurry's horse, made an awkward manoeuvre by wheeling about his men. His body of horse came in contact with his own foot, broke their ranks and created tremendous confusion. Seeing this, the Royalist Lord Gordon rushed Drummond's horse with his own party and put them to flight. Montrose followed hard with his foot, attacking the main body of Hurry's army, and routing them after an intense struggle. The veterans in Hurry's army, all experts and singularly well-trained soldiers who had served in Ireland, finding themselves for the most part cut off, fought manfully, opting to fight and be cut down in their ranks rather than retreat; but their comrades in arms, green levies from Moray, Ross, Sutherland and Caithness, fled in consternation. They were pursued for several miles and might all have been killed, the Royalists' cry of 'No quarter!' being followed by a stroke of the broadsword, had Lord Aboyne, flourishing a display of ensigns and standards taken from the enemy, not inadvertently halted the pursuers, who imagined that a fresh party of the enemy was coming up to attack them. In this way Hurry and some of his troops, the last to leave the field of battle, along with some stragglers, escaped danger and made it to Inverness by the following morning. As the loss of the battle was evidently due to Captain Drummond, who was accused of having betrayed the army and, it is said, admitted to having spoken with the enemy after battle had commenced, he was tried by court martial at Inverness and summarily shot.

The news of this fatal bloody battle soon spread over the north. The number killed on both sides was variously stated. The Covenanters were reported as having lost anywhere from 1,000 to 3,000 men, while Montrose was said to have lost at worst 200 men and at best only 'some twenty four gentlemen hurt and some few Irish killed.' There is no doubt Montrose knew the value of such returns. The cry of 'No quarter!' was now familiar after each victory, as the Royalist general's men took their usual advantage of 'killing everybody they could overtake, and yielding quarter to none.' The clans who had joined Hurry suffered considerably, particularly the Frasers. Sir James Fraser of Brea, 'The Marques of Argyle's Creature', had induced the men of the Fraser clan to fight Montrose and, besides unmarried men, lost eighty-seven married men amongst his casualties. How often after, Lovat would chide and challenge his brother Sir James for his forwardness in the quarrel, to lose so many of his kinsmen fallen in this battle. Montrose had taken sixteen standards from the enemy, along with their baggage, provisions, ammunition, and a considerable quantity of money and valuable effects.

Alford, Aberdeenshire, 2 July 1645

Although he had defeated one Covenanter army at Auldearn, Montrose had to overcome Lieutenant-General Baillie's main force before he could move out of the highlands and into central Scotland. Alasdair MacColla returned to the west to raise reinforcements while Montrose and Baillie once again spent several weeks maneuvering across Moray and Aberdeenshire trying to gain a tactical advantage.

The two armies finally met early in July at Alford, 20 miles west of Aberdeen. While Baillie approached from the north, Montrose took up a strong position on Gallows Hill overlooking a ford across the River Don. He placed most of his troops on the reverse slope of the hill out of sight, with a small force on the crest in order to encourage Baillie to advance. As Montrose expected, Baillie thought that the Royalist troops were retreating and sent his cavalry across the ford to outflank them. As soon as most of the Covenanter horse had crossed onto the marshy ground on the south side of the river, Montrose ordered his whole army to advance to the crest of the hill. Unable to retreat safely, Baillie was forced to deploy close to the Don in an area of marshy ground, using hedgerows and wet ditches to strengthen his position. Both sides drew up in standard formation, with two cavalry wings and infantry in the centre. Baillie's army had 1,800 foot and 600 horse under the command of Lord Balcarres. Montrose had about the same number of foot but only 300 horse. Lord Gordon's cavalry were placed on the Royalist right wing, Lord Aboyne on the left. In the centre were the Irish foot commanded by Ma'nus O'Cahan and highlanders of the MacDonald, Gordon, Graham and Stewart clans, with a small reserve in the rear.

The battle started when Lord Gordon charged downhill against Balcarres' cavalry. A fierce fight ensued on the Royalist right wing. Balcarres held his ground until Nathaniel Gordon came up with his infantry to support his kinsman, instructing his men to get among the Covenanter horses and use their dirks to hamstring them. As the surviving Covenanter cavalry broke and fled, the Gordons turned to attack the flank of Baillie's infantry in the centre. Meanwhile, Lord Aboyne led his cavalry down the hill to outflank Baillie on the opposite wing while O'Cahan and the highlanders charged in the centre. Montrose brought up his reserve to the brow of the hill to give the impression of an overwhelming force and the Covenanter position collapsed. Up to 1,000 men were slaughtered as they tried to escape back across the ford. For Montrose, however, the victory was soured by the death of Lord Gordon, killed by a stray bullet from his own side during the rout of the Covenanters.

1 Charles I, Henrietta Maria, Princess Elizabeth and the Prince of Wales (later Charles II) in more peaceful times. (Library of Congress)

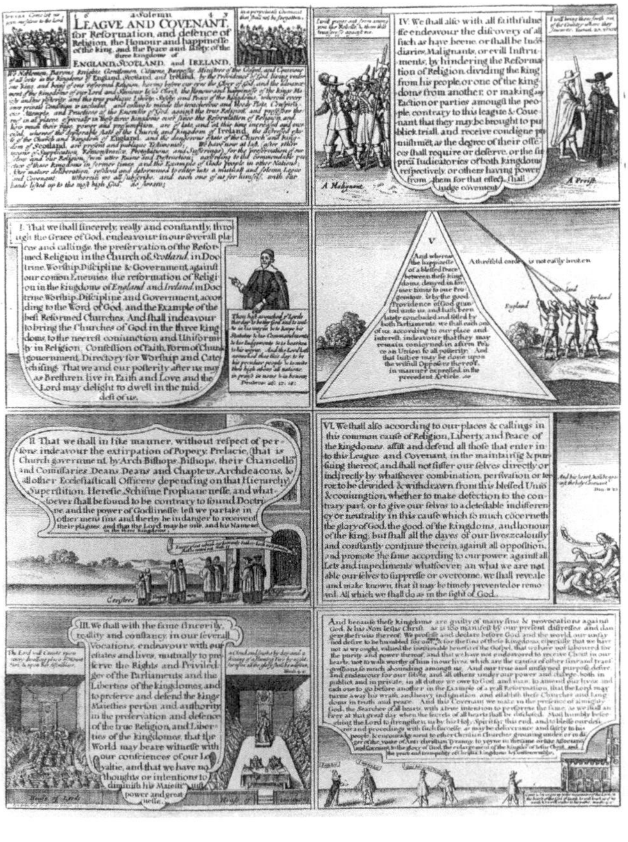

2 Broadsheet of the times advertising the benefits of the Solemn League and Covenant, to spread the kirk's one true religion throughout the three kingdoms. (Engraved by W. Hollar/The Bridgeman Art Library)

3 Illustration from a later period showing a somewhat romanticised version of the religious crusade many believed they were on. However, the religious fervour underwriting the military campaigns cannot be overemphasised. (From *Cassell's Illustrated History of England*/The Stapleton Collection/The Bridgeman Art Library)

4 Micklegate Bar, one of the principal gateways into the walled and fortified city of York, pictured in the late nineteenth century. (Library of Congress)

5 An 1819 illustration glorifying the Battle of Marston Moor (1644), showing the chaos that may have ensued when spirited but not particularly well-trained and often drunk young officers were led into a charge against the enemy. (By Cooper Abraham/Harris Museum and Art Gallery/The Bridgeman Art Library)

6 Army on the march at the Battle of Preston and Walton, 17 August 1648. A bridge like this would often have to be fought for before the enemy could destroy it, denying the opposing forces a crossing point. River crossings were more often fords, tree bridges or pontoon bridges created by the army prisoners. (By Charles Cattermole/Harris Museum and Art Gallery/The Bridgeman Art Library)

7 This is perhaps what Oliver Cromwell's redoubtable Ironsides may have looked like. The Scots' horse, in comparison, would have had much smaller mounts and the riders would have been more lightly armoured, with leather buff coats as opposed to back and breastplates. ('Cromwell at Dunbar, 1650' by Andrew Carrick Gow/Imperial Defence College/The Bridgeman Art Library)

8 William Hamilton, 2nd Duke of Hamilton, whose political and military expertise was not up to the task of raising the Scots in sufficient numbers to place Charles II on the throne of England. (*Lodge's British Portraits* (1823)/Ken Welsh/ The Bridgeman Art Library)

9 James Graham, Marquis of Montrose, upon his eventual capture by government forces, was led through the streets of Edinburgh to the gallows, 21 May 1650, looking like 'a groom going to his wedding'. (By James Drummond/© Scottish National Gallery/The Bridgeman Art Library)

10 Archibald Campbell, the self-serving Marquis of Argyll, charged with tracking and destroying the forces of James Graham, Marquis of Montrose – a command he was wholly unfit for. (From *Lodge's British Portraits* (1823)/ The Bridgeman Art Library)

A List of the Princes, Dukes, Earls, Lords, Knights, Generals, Maior Generalls, &c. and Colonells, of the *Scots* Kings party slaine and taken Prisoners,

By his Majesty DEATH the Hieroglyphix.

A PROCLAMATION.

DEATH.

REVELATION 13. 18.

A List of the Family from which CHARLES the second King of Scotland descended, that sat in the fatall Throne of Scotland, and came to untimely ends.

A List of the Earles, Lords, Knights, Generall Officers, and Colonells of the Scots KINGS party, slaine and taken Prisoners.

Lords taken Prisoners.

Lords slaine and dead of their wounds

Knights tooke Prisoners.

Knights slaine and put to death.

Generall Officers taken Prisoners.

Generall Officers slain.

Colonells taken Prisoners.

Colonells slaine.

Bishops, Magistrates, and eminent Clergy-men, Phisitians, &c taken prisoners,

Slain and put to death

LONDON Printed by Robert Ibbitson, 1652.

11 Broadsheet celebrating the crushing of the Scottish uprising to try to set Charles II of Scotland on the throne in England. The list of killed and captured included the ill-fated Duke of Hamilton, David Leslie, Middleton, Montgomery, O'Neil and others. (The Bridgeman Art Library)

12 The Lovats' chapel at Wardlaw cemetery, Kirkhill, Inverness. Hugh Fraser was interred in the Lovats' aisle after a funeral procession with full military honours marched him from Inverness in 1649. (Betty McRae)

Kilsyth, Stirlingshire, 15 August 1645

WHEN ALASDAIR MACCOLLA REJOINED him with more clansmen from the western highlands, Montrose was able to muster the largest army he had yet commanded, around 3,000 foot and 500 horse. After raiding for supplies in the north-east, the Royalist army advanced southwards towards Perth and established a base at Dunkeld. The Scottish parliament — driven from Edinburgh by a virulent outbreak of plague to Stirling and then to Perth — resolved to concentrate all available forces against Montrose. New levies were raised in Fife, the borders and south-western Scotland. Although the home army soon outnumbered Montrose's forces, the recruits were untrained and poorly disciplined. Lieutenant-General Baillie offered his resignation after the defeat at Alford, and parliament decided to recall Major-General Monro from Ulster to command all forces in Scotland. However, Baillie was obliged to continue his command until Monro's arrival. Meanwhile, the Committee of Estates, including the Marquis of Argyll, Lord Balfour of Burleigh and several leading clergymen, accompanied Baillie on campaign to offer him advice on strategy and tactics.

Montrose unexpectedly marched from Dunkeld to cross the River Forth and into the hills south of Stirling. With Montrose now threatening the Lowlands, the Covenanter committee urged an immediate pursuit. Montrose knew that the Earl of Lanark was marching from Glasgow with Covenanter reinforcements, so he turned to fight Baillie before Lanark could join him.

Montrose halted his army near the village of Kilsyth between Glasgow and Stirling. He drew up in fields that formed a basin amidst a surrounding ridge of hills. The Covenanters deployed on rising ground to the east of Montrose's position. With a rough slope separating the two armies, Baillie was content to hold his ground and await the arrival of the Earl of Lanark's reinforcements. The committee was concerned that Montrose might try to escape back into the highlands, so a flanking march was ordered along the hill crests to occupy Auchinrivoch ridge to the north of Montrose's position. This entailed marching the Covenanter army across the front of the enemy. Skirmishing broke out between some of Baillie's leading troops and the MacLean highlanders who were occupying a group of cottages on Montrose's left flank. The skirmish escalated as highlanders and Covenanters acted without orders to join the fray. Realising that the Covenanter line had become disordered as Baillie tried to re-deploy in battle order, Montrose sent Lord Aboyne's cavalry in to drive off the enemy horse and expose the infantry on the right flank. With the routing of the horse, the Covenanter infantry started to break and scatter. A few officers tried to rally their troops but the situation was out of control. The line collapsed under the onslaught of Montrose's attack. The last Covenanter army in Scotland was routed and slaughtered.

The Committee of Estates fled across the border to Berwick. The Earl of Lanark abandoned his newly-raised levies and joined them there. With no Covenanter army left to oppose him, Montrose was the master of Scotland. He marched in triumph into Glasgow on 18 August. Unable to advance to Edinburgh because of the plague in the city, he set up his Royalist headquarters in the burgh of Bothwell, in Lanarkshire, organised the release of all the Royalist supporters languishing in Covenanter dungeons, and issued a proclamation at Glasgow to summon a new parliament in the king's name.

8. Philiphaugh

News of Montrose's tremendous victory at Kilsyth soon reached Leslie, who promptly left the English at the Hereford siege, taking with him 4,500–5,000 horse to screen Leven's army and advance northwards. He reached Stourbridge a couple of days later, Uttoxeter on the 15th and rendezvoused with Sir John Gell's 1,600 horse at Ollerton the following day. On the 21st he rendezvoused with the horse of Poyntz, Rossiter and Thornhaugh, from where he moved on to Rotherham. A week later, he was at Northallerton, from where he advanced via Newcastle to Berwick by 6 September, continuing to press north via Dunbar, Home Castle, Haddington, and down the Gala Water to Sunderland, before arriving at Selkirk and the field of Philiphaugh early in the morning of 13 September.

Earlier, after the fall of Carlisle, the Earl of Dalhousie's horse, which had marched south from their Aberdeenshire quarters in March and probably served at the siege, apparently joined Leven's field army besieging Hereford. On 4 August, Routmaster Sir William Bruce arrived from Scotland in northern England with thirty-six troopers he was leading to Hereford. However, the regiment did not stay with Leven until the siege ended. Instead, it returned to Scotland under Lieutenant-General. Leslie and fought at Philiphaugh. Dalhousie's was reckoned to number at that time only around 320 troopers. In February Dalhousie's and Hamilton's regiments had gone to pieces after being quartered in Aberdeen through the winter,[89] and this was confirmed not only by their low turnout at Philiphaugh, but by a later muster report of 11 December 1645, which noted that the regiment comprised 324 troopers but had only eighty-four horses fit for service. Dalhousie's regiment was almost certainly therefore left in reserve at Philiphaugh.

Whether or not Hugh Fraser's regiment proceeded south to Hereford after Carlisle had fallen, it is certain that Fraser's men crossed the mountains again. In late August or early September they joined Leslie as he rode into Scotland with his force of cavalry to confront Montrose. Accordingly this regiment too, amounting to some 400 dragoons, was engaged at Philiphaugh on 13 September.

Soldiers of Colonel James, 1st Lord Coupar, his Strathearn foot, an infantry regiment some 700 strong, after serving on the Hereford campaign, marched to Scotland to take part in this battle. Whether the whole regiment fought at Philiphaugh is uncertain. It was the only infantry regiment known to have been present, yet had Leslie been willing to slow his march to infantry pace, there is no reason why he should not have brought other regiments with him also. It is possible that the unit's participation may have been limited to a party of dragooners – musketeers temporarily mounted on horseback to speed their march – and there are references to such a unit, led by a Captain Grierson, in the ordnance papers. The size of this unit, however, is in some doubt.[90] There are certainly numerous references to Lord Coupar's dragoons from this date on: in October, Coupar's dragoons were amongst a force of about 1,600 horse and dragoons sent north to Aberdeenshire under Middleton; in November some of their men[91] were used to 'stiffen' the Glasgow Militia unit and by mid-December the unit was stationed at Perth – possibly numbering as many as 480 men. Montgomery's horse, 600 troopers and officers, also faced Montrose at Philiphaugh, as did the Earl of Lanark's horse – comprising both horse and dragoons which had entered England as part of Callendar's army. Like many other units, Lanark's had virtually disappeared for months, only to re-emerge from the fog of war in September when it served at Philiphaugh.[92] Other units identified as serving in this campaign include about forty troopers of Harry Barclay's (still incomplete) horse regiment; Middleton's horse[93] and possibly the Earl of Eglinton's horse.

After Kilsyth, the king had heaped honours on his successful General Montrose. He was made lieutenant-governor of Scotland, and invested with all the prerogatives of royalty. But his power was insubstantial and to be of short duration. The unrestrained behaviour of his soldiery had rendered his cause universally abhorrent. After the Gordons had retired north; his highlanders, who had previously been deserting in small numbers with all the booty that they could collect, suddenly announced their intention to return north to their own territories in order to repair their houses, which had been reduced to ruins by enemy attack, and to stock up on provisions for their families for the coming winter. To persuade Montrose to more readily comply with their application, they promised to return to his camp within forty days, and to bring some of their friends with them. Montrose saw that they were determined to leave regardless, so concealed his displeasure and granted their request. But when Sir Alasdair Macdonald also announced his intention to return to the highlands, Montrose could not hide his annoyance, and argued strongly against such a move, requesting he stay until they were 'absolute conquerors', promising to go north himself to put down Argyll and his party as they deserved, at the same time declaring that to go their separate ways at this point must be the occasion of the ruin of them both – but all to no avail.[94] The loss of such a large part of his force, and the flower of his army, was exasperating for Montrose, who now depended upon reinforcements expected from England to bolster his numbers.

From Bothwell, where he was camped, Montrose sent the Marquis of Douglas to gather levies in his own territory. At the same time, Montrose began to shape his plans for the southern parts of the kingdom and sent to the Earls of Hume, Roxburgh and Traquair, who were very powerful on the borders, to invite them to come and give proof of their zeal and affection for the king's service. The reply received was an invitation to come to the borders, which invitation Montrose accepted. In a very short time, Douglas made considerable levies and, according to his orders, marched to Galashiels to give an opportunity to the noblemen of the south borders to take the field. From Calder, continuing his march with the small remains of the army, Montrose passed close by the city of Edinburgh and came to Galashiels, where he found that most of the troops which Douglas had just raised had already disbanded themselves, despite the efforts which that lord and others that had joined him had taken to keep them. But to make up the loss the Earl of Traquair came to him and, with great zeal and many demonstrations of his prosperity and stength of arms, offered his service. He also sent his son, the Lord Linton, at the head of a fine troop of horse.

By way of forcing the lukewarm lords either to support or oppose him, Montrose marched to Kelso, intent on seeing Roxburgh and Hume, from whom he had lately heard nothing. He arrived to receive news that both Hume and Roxburgh had been taken prisoner by Lieutenant-General Leslie, and carried to Berwick. There seems to have been reason to believe that their capture may have been with their own connivance, 'for by this means' as Wishart says, 'that crafty old fox Roxburgh (who had Hume under his girdle), conceived that they might both ingratiate themselves with the Covenanters, as freely committing themselves into their protection, and yet keep in the king's favour by appearing to fall into Leslie's hands against their wills'.

It is allowed that certain – probably the greater portion – of the border nobles viewed Montrose with considerable aversion, which in some cases approached open hostility. Remarking on this, Sir Walter Scott says:

> 'Without imputing, with Wishart, absolute treachery to the border nobles, it may be allowed that they looked with envy upon Montrose, and with dread and aversion upon his rapacious and disorderly forces. Hence, had it been in their power, it might not have altogether suited their inclinations to have brought the strength of the border lances to the support of the northern clans.'

At Kelso Montrose found himself disappointed not only of local support, but of the party of horse which the king had promised should be sent to him out of England. Worse than all, was the news of the arrival at Berwick of General David Leslie at the head of several thousand experienced and disciplined troops, called home on the urgent representation of the Scottish parliament. Montrose, while he had no certain news of Leslie's disposition, estimated that his chief strength would be in his horse and it was for this reason that he opted to shun the plain country as much as possible. From Kelso, he marched south to Jedburgh, desperate for support from over the border and, being disappointed, turned west into Nithsdale, Annandale, and Ayr, where he had the prospect of recruits. On 12

September he reached Selkirk, and, on the large level plain of Philiphaugh, he found, it seemed, a secure field for the encampment of his infantry.

About 2 miles above Selkirk the Yarrow stream joins the Ettrick, between this and the town to the north, skirting the left bank of the Ettrick, is a plain about 2 miles in length and between a quarter and half a mile broad. The considerable range of hills between the Yarrow and Tweed serves as a defence on the north; while on the west it is bounded by the thickly wooded height known as Hareheadwood; and on the east lie the Philiphaugh and Linglie hills, extending nearly to the river. Arriving here on ground so admirably adapted for the security of his troops, and so well defended on either side, Montrose had dug trenches, and stationed part of his army on the ground which his skilful eye perceived as both the best and safest he could find in a part of the country where the local people were unfriendly to his cause.

There can be little doubt however that his dispositions were not those of a skilful general. Misled by reports that Leslie had marched north to intercept his supposed retreat into the highlands, Montrose does not seem to have conceived that an attack was probable. The cavalry were bivouacked on the Selkirk side of the Ettrick, while the greater part of the infantry remained on the Philiphaugh grounds – the side remote from Selkirk. This separation of his horse and foot, so dependent upon each other for support, was a fatal error. Nor did he observe his usual custom of personally placing the sentinels and instructing the watch. Having entrusted these duties to reliable officers, and left instructions for the rendezvous next morning at Philiphaugh,[95] he retired to his quarters in a commodious house close by the west port of Selkirk. On the haugh, part of his foot were already encamped, their headquarters being the house and offices of Philiphaugh, which then stood near the site of Lauriston Villa.

Here the few cannon Montrose possessed were planted so as to command the valley and flank the road up the river. On the bank from Leslie Cottage by Beechwood and Thirladean, other companies were bivouacked, while the horse were mainly quartered in or near the town.

While the king's troops rested in supposed security, a capable and wily foe was rapidly approaching. On Thursday, 11 September, David Leslie had made his rendezvous with the shires of east and west Lothian on Gladesmuir, his horsemen, 'being about 4,500, besides some horse sent south, and dragouners, having come to Scotland on the previous Saturday from England'. On the 12th Leslie pitched camp at Melrose, the existence of a bridge over the Tweed near the place being the principal reason. He is said to have spent the night in a house called the West Port; but the coincidence is perhaps too remarkable that Montrose's accommodation was the West Port house in Selkirk. In fact, if a narrative ascribed to Covenanting officials at Haddington three days after the battle for transmission to England is to be believed, Leslie had little enough time for sleep. He is said to have come in contact with Montrose's outposts that very night. On the day Montrose marched from Jedburgh, Leslie, having already given orders to his army to march north, suddenly disregarded the instructions from his political chiefs, stopped his march north, wheeled left, and marched towards Teviotdale and Mers, and down the Gala Water. He had newly received letters giving him notice of the low and impaired state of Montrose's army and an accurate estimate of the Royalist forces at only 500 foot, mostly Irish, plus some newly raised troops of horse – exposing their numerical weakness and their discontent due to long arrears of pay, and the opportunity that, were he to strike quickly, Montrose might easily be surprised and destroyed. Whether or not there is any truth in the suspicion that Traquair was the man who furnished this information, it seems to be fact that during the night his son, Lord Linton, had left Montrose's camp with the troop of horse he had brought, when the marquis was descending the vale of Gala. The actual course of the conflict, however, cannot be identified with any certainty, as the accounts given by sympathisers on either side are so conflicting.

Wishart, Montrose's chaplain, for example, says that the marquis, after earnestly exhorting his officers 'to have the more care, lest the enemy, who were very strong in horse, should surprise them unawares', was so occupied with writing letters that he did not sleep at all that night:

> And sending ever and anon to the Captains of Guard – men that were skilful soldiers and known to be so in foreign countries – such uncertain noises as were brought to him of the enemies' approach, they being deceived either by the negligence of their own scouts or their own misfortune, very confidently sent him back word that there was no enemy in these parts nor in the country thereabouts. At day break, some of the best horse, most acquainted with the country, were sent out again to scout; they also brought word that they had been ten miles about, had diligently examined all by-ways, and rashly wished damnation to themselves if they could find an enemy in arms within ten miles. But afterward it appeared when it was too late, that the enemy, with all their forces, were then scarce four miles from Selkirk, and had lain there all night in their arms … And truly that morning being very misty gave no small advantage to the enemy, whom at last Montrose's frightened scouts discovered to march towards him all a full body at such time as they were not above half a mile off. Rebel accounts have Captain Blackadder bursting in upon Montrose at breakfast 'in a great fright' with the news that Leslie was almost upon them.

> Montrose, mounting the first horse he could light on, gallops into the field appointed for the rendezvous that morning, where he finds a great deal of noise, but no order. The cavalry being but little acquainted with their duty, and lying already dispersed in their quarters, where they dreamt more of baiting their

horses than maintaining their lives and honours, upon the first alarm which they received from the enemies' trumpet, ran disorderly up and down they knew not whither, but never came in the fight. Yet there were a few, no more than 120, for the most part noblemen or knights, who made all speed, and gallantly undertook to make good the right wing. Nor did the 500 foot make a good appearance, for many of them, looking after their own private business among the carriages, and by that unreasonable care of saving, lost themselves and all they had. And, which spoiled the matter, which was bad enough before, most of the commanders were absent and never came into the field. Besides, the enemy coming on so speedily, left them no time for deliberation. The enemy, therefore, who were 6,000 (whereof most were horse out of England), furiously charging Montrose's right wing, were twice gallantly received and repulsed with no small loss. Nor could they make that noble troop give any ground, or break through it, until at last, laying along those few foot that withstood them, they broke in upon the left flank where there was no horse. By this, 2000 horse, whom the enemy had sent over to the other side of the river (possibly having branched off from the main Scots' advance, south through Selkirk, and right, round Howden Hill to strike northwards upon Montrose's forces from the south, in a pincer style assault with the main force attacking from the north-east) , were gotten on the rear of those noble gentlemen, who, being hemmed in on every side, and galled with the enemies' shot at distance, lest they should fall for nothing and unrevenged, withdrew themselves, everyone the best way he could. But the foot, who could have little security by flight, fighting a good while, stoutly and resolutely, at last upon quarter asked and given for their lives, threw down their arms and yielded themselves prisoners. According to the Covenanters' account, on the other hand, Lieutenant-General David Leslie with his forces advanced upon Friday the 12th within 3 miles of the enemy, who were quartered in Philiphaugh.

That night he sent out two parties who fell in upon their quarters, killed some, and gave the alarm, which made them continue all night in arms; and ours did the like. The morrow our forces marched towards the enemy and came within view of them about ten in the morning. According to their (Montrose's) usual manner they had made choice of a most advantageous ground wherein they had entrenched themselves, having on the one hand an impassable ditch, and on the other dykes and hedges; and where these were not strong enough they further fortified them by casting up ditches, and lined their hedges with musketeers. After viewing one another, there came out three horses from each side; and after skirmishing very gallantly about a quarter of an hour, the enemy's three were beaten in. After this the enemy sent out a party of 200 musketeers, who were forced to retreat by ours in great disorder, whereupon the van of our forces advanced, and for almost an hour (being between 11 and 12 o'clock) it was hotly disputed, our

> horse endeavouring to break through, and the enemy with great resolution maintaining their ground. At length, General Leslie charging very desperately, upon the head of his own regiment, broke the body of the enemy's foot, after which they went all in confusion, and the horse wanting their foot, not able to great opposition. The foot were all cut off and taken, whereof 100 were Irish, who were all since shot at a post. Of the foot and horse it is conceived there are between two and three thousand killed.

These narratives, giving as they do much the same account of the fight at close quarters, contradict each other vitally as to whether or not the attack was a surprise. By the Covenanters it is asserted that both forces were on the alert, all night, whereas Wishart maintains that Montrose and his troops were unaware of Leslie's advance until daylight, when there was only half a mile between them. There is no reason to believe that the chroniclers on either side made wilfully misleading statements, however, and local tradition goes some way to show how both may have written in perfect good faith.

After he crossed the Tweed, Leslie seems to have gone a mile or so up the river before he halted. Scouts sent to feel for the enemy and ascertain his position soon came upon Montrose's outposts, and appear to have returned with news of the foe being close at hand. Leslie, good general as he was, kept his men ready for emergencies all night; and no doubt supposed as much was being done in the other camp. Montrose seems never to have been properly informed of this preliminary brush, the reports reaching him being probably 'the uncertain noises' which Wishart admits were brought of the enemy's approach. His officers may have been misled as to the quality of the horsemen that had killed some of the advanced guard – thinking perhaps they were men of the district, who were known to be sufficiently disaffected. At all events, the Royalist commander relied on the reassuring reports which reached him rather than on the 'uncertain noises' and set himself to pen dispatches to the king. Nevertheless, it seems hardly likely he would deprive himself of a whole night's sleep to write a letter, and one may suspect that though he neglected to satisfy himself personally about the unsettling rumours, he felt too apprehensive to retire to rest.

Leslie spent the night in laying plans of attack, in which he was materially assisted by friendly people of the countryside, particularly an individual who lives in local history under the name of 'Will.' Acting on the advice of this man, himself an old soldier, Leslie sent a strong body of horse – led by Lieutenant-Colonel James Agnew of Lord Kirkcudbright's – over a dip in the bank that separated his advance guard from the River Ettrick, and still known as 'Will's Nick', with instructions to follow their guide, Will, up Netley Burn, wheel to the left round Linglee Hill,[96] and then fall upon the flank of Montrose's army. Under cover of a thick mist which filled the entire valley at daybreak, this movement was carried out without attracting the enemy's notice,

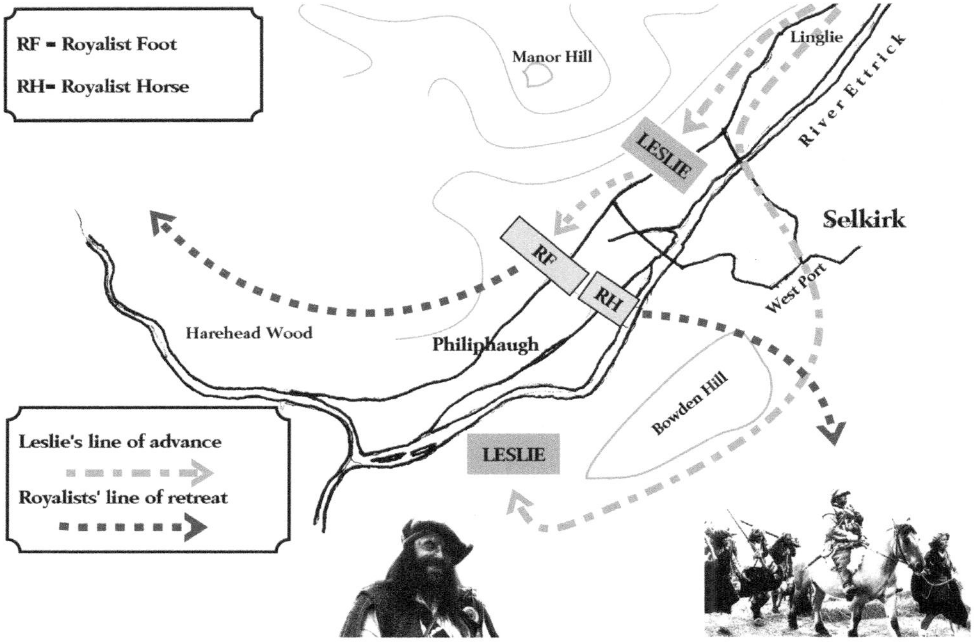

and after pausing a sufficient time to let his flanking force get well round their route, Leslie ordered a general advance of his remaining troops. Even this movement surprised Montrose. It was all he could do to mount the first horse he saw, gallop down the steep brae from Selkirk, and reach the haugh in time to direct the first dispositions of his troops. It was too late; confusion and panic reigned in the army, which, at the best, did not amount to a third the number of Leslie's, and was greatly inferior in freshness and discipline: but he made a gallant effort to retrieve by hard fighting what he had lost by bad generalship. To oppose the advance of Leslie's compact legions, he was able to get into order a small body of horsemen under Lord Ogilvy and Colonel Nathaniel Gordon, and a few companies of foot – perhaps only 200 infantry – even Laghtnan and O'Cahan being able to assemble only half or less of their forces, as many even of the Irish veterans were apparently intent only on saving their personal baggage. The former he constituted his right wing resting on the river, and the latter his left wing, flanked by a steep bank. For a while the few horsemen, for the most part loyal nobles and gentlemen, as brave as they were skilful, succeeded by a tremendous effort in holding up the advance of the well-trained bands of Covenanters; but in the end 'Providence declared itself on the side of the stronger battalions'.

Montrose's left wing gave way, swinging round upon the farmhouse, from where their guns, planted on the high ground, began to play upon the enemy's soldiers as they marched up the valley to the help of their comrades. About this time the Royalists, becoming aware of the column sent round by Linglee (Howden?) Hill to take them in flank and rear, realised that all was lost, and *sauve qui peut* became the order of the day. Many mounted troopers recrossed the Ettrick,[97] and along with those who had not yet reached the field of battle, dispersed in different directions. Montrose himself seems to have made up his mind to sell his life dearly in a last heroic charge; but his staff, reminding him of the service he might yet give to King Charles, persuaded him to try and hack his way to safety. Closing up in one compact squadron, these patrician cavaliers of dauntless heart and strong right arm literally hewed a path through the encircling foe, and, gaining the high ground, made over Minchmoor Hill towards Peebles.[98] On the way they were joined by numerous stragglers, who had left the field before them, Montrose with his mounted men forming a rear guard to protect those retreating on foot until the enemy's cavalry gave up pursuing. It is said that Captain Bruce and two cornets with standards of the Covenant, pursuing the retiring cavaliers too closely, were actually made prisoners by Montrose, who, after treating them courteously, dismissed them on their promise to set loose prisoners of equal rank and number.

***

The last shot had been fired on the field of battle. A large body of Irish who marched under Montrose had retired to an eminence, where they held their ground in spite of a heavy fire until Stuart – their adjutant – negotiated a surrender, by which Leslie undertook to give them quarter if they laid down their arms. This being done, they were removed to a level field under guard. According to Bishop Guthrie (no friendly critic of the Covenanters), a scene ensued almost too revolting for description:

> Then did the churchmen quarrel that quarter should be given to such wretches as they, and declared it to be an act of most sinful impiety to spare them, wherein divers of the noblemen complied with the clergy; and so they found out a distinction whereby to bring David Leslie fairly off, and this it was, that quarter was only meant to Stuart the adjutant himself, and not to his company: after which having delivered the adjutant to Middleton to be his prisoner, the army was let loose upon them, and cut them all into pieces. [This piece of ground, near Newark Castle, is still known as 'Slain Man's Lea'.] With the whole baggage and staff, which was exceeding rich, there remained none but boys, cooks, and a rabble of rascals and women with children in their arms; all those without commiseration were cut in pieces; whereof there were 300 women that, being natives of Ireland, were the married wives of the Irish; there were many big with child, yet none of them were spared, but all were cut in pieces with such savage and inhuman cruelty as neither Turk nor Scythian was ever heard to have done the like; for they ripped up the bellies of the women with their swords till the fruit of their womb, some in embryo, some perfectly formed, some crawling for life, and some ready for birth,

> fell down upon the ground weltering in the gory blood of their mangled mothers. O impiety! O horrible cruelty! Which Heaven doubtless will revenge, before this bloody, unjust, and unlawful war be brought to an end.

Wishart, in his memoirs, states of the incident that a Covenanting minister, David Dickson, 'The Bloody Preacher', who was present at the execution observed, 'This wark gaes bonnilie on.'

It is certainly not in question that the slaughter of prisoners took place. Whether they were promised quarter on condition that they laid down their arms is perhaps not so clear. Firmer evidence that quarter was promised should be proposed before such serious accusations are charged against the government troops.

Incredibly brutal as this conduct appears, it is confirmed beyond doubt in the official narrative, which curtly states that of those taken 'were 100 Irish, all since shot at a post,' and adds that 'since the battle divers of the enemy's soldiers are killed.'

A number of the Covenanters set to plundering the baggage and so failed to pursue about 250 Royalists that fled the field, missing the opportunity to capture their colours, as one Irish foot soldier who had carried the colour, tore it off its staff and, putting it around himself like a scarf, made his way with drawn sword through a squadron of horse and successfully carried the colours to Montrose who took him into his own Life Guards and allowed him thereafter to carry that 'glorious mark of his valour and fidelity.' William Hay, brother of the Earl of Kinnoul, who carried the standard and who had been seriously wounded at the Battle of Alford, did the same and, having hidden himself in England until the banks of the Tweed were quiet, returned, accompanied by Captain Robert Tower, and brought that standard back to Montrose in the north.

Among those who escaped the battlefield only to be taken by the country people and delivered up to their enemy, were the Earl of Hartfell, Lord Drummond, Lord Ogilvy, Sir Robert Spottiswoode, Sir Alexander Leslie of Auchintoul, Sir William Rollock, Sir Philip Nisbet, William Murray, brother of the Earl of Tullibardine, Alexander Ogilvy, yr., Colonel Nathaniel Gordon, and Mr Andrew Guthrie, son to the Bishop of Moray.

Among those who fought their way out with Montrose were the Marquis of Douglas, old Lord Napier and his son the master of Napier, Lord Erskine and Lord Fleming. Having shaken free of their pursuers, and being secure from molestation, the Royalists marched leisurely along, without a halt, until they reached Traquair House, the residence of their professed sympathiser. Montrose asked to see the earl and Lord Linton, but both were denied to be at home, 'although,' says Wishart, 'some gentlemen of honour and credit have affirmed they were both in the house.' When, later on, Traquair with characteristic effrontery, congratulated the Covenanting leaders on their victory, his own daughter was so shocked that she 'checked him for it as far as filial modesty would permit.' From Traquair the fugitives continued west, crossing the

Tweed at Howford, and following the road by an avenue of old elms which led to the tower of Ormiston. From there Montrose went by an old road along the high ground to Peebles, where he arrived at sunset, and rested several hours. By daybreak they had crossed the Clyde at a ford to which they were all conducted by Sir John Dalziel, and where, to the great joy of all, they were joined by the Earls of Crawford and Airlie with 200 horsemen who had escaped by a different road – probably by the valleys of Yarrow and Megget.

Montrose continued north into the highlands to raise 400 Athole men, while yet again the Marquis of Huntly refused to co-operate with his efforts to recover the king's fortunes in the north. Notwithstanding the evasions of the Marquis of Huntly, Montrose succeeded in inducing the Earl of Aboyne to join him at Drummuir, the seat of Lord Forbes, with a force of 1,500 foot and 300 horse, all of whom appeared to be actuated by the best spirit. To remove every unfavourable impression from the mind of Montrose, Aboyne assured him with great frankness that he and his men were ready to follow him wherever he should be pleased to lead them; that they would obey his orders; and that his brother, Lord Lewis, would also speedily join him, as he soon did, with an additional force.

On receiving this reinforcement, Montrose turned south and marched towards Mar, where he was to be joined by the forces of Lord Erskine; but he had not gone far when Lord Lewis Gordon, under some pretence or other, returned home with a substantial number of horse, promising to return the following day. The desertion of Lord Lewis had a pernicious influence upon the rest of Aboyne's men, who, before the army had reached Alford, were greatly diminished by desertion. When the rest showed a great unwillingness to continue the march, and desertions continued, Aboyne requested a leave of absence, claiming that his father had commanded him to return to defend his possessions [from] a party of the enemy who were in Lower Mar, and who were threatening to attack. Aboyne's demand astonished Montrose, who protested, giving many reasons why he should remain – that Aboyne's apprehensions of danger were groundless, as, with the exception of a few troops of the enemy's horse quartered in Aberdeen, there were no other forces in the north which could disturb his father's possessions, and that these horse were too weak to attempt anything – that by marching south, the seat of war would be transferred from the north country, and that, in this way, the Marquis of Huntly would be relieved altogether of the presence of the enemy – that it would be impossible to join the Royalist forces, which were on their way from England, without crossing the Forth, and that it was only by adopting that step that they could ever expect to rescue their brave friends from the jaws of the Covenanters, and save their lives.

Aboyne did not attempt to answer these points, made with Montrose's peculiar energy, but he requested him to send representatives who had influence with his father to acquaint him with them – Donald, Lord Reay, at whose house Huntly had lived during his exile in Strathnaver, and Alexander Irvine, younger of Drum,

Huntly's son-in-law, both of whom had been indebted to Montrose for their liberty, were therefore sent by him to the Marquis of Huntly, as the most likely people he could choose to persuade Huntly to allow Aboyne to stay with the army. But all their entreaties were to no avail. Lord Reay was so ashamed at the failure of his mission that he declined to return to Montrose; and Irvine, who brought some evasive letters from Huntly, frankly declared to Montrose that he could obtain no satisfactory explanation from his father-in-law of his real intentions, farther than that he remained firm in his resolution that Aboyne should return home immediately. After declaring that he parted from Montrose with reluctance, and promising to join him within a fortnight with a force even larger than that which he had recently brought, Aboyne returned to his father.

Montrose continued his march through Braemar and Glenshee into Athole, where he obtained an accession of force. Shortly after, he was met by two messengers – Captain Thomas Ogilvie, younger of Pourie, and Captain Robert Nisbet – with orders from the king, desiring Montrose to join Lord George Digby, near the English border, as soon as possible. Montrose immediately sent the messengers north to the Marquis of Huntly, to advise him of the king's wishes, in the futile expectation that the use of his majesty's name would encourage him to send Aboyne south with reinforcements.

As soon as the members of the Committee of Estates, who had taken refuge in Berwick, heard of Montrose's defeat at Philiphaugh, they joined Leslie's army, which they accompanied to Edinburgh, and there conceived those measures of retribution against the Royalists who had fallen into their hands.

Concerned that Montrose might still be able to avenge the blood of his friends, the committee did not immediately carry out their sentence upon any of them; but hearing of the division between Montrose and Huntly and the desertion of the Gordons from their ranks, they thought they might now safely venture to immolate a few victims at the shrine of the Covenant. Accordingly three of the prisoners were ordered for execution; Sir William Rollock, Sir Philip Nisbet, chief of that name, and Alexander Ogilvie, younger of Inverquharity, a youth not yet 18 years old, who had already shown great signs of ability. This fine young man was sacrificed just to gratify the malignant animosity of Argyll and the Ogilvies. Sir William was executed at the market-cross of Glasgow on 28 October, and Sir Philip and Ogilvie suffered at the same place the following day. Wishart tells a tale of Sir William Rollock's condemnation which shows the ferocity and fanaticism of the times. He says that the chief crime laid against Sir William was that he had not perpetrated a deed of the most villainous and atrocious nature. Having been sent by Montrose with some dispatches to the king, after the Battle of Aberdeen, he was captured by parliament forces and would have been immediately executed, except that Argyll used all his efforts to engage him to assassinate Montrose, and who by threatening immediate death and promising very high rewards, prevailed on him to undertake that treacherous piece of work, for which, however, he secretly entertained the utmost abhorrence. Having obtained his liberty by agreeing to the scheme, he returned straight away to Montrose and revealed the whole matter to him, begging him at the same time to look to his own safety; as it could not be presumed that he, Sir William, was the only person who had been approached in this manner or that others would equally detest the deed, but that some persons would undoubtedly be persuaded to attempt the plan.

Two Irish commanders – Colonel O'Cahan, who had distinguished himself by his bravery at the Battle of Fyvie, and Major Laghtnan, another brave officer – were taken after Philiphaugh into Edinburgh and hanged without trial, at the Castle-Hill gibbet. Just being Irish was sufficient reason. This hatred of the Irish by the Covenanters was not confined to these individuals. As well as Royalist claims of the Covenanters' slaughter of non-combatants and helpless women at the scene of the battle itself, Wishart asserts that certain of the loyalists captured near Linlithgow after the battle by the Covenanters in their march west towards Glasgow – a body of helpless Irish women and children who, after the loss of their husbands and fathers at the battle, were now making their way home to their own country – were by order from the 'Rebel Lords' (the heads of the Covenanters) thrown headlong off a high bridge over the Avon, and any men, together with their wives and sucking children, drowned in the river beneath; any that swam toward the side were beaten off the bank with pikes and staves, and thrust down again into the water. Montrose was never more troubled than at this news. The Covenanting army continued its march to Glasgow, where a convention of estates was held, to decide upon further measures and consider how best to show their gratitude to Leslie.

The Committee of Estates awarded General Leslie 50,000 merks for his service, and to have fought on the same side at the famous battle was long regarded as a claim to consideration and advancement. Leslie himself, five years after his rout of the king's forces at Philiphaugh, found himself leading the Scots against Cromwell at Dunbar, and was taken prisoner while fighting for Charles II at Worcester. It is said that when the king created him Lord Newark, Leslie's father, a staunch loyalist who had never swerved, observed that 'Davie should rather have been hangit for his auld work.'

To the officers and soldiers of the ten regiments of horse and dragoons under Leslie[99] the estates decreed an extra month's wages, but it is clear from numerous petitions presented to parliament up to the Restoration that the Covenanters' gratitude was in advance of their Exchequer. Most of these grants were payable out of fines placed upon such as had assisted Montrose. An act, passed four months after the battle, subjected to loss of from four to six years' rent such as had 'been present at the Battle of Philiphaugh, or had executed orders to promote the service of the rebels, or had raised or forced others and carried them along to the said battle,' and against whose persons parliament had 'not thought fit to proceed to death.' Pringle of Blindlee, who was fined 10,000 merks, got off on paying 7,000 merks to Colonel

Hugh Fraser's regiment. Finally, in 1647, 'for payment of the assignment for service at Philiphaugh,' a special levy was made upon the shires and burghs of the kingdom, Selkirkshire being assessed at £1,278 and the burgh at £126; but even this proved insufficient.

In December 1645, the Estates of Parliament dealt with a supplication by the town of Selkirk for payment of 3*s*. Scots 'a day, for the bygane intertinement of euerie ane of the prisoners eftirspecifit,' and further, praying to be relieved of said prisoners in time coming (after which were listed twenty-eight Scots and ten Irish men and women).

The estates empowered Sir John Murray of Philiphaugh, Sir William Scott, younger of Harden, and the magistrates of Selkirk to identify if the Irish were at Philiphaugh on the day of battle, or were in company with the rebels – with power after trial to 'cause summarily put to death and execution without further delay the foresaid four Irish men and six Irish women without any process of law or putting of them to the knowledge of an assize'. This, the estates 'ordained the Commissioners' to do; and instructed them to 'sit as justiciaries for trying the other prisoners in the jail of Selkirk,' with power to sentence them to punishment, death, or liberation. Monies spent by the magistrates in 'entertaining' the prisoners were to be recovered from the excise within the burgh. Similar powers were given to the magistrates of Jedburgh to punish Irish prisoners in their tollbooth, the same fate being decreed against those in custody at Glasgow, Dumbarton, and Perth. It is said that Leslie, who would rather have saved these wretched mercenaries, was over ruled by the bloodthirsty Covenanting clergy – the same who after the battle had impiously urged the massacre of the surrendering Irish by quoting texts from the old testament – 'Thine eye shall not pity, and thou shalt not spare,' – 'What meaneth this bleating of sheep in my ears?' etc. The four men and six women in Selkirk tollbooth were shot in the marketplace three months after the battle. It does not seem that extreme measures were taken against common soldiers of Scottish birth captured at Philiphaugh; but it was far worse for those of high rank. Parliament would have had pity; but the General Assembly of Ministers of Christ, on 5 December, sent the High Court a remonstrance demanding justice upon delinquents. At the same time petitions from provincial Synods were presented, praying 'parliament would hear the voice of their brethren's blood, would execute impartial justice on the malignants now in bonds, and purge the land from blood-guiltiness.' Of the distinguished Royalists who lost their heads to satisfy the demands of the clergy, only one, William Murray, a brother of Lord Tullibardine, can be said to have suffered justly. Fleeing from the field of Philiphaugh, and maddened probably by what he had heard of the preachers' cruelty to his Irish comrades, he had, according to his indictment 'most cruelly murdered one of Christ's ministers and servants, Mr. Robert Brounley's, minister at (Kirkton), being living at home at his own house in a most sober manner.' Besides civil penalties, ecclesiastical punishments were brought to bear on enemies of the

Covenant. In 1646 George Tait of Pirn, the Laird of Hawkshaw, and others, had to occupy the stool of repentance for 'complying with James Graham'.

At the time of the battle there was just a ford crossing the Ettrick for traffic to and from the town. The people of Selkirk flocked to the top of the bank overlooking the ford to see the battle and during the contested passage of the ford, in which General Leslie was successfully held in check for some time; one of his regiments' pipers stationed on the steep overhanging bank, stimulating his fighting friends on the other side of the river, was felled by a Royalist bullet and rolled, dead, over and over into what is now called 'The Piper's Pool'. One story – that the piper was a Royalist and played the tune of *Whirry, whigs awa', man* – has been supplemented to the effect that he was Piper of Soney, and had been ordered by Montrose to play all day with a promise of liberal payment in the event of victory. Hence the saying:

He is like the Piper of Soney-
Play'd a' day and gat nae money.

Another incident is told of a highland woman, who having been widowed in the fight, implored one of Leslie's troopers to take her over the river behind him; and who, when halfway across the stream, plunged a poniard into the good-hearted soldier, dropped him into the water, and galloped off with his horse.

Most stories, however, relate to hidden or abandoned treasure. On the morning of the day of battle, it is said, the Earl of Traquair left home with a large sum of money for the payment of Montrose's forces, accompanied by a blacksmith, one of his retainers. As they crossed Minchmoor, they were alarmed by firing which the earl took to be Montrose exercising his forces, but which his attendant, from the constancy and irregularity of the noise, suspected was the sound of an engagement. As they came below Broadmeadows, upon Yarrow, they were met by retreating Royalists, hotly pursued by Parliamentarian troopers. The earl turned and fled, but his horse, jaded with the weight of dollars which he carried, refused to take the hill; so that the earl decided to swap mounts with his attendant, leaving him with a breathless horse and bag of silver, to shift for himself, which he is supposed to have done very effectually. Some of the soldiers, attracted by the appearance of the horse and trappings, gave chase to the smith, who fled up the Yarrow; but finding himself weighed down by the treasure, and unwilling for it to be taken, flung it into a well or pond, near the Tinnies, above Hangingshaw. The farmer of Tinnies, on hearing this story a century and a half later, ransacked the well, but without success. Curiously however, a number of silver coins of the appropriate period were later turned up under the plough on a haugh on the Tinnies and ended up in the hands of Sir Walter Scott. This was, however, a small treasure compared with what some farm labourers later discovered while digging in the neighbourhood of the battleground – numerous silver coins, which the owner had clearly not been able to retrieve during their flight.

Sir Walter Scott, with all dramatic effect, gave some friends, as they rode up Yarrow, the history of a local family who had treated with kindness a young officer of Leslie's army before the conflict. When parting from them to join the troops, he took out a purse of gold, and told the good woman he had a premonition he would not see another sunset, in which case wished his money to remain in her kind hands; but, if he should survive, he had no doubt she would restore it honestly. The young man returned mortally wounded, but lingered a while under her roof, and finally bequeathed to her his purse and blessing. Montrose is credibly reported to have flung his military chest in 'the Meyster (treasure) Pool,' near the Harehead Wood; 'telling the devil to keep it till he came back to seek it.' This pool was drained many years later, and nothing found in it but a Lochaber-axe. Another possible fate is recorded of the same chest. The person carrying (!) it threw it into a house at Foulshiels, and while the only inmates, an old man and his wife, were still disputing what they should do with the money, Leslie's men came up and appropriated the whole lot. On various occasions, and at various places, considerable quantities of coin have been recovered from holes where they had been hidden in haste by Montrose's quartermasters. In 1770 a very rich deposit seems to have been come upon by labourers at work on Philiphaugh estate; and in January 1845, the plough turned up about 200 silver coins. Money of the seventeenth century was found in a field, now called the Treasure-field, close by the road leading over Minchmoor.

In Haliwell House Museum in Selkirk there is preserved an old flintlock gun, used in the battle.

The loot which fell into the hands of the Covenanters, and also, there is reason to believe, of certain plundering burgesses of Selkirk, was large and valuable. Three little silver lockets said to have been found in Montrose's baggage were doubtless meant as decorations for specially meritorious service in the king's cause: heart-shaped, carved on one side with a long straight sword, and below it a winged heart; and on the other a heart pierced through with darts and the motto, 'I live and dye for loyalty.' The inside of the lid bears the words, 'I mourn for Monarchy,' and the other half of the locket bears a finely executed portrait in relief, possibly intended as a likeness of Montrose, but more likely representing Charles II as Prince of Wales. Charles would have been about fifteen and in exile in France at the time of the battle and the face on the portrait is quite young and with a ribbon, like the ribbon of the garter, round the neck. The portraits, if not the lockets themselves, may have been sent for by Montrose out of France, while the mottoes and devices are certainly creations of Montrose himself.

The following ballad written on the battle, doubtless by a stern supporter of the Covenanters more familiar perhaps with the sword than the pen, rejoices over the defeat of the marquis – the impersonation of all evil to the government forces, the more so from his having been one of the keenest of their partisans before switching his allegiance to the king's cause. Possessing little artistic merit, it is considered to be, on the whole, an accurate account of the event and so worth reproduction:

THE BATTLE OF PHILIPHAUGH

On Philiphaugh a fray began,
At Haresheadwood it ended;
The Scots out o'er the Graemes they ran,
Sae merrily they bended.

Sir David frae the border came,
Wi' heart and hand came he;
Wi' him three thousand bonny Scots
To bear him company.

Wi' him three thousand valiant men,
A noble sight to see!
A cloud o' mist them weel conceal'd
As close as e'er might be.

When they came to the Shaw burn,
Caid he,'Sae weel we frame,
I think it is convenient
That we should sing a psalm.'

When they came to the Lingly burn,
As daylight did appear,
They spy'd an aged father,
And he did draw them near.

'Come hither, aged father!'
Sir David he did cry,
'And tell me where Montrose lies,
With all his great army.'

'But first, you must come tell me
If friends or foes you be;
I fear you are Montrose's men,
Come frae the north country.'

'No, we are nane o' Montrose's men,
Nor e'er intend to be;
I am Sir David Lesly
That's speaking unto thee.'

'If you're Sir David Lesly,
As I think weel you be,
I am sorry ye hae brought so few
Into your company.

'There's fifteen thousand armed men
Encamped on yon lee;
Ye'll never be a bite to them
For aught that I can see.

'But halve your men in equal parts,
Your purpose to fulfil;
Let ae half keep the water side,
The rest gae round the hill.

'Your nether party fire must,
Then beat a flying drum;
And then they'll think the day's their ain,
And frae the trench they'll come:

'Then, those that are behind them, maun
Gie shot, baith grit and sma';
And so between your armies twa
Ye may make them fa'.'

'O were ye ever a soldier?'
Sir David Lesly said;
'O, yes; I was at Solway Flow,
Where we were all betray'd.'

Again I was at curst Dunbar[100]
And was a prisoner ta'en;
And many a weary night and day
In prison I hae lien.'

'If ye will lead these men aright,
Rewarded shall ye be;
But if that ye a traitor prove,
I'll hang thee on a tree.'

'Sir, I will not a traitor prove,
Montrose has plundered me;
I'll do my best to banish him
Away frae this country.'

He halved his men in equal parts
His purpose to fulfil;
The one part kept the water side,
The other gaed round the hill.

The nether party fired brisk,
Then turn'd and seem'd to rin;
And then they a' came frae the trench,
And cry'd 'The day's our ain!'

The rest then ran into the trench,
And loosed their cannons a';
And thus, between his armies twa
He made them fast to fa'.

Now, let us a' for Lesly pray,
And his brave company!
For they hae vanquish'd great Montrose,
Our cruel enemy.

(Traditional Border Ballad)

In 1810, excavation work at a school near Newark uncovered large quantities of bones and skulls. The field is known as Slain Man's Lea.

***

In late September Leven's army had been quartered in the North and West Ridings of Yorkshire, from where, later that same month, Leslie advanced to St Andrews. In October he moved to Glasgow, and then into the Carse of Gowrie to reach as far as Forfar before heading south.

On 2 October, Leven's army headquarters were reported as being at Stokesley with foot and horse in Clevelandshire. His army moved to Northallerton in November and on the 15th was at Bramham Moor prior to his march south via Texford to Newark.

About this time, Montrose crossed the Forth and entered Lennox with a force of 300 horse and 1,200 foot, and took up his quarters on the lands of Sir John Buchanan, an ardent Covenanter, from where he sent out his cavalry every day, who hovered about Glasgow and plundered the neighbouring country without opposition, although the Covenanters had a force of about 3,000 cavalry in Glasgow and the neighbourhood. When Montrose heard of the execution of his friends, his heart was filled with the most poignant grief, and he longed for a suitable opportunity to avenge their deaths, but he was too weak to venture upon any attack. He sent repeated messengers from his headquarters to Sir Alexander Macdonald to join him; but after hovering several weeks about Glasgow, like a hawk ready to pounce upon its quarry, he had the mortification to find that Macdonald had no intention of ever again returning to him, and that his expectations of being joined by the Earl of Aboyne were to be equally disappointed.

Shocked when rebels had unexpectedly reappeared before Glasgow only a short time after, having apparently been defeated at Philiphaugh, the estates ordered the fortification of the burgh on 6 November. All fensible men in the presbytery of Glasgow were to begin work on the following Monday, working until noon on Saturday. The Sabbath was of course to be left free for matters spiritual, and then the fensibles of Paisley and Hamilton were to take their turn from 17 and 24 November respectively, being followed in succeeding weeks by those of Irvine, Ayr and Lanark. The Glaswegians themselves were to labour alongside the countrymen on Mondays and Saturdays, and the works were scheduled to be complete by 20 December. In the meantime the burgh depended for its defence upon a militia regiment led by Colonel George Porterfield and Lieutenant-Colonel William Dick. The unit had earlier been conspicuous by its absence in the weeks after Kilsyth, and as Porterfield and some of his officers were evidently seconded from the general of the artillery's regiment (now commanded by Lindsay of Bellstanes), it is evident that some stiffening had been necessary. Further stiffening was provided by the remains of Cassillis' regiment of foot, together with Lord Coupar's dragoons and Sir John Browne's horse and dragoons.

Lanark's horse and dragoons meanwhile were still in Clydesdale, and Colonel Robert Montgomery's (formerly the Earl of Eglinton's) regiment of horse was quartered in Renfrew and Ayr. The greatest concentration of troops was, however, around the Forth crossings; Dalhousie's regiment together with Argyll's and Callendar's troops was in the Stirling area, while Lord Montgomery's and Colonel Hugh Fraser's regiments lay in Clackmannan. Lord Kirkcudbright's regiment was pushed forward to Baillie's old camp at Bridge of Earn, where it could maintain contact with the Earl of Moray's regiment watching the highland passes out of Atholl, with Sir James Lindsay of Bellstane's regiment of foot at Falkland in Fife and with the Dundee garrison under a Colonel Lyell. This last comprised a militia regiment under Lyell and Colonel George Milne's dragoons. Stirling itself was of course well-garrisoned with the remains of Baillie's army, but to the north, only Perth, Dundee, Inverness (and shortly St Andrews where the estates were to move to escape the plague) were garrisoned, and generally lightly at that. Clearly this state of affairs was not satisfactory and, while Leslie's regiment was ordered south, Middleton[2] remained in Scotland, was appointed to command the army in Scotland – in place of Robert Monro,[3] left to the Irish bogs – and make the necessary preparations for yet another expedition into Aberdeenshire. The forces made available for this expedition were not great in number – two horse regiments and two dragoon regiments (approximately 1,880 horsemen) including 450 Fraser's, 480 Coupar's dragoons, 350 troopers of Kirkcudbright's horse, 600 of Montgomery's horse, and Lanark's horse – and the fact that this small force proved capable of completing the task successfully shows the extent to which the rebels' cause had been overwhelmed.

This force reached Aberdeenshire in October. It was felt that those units which had already been mauled by the rebels had done enough, and as soon as they were strong enough to go were sent back to join Leven's army in England. In their place, two regular infantry regiments recently returned north from England with David Leslie, Colonel William Stewart's Galloway regiment and Viscount Kenmure's were lying in Forfarshire by mid-December; the first at Arbroath and the second at Montrose (Lord Coupar's men were ordered to Perth at the same time but do not appear to have taken much part in the subsequent operations).

On 31 October 1645, Colonel Hugh Fraser received permission to convert his regiment of dragoons into one of horse on its return to England. After leaving St Andrews, this regiment and the rest of Middleton's force ravaged the Earl of Mar's estates at Alloa then travelled north to quarter in Aberdeen for four days before proceeding to Banff in search of Royalist forces. On his approach the Gordons lifted their siege of Spynie Palace. Middleton's men quartered on the lands of the Earl of Erroll, Stewart of Ardoch, Burnett of Leys and Burnett of Craigmill, and in Turriff, remaining in Scotland until December.

Supply problems vexed these regiments. Major William Stewart of his regiment had a tenant's house timbers burnt in Turriff. Troopers stole food from Stewart of Ardoch and his tenants and also from tenants in Easter Seggiden. Forty-two men of the regiment quartered on Haldane of Gleneagles' estates, where they destroyed crops and stole a horse. The Earl of Erroll and others in Turriff complained of general plundering by Fraser's in a report made eighteen months later. Captain David Kennedy's troop was accused of stealing grain. On the way south, men of the regiment seized £3 from a tenant of Erroll. The dragoons, with Kirkcudbright's, remained in Aberdeen for 24 hours before continuing south, leaving Aberdeen an open city. Their exaction on the burgh and that of Coupar's dragoons for five days quartering totalled £3,345. The tenants of Erroll, Lord Coupar, Stewart of Ardoch and Archibald Thompson also complained about Lanark's horse plundering food and money and about the cost of their quartering, while some of Montgomery's horse were accused of being involved in crop destruction.

With the end of this campaign Fraser's men were scattered into garrisons in the Mearns, Angus and Perthshire, and later moved to west Fife, Clackmannanshire and Perthshire with Montgomery's horse, while Kirkcudbright's horse was assigned quarters around the Bridge of Earn. Two weeks later the horse unit (Fraser's – now horse, but still frequently referred to as dragoons) was ordered to cease quartering in Fife.

On 31 October 1645, with the immediate threat to Glasgow having receded, Leslie was ordered south with his and most of Middleton's regiments of horse, and reached England by late November, where they were to serve at the siege of Newark, while Leven's regiment remained in Scotland until December. After Leven returned to Scotland during the siege, Leslie was to become commander-in-chief of the Scottish forces there.

In early December thirty-two troopers and six officers of Fraser's were selected to serve as part of a commanded party of cavalry under Cornet Calhoun of Dalhousie's horse at the siege of Newark. They, along with twenty troopers of the Earl of Lanark's horse, a number of Eglinton's horse and thirty-seven troopers from Montgomery's, reached the besiegers' camp at Nottingham on 11 December and remained there until the town fell in May 1646. Routmaster George Hepburn led a commanded party of ten troopers of Dalhousie's. A party of twenty-six commanded horse from Kirkcudbright's reached the force besieging Newark by 17 January 1646 when a muster of the Army of the Solemn League and Covenant was held there at Muskham Moor, consisting of nine foot regiments, ten horse regiments, two companies of dragoons and thirteen troops of horse. The troop of thirty-eight Fraser's was described in the muster roll as 'lately dragoons and are not yet armed as troopers; more than that, there's some (i.e. not many) have pistols by their sides, nor have they horses fit for troopers'.

On 13 and 15 December the estates ordered the Strathearn foot (sometimes having been described as dragoons) to march to Perth immediately and to remain there until further instructions, which were sent out on the 16th when the regiment was ordered to Montrose, and to replace the garrisons formerly manned by Fraser's in Perthshire, Angus, and Mearns. By 16 December Fraser's regiment was back in Aberdeen, only to be ordered on that date to return to England via Mearns and Angus. By January 1646 the regiment, now of horse, had reached Yorkshire, where, from 27 January until 1 March, they were free quartered and billeted in Yorkshire. Until now the regiment had covered itself in glory. That changed during this occupation of England.[101]

9. The Siege of Newark

On 4 October the king reached the town of Newark, where he was loyally received. Sir John Gell wrote to the speaker from Derby that 'the king with 2000 horse in his army, of which 1500 were fighting men, has passed our garrison today, about 8 miles distant, en-route to Newark. Most of his army now is Irish. Those of any religion at all have run away, of whom we have two. Commanders now with the king are; Gen. Gerard, Sir M Langdale, Sir William Vaughan, and Lord Loughborough. There is no other commander of note with him.' On 6 October, the king wrote 'from our Court at Newark' to Sir Gervais Lucas, governor of Belvoir Castle, requesting he provide accommodation for Gerard's horse – about 300. The Committee of Parliament was on the alert, and the same day sent orders to General Poyntz to follow the king, 'both to prevent his plunder of the country, and to hinder his recruiting'. Sir H. Vane Jr described the king's force as 'tattered and tired' and in a further letter to Poyntz, the Committee stated: 'We have certain intelligence that the king is about Newark, and by his own letters which were intercepted we know he intends to put his horse into the garrisons thereabouts for some time. If our forces come up he might find some difficulty to get them together again.' Clarendon wrote that what persuaded his majesty to go to Newark instead of Worcester, was the advice of Lord Digby, who did not wish him to meet Princes Rupert and Maurice, and whose standing with the king was so great that his advice was heeded over the opinion of any other.

On 5 October Digby wrote to Lord Byron, 'His Majesty is advanced as far as Newark'; the reasons he gives being very different from those suggested by Clarendon – 'We hope it will have the wished result of drawing the rebels' great body of horse from the Welsh side of Chester.' In another letter he gives other considerations which drove the king in this dark hour of his fortunes to remain with his Newark Cavaliers. In a letter to Lord Jermyn on 10 October, he says, 'We rest about Newark the unlikeliest place to be besieged, and the strongest if it be, and from whence the king may not be hindered from marching away with his horse at any time.' Clarendon says, 'When the king came to Newark, he betook himself to regulating the disorders of that garrison, which by their great luxury and excesses in a time of so general calamity had given scandal to the Commissioners and to all the country. The garrison consisted of about 2000 horse and foot, and to those [small numbers] there were about four and twenty Colonels and general officers, who had all liberal assignments out of the contributions, according to their qualities; so that though that small county paid more than any other of that bigness in England, there was very little left to pay the common soldiers, or to provide for any other expenses. This made so great a noise that the king found it absolutely necessary to reform it, and reduced some of the officers entirely and lessened the pay of others, which added to the number of discontented which was very much too numerous before.'

A newspaper for the period 10 to 17 October details the arrangements for the encamping of the Scottish Army outside Newark, and states that a letter had been received from Colonel Rossiter concerning the king at Newark, and of some encounters between him and the enemy, and a letter intercepted by him going from the king to Sir Gervais Lucas, Governor of Belvoir, requesting that Lucas provide for General Gerrard's 300 horse, by levying and bringing in provisions for both horse and men.

Charles also wrote to Sir Edward Nicholas, advising that 'Sr. Tho. Glemham will be come to you, whom I have commanded to take particular care of purging Oxford of mutinous and disaffected persons. Least he should not be bold enough, having yet but a verbal command, I thinks fit now, that you should show him this, under my hand, that my pleasure herein be duly executed, whomsoever it may concerns.'

On 14 October Sir John Gell writes that the king is still at Newark, making a show of taking up winter quarters. 'He hath appointed the country people to come into Newark this day to be healed of the "King's Evil."' (The practice of touching for this ailment prevailed from the reign of Edward the Confessor to that of Queen Anne, and it must have been a curious sight to see the scrofulous sufferers of the district gathering together in Newark, eagerly awaiting the touch of the royal hand, accompanied perhaps by a small gold or silver coin called a touch-piece, though his majesty possessed little enough silver or gold in these anxious days.)

News arrived that Montrose had beaten David Leslie and was marching towards the border with a strong army, so the king decided to move north to join him, and after ten days at Newark, proceeded to Tuxford-le-Clay and then on to Welbeck. Here, to his utter dismay, he learned there was no truth in the rumour, and that Montrose was in retreat. Sending Digby in command, with Sir Marmaduke Langdale as his chief officer, and 1,500 horse to try to join forces with Montrose, the king and 800 of his horse guards, plus the 300 troopers belonging to Lord Gerard, marched back to Newark.

Digby's forces met with defeat and disaster, and the king decided that, as Poyntz had reached Nottingham, and Rossiter with all his forces was at Grantham, it was perhaps time to leave Newark, and retire to Oxford. However, before he could leave Newark, he had to endure an indignity from his friends, sharper than any meted out by his enemies, which without doubt caused him more grief and distress. According to Clarendon, Prince Rupert, who had swept down on the enemies of Newark with his troops 'like a whirlwind on the trees' when the town had been hard-pressed, was determined to visit his majesty to clear his name of accusations levelled against him for the loss of Bristol. He had been charged with 'a gross dereliction of duty' and 'a mean action', and naturally such accusations from the highest sources were more than a brave soldier such as he could bear without indignant protest. With his brother Maurice and 120 officers who attended him, he arrived at Belvoir Castle (fighting Rossiter on the way), and shortly, despite a message from the king requesting he remain at Belvoir, he came to Newark. Lord Gerard and Sir Richard Willis met him about 2 miles from town. Clarendon writes:

> About an hour after, with his train, he came to ... Court, found the king, and without ceremony told his Majesty that he was come to render an account of the loss of Bristol, and to clear himself of those imputations which had been cast upon him. The king said very little to him; but meat being brought ... went to supper, and during that time asked some questions of Prince Maurice without saying anything to the other. After he had supped, he retired to his chamber, without admitting any further discourse, and the Prince returned to the Governor's house, where he was well treated and lodged. However displeased he may have been, the king thought he should listen to what Prince Rupert had to say, as he might need the Prince's services to assist in any escape from the place, which was looking more likely. So he chose to hear his defence the next day, which the Prince made with many protestations of innocence, and how impossible it was to defend the fort after the line was entered. The king did not believe his nephew to have any malicious design against his service, and had no intention to aggravate the situation so, after a day or two's consideration, had a short declaration drawn up by which Prince Rupert was cleared from any disloyalty or treason in the rendering of Bristol, but not of indiscretion.

Differences, however, did not end here. The governor and the commissioners were (according to Clarendon) on such bad terms that the king thought it wise to remove the governor from his office, and sending for him (Sunday 20 October), offered to make him captain of his horse guards, at the same time telling him that he proposed to leave Lord Bellasis Governor of Newark, 'who being allied to most of the gentlemen of the adjacent counties, and having a good estate there, would be more acceptable to them.' Sir Richard was much troubled, and said his enemies would triumph at his removal, to which the king replied that a man could not be looked upon as disgraced who was placed so near his person.

The king then left his chamber, and went to church. When he returned, he sat down to dinner, his lords and other servants retiring similarly to their own lodgings. Before the king had dined, Sir Richard, with both princes, Lord Gerard, and twenty officers of the garrison, entered his chamber. Willis addressed the king, saying that what had been said to him in private was now the public talk of the town, and very much to his dishonour. Prince Rupert declared that Sir Richard was being removed from his position for no fault other than for being his friend, and Lord Gerard added that it was the plot of Lord Digby, who was a traitor, and would be proved so. The king was so surprised with this behaviour that he rose in some disorder from the table, intending to go into his bedchamber, calling to Sir Richard Willis to follow him, who answered loudly that he had received a public injury, and therefore expected a public satisfaction. This, with what passed before, so provoked the king that with great indignation he commanded them to leave his presence. The next morning passes were sent to them, and in the afternoon they left town, with 200 horse.[102] Pepys, in his 'Diary', fills in details of which Clarendon was unaware: 'the king, having newly put Prince Rupert out of his generalship, upon some miscarriage at Bristol, and Sir Richard Willis from his governorship of Newark … and put in … Bellasis, the great officers of the king's army mutinied, and came … with drawn swords into the Market-place … where the king was; whereupon the king said, "I must horse," and … cried to the head of the mutineers – Prince Rupert, "Nephew, I command you be gone." So the prince in all his fury and discontent withdrew, his company scattered', and shortly after left the town, the king looking out of a window and weeping to see them as they went.[103] After this interview Rupert rode back to Belvoir Castle with 200 officers and gentlemen who now gave up the Royalist cause as hopeless, resolute on going overseas. From Belvoir he went to Wiverton, and on the 29th, after some days' reflection, addressed a letter to parliament, stating that, along with his brother Maurice, Lord Hawley, Lord Gerard, Sir Richard Willis, and many officers and gentlemen of quality, he had decided to leave the kingdom, and asking for a pass either to enable them to go beyond the seas or to retire to their houses, 'as shall be most to their conveniency.' The application was read in the commons on 31 October, and both houses agreed to grant the passes desired. So, almost within sight of the spot where the king had first raised his standard, many of his ablest and bravest friends finally decided that they must lay down their arms.[104] Lord Bellasis, to whom the governorship of Newark was entrusted in succession to Sir Richard Willis,[105] was a man of great energy and bravery, with local associations that gave him considerable influence in the district. He was the second son of Thomas, first Viscount Fauconberg, and had been raised to the peerage in 1644 as Lord Bellasis of Worlaby, in the county of Lincoln. He had taken an active part in the campaign from its commencement, had supplied six regiments of horse and foot at his own expense, had fought at Edge Hill, Newbury, and Naseby, and had been present at the sieges of Reading and Bristol. He held property at the little village of Holme, near Newark, and owned a substantial residence there, which had previously belonged to the family of Barton, from whom he inherited it. Under his efficient leadership the garrison was reorganised and preparations made to resist another and more formidable siege than any that the town had previously undergone.

Dispatches show the preparations being made by parliament for the final siege of the town: 22 October … 'There is now a very great force of horse in our county with General Poyntz to besiege Newark, but the extreme poverty of the miserably harassed countryside, so long under the power of potent enemies, and forced to entertain forces both for and against parliament will not permit any delay in supplies from adjacent counties or elsewhere. We therefore desire the House to give us speedy and timely assistance.'

Same date, from Southwell, requesting 'that if Newark is to be besieged this time, a standing Committee be appointed out of the neighbouring counties to oversee and provide for the army, and that it may be maintained by the counties of Derby, York, Leicester, Rutland, and Lincoln, and that what foot shall be required for this campaign be sent promptly, otherwise the country may all be consumed before the work is even begun, and stating the impoverished state of the county and army. The King and Princes are still in Newark. General Poyntz lies at Southwell with our horse and foot and some other horse of Yorkshire, Gloucester, and the London Brigade. Welbeck is also besieged. Colonel Rossiter is now at Bingham, but we cannot approach closer to Newark without foot.'

Four days later, Nottingham … from General Poyntz (Addressed 'at the sign of the Pear in the little Centrey at Westminster'), advising of the extreme shortages of match and powder, and asking that necessary quantities be provided, plus money to replace horses and arms lost in the present expedition, and … that the neighbouring counties might quickly be made to contribute to the maintenance of the armed forces gathered in that county.

A Mr Thompson seems to have visited the committee to discuss the surrender of the town, and the committee promptly instructed Colonel Poyntz to offer favourable terms, but nothing came of it, and there is no evidence that Thompson, whoever he may have been, had any authority to negotiate. To the contrary, all evidence pointed to a resolute determination to fight to the bitter end. The committee, writing to Poyntz on 1 November, says, 'We know no more of this gent than what we learn from Major White's letter, and therefore desire you to take care that you be not by sharp practice brought into any danger under the pretence of a treaty. But if you find there may be any use made of him for the gaining of that place (Newark), you shall proceed as you see cause. If you shall proceed with this to the town, you may promise them security for their persons and estates, and that either the fortifications shall be slighted, and then there will be no need of any Governor, or if there be a garrison continued there the Governor shall be such a person as against whom there can be no just exception.' This is the last heard of the matter. On 4 November the committee, deploring the withdrawal of the Yorkshire horse, tells the York Committee, 'For want of your forces, Col. Poyntz is forced to retire to Nottingham.' The night before, on 3 November, the king, accompanied by about 500 horse, left Newark, to make his way as rapidly as possible to Oxford, which was holding out bravely in the defence of his cause. Clarendon gives an account of the king's departure: 'Order was given that all should be ready in the Market Place at ten o'clock at night. By that time the horse were all there, and were in number between 400 and 500 of the Guards and of other loose regiments; they were all there put in order, and every man was placed in some troop; which done, about 11 o'clock they began to march; the king himself at the head of his own troop marched in the middle of the whole body. By three o'clock in the morning they were at Belvoir.' It was thought the king got out of Newark the Monday night before parliament's forces could completely encircle the town. Several parties of Royalists were abroad at the same time, and gave the alarm to some of the besiegers' quarters, while that party with which his majesty rode made their escape, but parliament forces claimed they captured over forty prisoners that night, Colonel Rossiter quartering on the south side of the town and Colonel General Poyntz on the north.[106] On 6 November, the committee wrote to Poyntz saying they were informed the king had returned to Oxford. They desired him to send back the London horse, and to use the rest 'to block up Newark'.

John Twentyman, who lived through these turbulent times and wrote an account of what he saw at Newark, has provided information about these events. He counts the first brisk attack in 1641 as the first siege, the more vigorous attack under Sir John Meldrum as the second, and the final assault of the Scots and English forces in 1645–6 as the third. He says: 'after Sir Richard Byron succeeded Sir Richard Willis to be governor, who for his misdemeanour was removed, the third and last siege was anno. 1645(6).' John Bellasis, now Lord Bellasis, was governor. The king's army decaying, and not able to keep the field, many took themselves to the strongest garrisons, and there was built at the Spittal a very noble and strong work, which the townsmen kept, and built up a house of three or four bays of buildings in the middle of it. They called it the king's sconce, and later the royal sconce.[107] At the Mill-gate end, upon the south, above Markhall Bridge, there was another very noble work called the queen's sconce. The loyal townsmen kept the king's sconce, and were formed into a regiment. Edward Twentyman, the eldest or first captain of that regiment, died of a gangrene which followed upon a cut on his toe a little before the surrender. It was a strong garrison now, and kept the enemy a great distance from them. They were well provided for the siege, and were strongly beleaguered by the Scots and others of the parliament force.

What led to the great gathering of troops around Newark was a determination on the part of parliament to conquer the town. Disaster had befallen the Royalist cause everywhere. Montrose was defeated in Scotland, Fairfax had relieved Taunton and stormed Bridgewater and Bristol, the royal troops in Cornwall who had until recently held their own were dispersed, and of the remaining garrisons, only Oxford and Newark were of any strength. The king's army was no longer able to keep the field, and all that remained for the victorious party to do was to secure, if possible, the king himself and to reduce Newark and Oxford. While Fairfax attacked Oxford, two great armies – one English and one Scottish – gradually concentrated around Newark. State papers show how these forces were gathered, and what importance parliament attached to their action. The committee of both kingdoms, writing on 31 October to the committees and governors adjacent to Newark, states that the king is still in Newark, where he is watchfully blocked up, and if a sufficient number of foot is brought up quickly, the reduction of Newark might be readily achievable, the garrison being few and discontented. After pointing out that the taking of the stronghold, especially at this time, will not only put an end to the plundering and spoil of the adjacent counties, and the frequent and chargeable alarms of the rest of the Association, but in all probability might end the war, the Committee says that an order is given for various forces to march with all possible expedition, the season being so far advanced, for this service against Newark. As Lord Gerard wrote from Belvoir Castle, 'Here are armies upon armies for Newark.'

***

As described earlier, the king, despite the watch kept on his movements, had no difficulty in leaving the town; but before he left an effort seems to have been made to open up friendly negotiations with the Scots, with a view to secure their influence on his majesty's behalf. This is worth noting, as it shows that the king entertained some hope of co-operation with his Scottish subjects, and helps throw light on his motivation when he decided, a few months later, to place himself in the hands of the Scots' Army before Newark. On 15 October a communication was read in the House of Lords from the committee of both kingdoms at Berwick, enclosing a letter from Lord Digby to the Scottish generals, as follows:

> To the right honourable the Earl of Leven, General, and the Earl of Callendar, Lieutenant-General of the Scots forces now in England.
>
> My Lords,
>
> Having formerly written to your Lordships, by His Majesty's command, upon a subject highly importing the peace and happiness of all His Majesty's Dominions, I am again commanded to tell your Lordships that, in confidence of the good effects thereof, His Majesty is, through many difficulties, advanced hither to Newark, with a considerable body of horse and doth earnestly desire that he may receive, with expedition, an answer to what was then proposed by,
> My Lords,
> Your Lordships most humble servant,
> Newark, Oct. 4, 1645. GEORGE DIGBY

The committee reported to the house on 8 October that a trumpeter came from Newark with this letter, that it was opened at Northallerton by the general of the artillery, who commands in chief there, that he sealed it again, and sent the trumpeter, with a servant of his own, to the general, who, hearing what it was, would not open it until he sent for the Marquis of Argyll and the Earl of Lauderdale and Lanark. They immediately brought it to the Commissioners of the Parliament of England, and it was resolved to send it to be communicated by the lords to both houses. The general protests he never saw any other letter. Enclosed with this was Lord Leven's reply 'to the commander in chief with the forces now with His Majesty,' stating that no previous letter had come into his hands, but if it had, he should have addressed it to the parliaments of both kingdoms or their commissioners, 'as only capable of receiving and answering such propositions.' At the same time a deposition sent from Nottingham reached the house as follows:

> George Biggin of Eakring, informed Mr. Hawden of Tixford, minister, that a trumpeter belonging to Colonel Eyre of Newark, passing through Tuxford on Sunday, the 5th of October, in the presence of Mr. Hawden, affirmed that he was going with letters from His Majesty and from Sir Richard Willis, Governor of Newark, to General Leven, with hopes to bring him back with his army to Newark for the king, with as much joy as ever he did come for the parliament, and Mr. Hawden saw two letters in the hand of the trumpeter. And two Scotch gentlemen being at Tuxford with Mr. Hawden the same day, he affirmed to them that the king and General Leven had long been in treaty, and he did not doubt that it was effected, and that this letter would bring him back.
>
> Taken at Nottingham, in the presence of us,
>
> FRA.
>
> THORNHAUGH.
>
> Oct. 6, 1645. CHARLES WHITE.

A scout's report also came from Oxford, stating that 'on Wednesday night, very late, a messenger came from the king to report that all forces of the Scots around Hereford have agreed to come over to the king, and that they are in as much joy for that as for the coming of the new governor.' The lords decided to send these papers to the commons, who had at the same time to deal with complaints from the north about the cost of maintaining the Scots there, and of their 'levying of taxes and raising of money upon the subjects of this kingdom.' There is no more information of any negotiations between the king's party and the Scots, but the latter were urged to give 'a positive and speedy answer touching their army's marching to besiege Newark,' and it was ordered that some gentlemen be sent into the City of London to borrow £30,000 towards their payment.

Meanwhile, the parliament, feeling it imperative to reduce Newark, were drawing around it one of the most powerful armies under their control. Colonel Rossiter with a strong force was quartered at Balderton, Colonel Theo. Gray at Coddington, Colonel Henry Gray at Winthorpe, General Poyntz at Farndon, and the Scots were to take up their quarters at Kelham, so as to complete the investment of the town and coerce it to surrender. The task was formidable, for Newark was as strongly fortified as military ingenuity could devise and indomitable industry secure. An old manuscript account says:

> At the south end of this maiden garrison stood the queen's sconce facing the Trent, and the king's or royal sconce was to the east, so that the whole town seemed invincible. It was 'well defended with men, arms, ammunition, and artillery, besides such strong bastions, earthworks, half-moons, counterscarps, redoubts, pitfalls, and an impregnable line of earth and turf pallisaded and stockaded, and every part so furnished with great guns and cannon, that this bulky bulwark of Newark represented to the besiegers one entire sconce, and the two Royal forts formidable flankers; nor was there a tree to hinder the prospect.'

Any houses which had stood in the way of increasing the fortifications had been removed, as an entry in the Corporation Minute Book dated 23 September 1645 shows:

> Whereas there is a small tenement, consisting of two bays of building, lately erected upon the town's land, at Milne Gate, and near the river of Trent, by Thomas Waite, deceased, which said tenement is, by order of the general and commissioners, appointed to be taken down for the strengthening and better fortifying of the bulwarks there. We, therefore, the Mayor and Aldermen of the town of Newark, whose names are subscribed, do hereby authorise and appoint James Waite, executor of the last will and testament of the said Thomas Waite, his father, to take down the said tenement, and the same to re-edifie upon some part of the ground belonging to the Corporation, so soon as the same may or can be done with conveniency.

The king's sconce was situated on rising ground near the edge of the water, and a short distance from St Leonard's Hospital. The queen's sconce stood in a field off the Farnon Road, opposite the Spring House. While the king's sconce kept Gray's forces at Winthorpe and Coddington on the alert, the queen's sconce commanded the headquarters of Poyntz at Farndon and Rossiter at Balderton, as likewise their field positions.

The defensive works consisted of about twenty bastions,[108] each connected by a curtain wall. They began at the River Devon, 3 furlongs and one perch (606m) north and south from the castle, and completely surrounded the town from those points. The whole line of defence was 17½ furlongs (3,520m), or nearly 2¼ miles; its distance from the queen's sconce was 330yd (302m), from the centre of the marketplace to the extent towards Balderton 500yd (457m). A deep ditch ran parallel to these works, which the besieged normally had filled with water. The bridge over the Devon was defended by an iron turnpike, or kind of *chevaux de frieze*,[109] besides which there was a strong redoubt, at the distance of a furlong (201m) in front, on the road to Kelham. This, with the king's and queen's sconces, formed the outworks. There had been a fort at the Crankleys, but that was now within the enemy's lines. Muskham Bridge was still broken down after Prince Rupert's earlier relief of the town, and the bridge at Kelham was in the same state, the passage being occupied by a bridge of boats.

While the besieging forces were assembling, the Parliamentarians assaulted any minor garrisons that remained loyal to the king, amongst others Shelford, gallantly defended by young Stanhope. The committee of both kingdoms, writing to Sir Thomas Fairfax, state: 'On Monday last (November 3), Col. General Poyntz summoned Shelford Manor house, a garrison between Nottingham and Newark, and received a peremptory denial, upon which he fell upon it on all sides and carried it by storm, most of those within, which were the Queen's regiment, being put to the sword. There are 4,500 foot ordered to reinforce Col. General Poyntz for the besieging of Newark, some of which forces are upon their march.'

A short letter dated 5 November says that 'Since the taking of Shelford garrison, news came that, on Monday evening, the king got away with three hundred horse between Belvoir Castle and Col. Rossiter's guards, but to where it is not known.' It adds that General Poyntz was drawing against Werton House, which in a few days he hoped to reduce with the 4,500 foot ordered to him for the siege of Newark. They were to have their rendezvous at Grantham and Southwell the following Friday.

The winter seems to have been very severe, adding to the difficulties and sufferings of both besiegers and besieged. Ditches were frozen, and due to drought the water was very low in the river, enabling the enemy to approach the town's works, so that there was some hope of taking Newark 'without a storm'. The troops, however, came up slowly. Colonel Poyntz wrote on 9 November to William Lenthall from Bingham that since reducing Shelford, 'it pleased God to assist us in the gaining of Wiverton House, the strength of which moved me to give them fair quarter to march away with bag and baggage. As the foot ordered to me for the siege of Newark have not yet come from the Eastern garrisons I have had to delay going against it. The garrisons of Welbeck, Tickhill, and Bolsover are disgarrisoned by consent. I never received anything for intelligence, and am more than £400 out of purse.'

The House of Commons had ordered 'that 200 barrels of powder, with bullets in proportion, and a double proportion of match be furnished for the Scots army, in case they shall be before Newark by the 1st November.' This date, however, passed without their appearance, but a letter was received on 12 November intimating that they would speedily advance, 'though the men had neither money to keep themselves, nor clothes to protect them from the injury of the weather.' The Scots arrived at the end of November, and took up quarters in the fields between Newark and Kelham.

The Earl of Leven reported his arrival in November, and a joint committee of English and Scottish Commissioners was appointed to direct operations.[110] Muskham Bridge was seized on 26 November. Here is the Earl of Leven's dispatch:

> Upon the 26th of this instant November, having come to this place, within a mile of the Town, I caused to draw a Line [dig a trench] close to Muskham Bridge, whereupon I placed Musketeers, and sought all means to cross the river, and storm the sconce upon the other side; but the Enemy, apprehending the Design, sallied out yesterday morning before the Break of Day, [from the fort at the other end of the bridge, controlling it] and attempted to cut off the bridge, from which they were beat off by our Musketeers with little loss. Afterwards they set fire to the drawbridge, but our forces falling on, beat them back and extinguished the fire, which made them forsake their Works; so that we are now masters both of bridge and sconce. The Scots now camped at the island sconce beyond the bridge.
>
> Tuesday 2nd December. The Scottish army, about 7,000 horse and foot, quartered on the north side of Newark, while the English were on the south, the plan was to cut off the river from Muskham Bridge, which once done, would stop the Royalists from drowning the meadows, and safeguard the Scots' approach to the enemy's works, if forced to storm them [sic].[111] The works are very strong.

A previous dispatch had announced that the Scots had taken 'Musco' Bridge, and another party had seized the Mill Fort not far from the town, so that the Scots had blocked the garrison up on the north side, and Colonel General Poyntz and General Rossiter on the south.

Though very closely invested, the Newarkers made many desperate and successful sallies to keep themselves supplied with provisions. The Parliamentarians made accusations that the Newark forces endeavoured, with all possible diligence and the exercise of violence and cruelty, to fetch all the provisions they could out of the country into the garrison, carrying away as prisoners men out of those towns where they had not paid all their taxes and arrears; and if they were not brought in within eight days after, the enemy sent out parties to fire their houses and make total destruction of all they found, as may be seen by this warrant directed to the constables, etc. of Ossington.

> I do much marvel that you have no more care of me nor yourselves, but let your assistants run far, but now I have got two of your inhabitants, I wish you, as you

> do tender the good of yourselves and them, that you would gather my assessment, which is £200, or else expect to hear from me in another way, for I assure you, by the word of a gentleman, whosoever is wanting or backward in this tax, I will protest (although he be my friend), yet I set fire to his house (as I live). Therefore, I command you not to fail, as you expect safety of your house and timely answer it at your peril. Given under my hand 10th November 1645.
>
> ROBERT DALLISON

Sir John Verney writes on 10 December that 'the Scots are outside Newark, and intend speedily to take it. The town is in great want, and various persons of note are daily making their escape out of it.'

Not only the besieged, but also the besiegers, were in dire straits through lack of money. The parishes around must have suffered severely, being squeezed by both parties for both money and provisions. The little village of Upton paid in weekly assessment to the Scots, who controlled the country around their camp, over a period of three months, a total sum of £69 6*s* 8*d*. The Common Council of London were asked to advance £30,000 by way of loan towards payment of the Scots' Army, and agreed on 6 December to do the best they could to raise the amount at 8 per cent interest. A further £6,000 was borrowed from the Treasurers of Goldsmiths' Hall, to be disposed of and paid to the Scottish forces, also in December. That same day, the committee wrote to Poyntz and Rossiter saying that they were informed provisions were being carried into Newark daily on the south side, and insisting they do everything to prevent this. Orders were issued in all directions for more troops. A writer of the period states by letters of the 14th that 'the Scottish Army still quarters about Muscombe Bridge on the north of Newark, and Colonel General Poyntz on the south with four troops of horse and 600 foot on the Lincolnshire side, about Belvoir, Colonel Rossiter, Major Lebunts, and Major Heynes, at Beckingham and Claypole, 500 of the Isle of Ely foot at Long Bennington; Major Gibbs, his regiment and Leicester foot, being 600, at Stoke; and when Lynn foot come up they intend to complete the quarters on the north-east. On Wednesday, 17th, about sixty Royalists sallied out of Newark at Captain Penn's quarters, who was then on his guard with about forty men, and who received them with much gallantry, killed four, and pursued the rest of them nearly to the enemy's works. This action speaks much of the valour of our men, but being too eager in the pursuit they unwarily fell into an enemy ambush, and twenty of them were taken prisoners.'

In addition to the above quartered troops, the Nottingham and Derby troops had established their posts at Farndon where, on the same date as the letter was written, a party of Newarkers sallied out against them. One Royalist officer 'in a bravado flourished as if he would challenge any man there to fight with him'. In the spirit of the medieval knightly contest, Colonel Thornhaugh at once spurred out and at the first charge dismounted his adversary, killed his horse and took him prisoner – for which, on his return he was hailed with a great shout of applause.[112] The start of 1646 saw the gallant garrison hard-pressed by their foes, and against great odds fighting as bravely and boldly as ever. A newspaper of 8 to 16 January 1646 printed that the Royalists had sallied out of Newark and fallen on Colonel General Poyntz's quarters at Stoke, aiming to surprise him. The Nottingham forces had until recently been quartered in the church, until such a great fire caught hold of the straw that they could not extinguish it before it had consumed everything that was combustible, and the following morning nothing remained but the walls; a sad picture to onlookers. This may have encouraged the enemy, as not long after, the besieging Nottingham forces (now reduced in number to around 800 horse and 200/300 Royalist foot due to many going to Nottingham for some purpose) sallied out of Newark and bore down on the major-general's quarters with so much fury and eager speed that his horseguard fled and, in the midst of their disorder, two of their horses fell as they passed through the turnpike. Because of this, no adequate warning was given of the enemy's arrival until they entered the quarters and Major-General Poyntz's own chamber, which they set about plundering. Poyntz, on being told of the enemy's raiding party on his quarters, returned immediately and clashed with them, reportedly slaying one with his own hand, which encouraged his soldiers to act with the utmost gallantry and resolution.[113] Many of the enemy were reported killed, nine taken prisoner, and over fifty wounded, while the parliament forces admitted to only three slain and seven hurt. The enemy retired 'in disorder' to Newark on hearing that Colonel Rossiter, with a body of 1,000 horse and foot, was coming down from Claypole towards them, though they did manage to take with them some prisoners of their own, as well as items plundered from the Major-General's quarters. Seeing that the Royalists had notice of their coming and were fleeing to Newark, Rossiter returned to his own quarters.

Immediately after this, General Poyntz's forces were strengthened by the addition of 2,000 horse and foot from Skipton, and 300 foot from Lieutentant-General Leslie, which was indicative of the alarm that had been caused by the fierce onslaught of the Newark forces on the general's quarters.

Many other skirmishes followed. A newspaper between 30 January and 6 February 1646 reported:

> The Royalists lately made a flourish upon the Scots' side, but did not much hurt or take any considerable person. They are very silent on the south side of the town, but we shall make them cry herelong, for there are now two more mortar pieces, cast by a bell founder of Nottingham, which will be very useful, not only upon the town but forts of Newark, especially in frightening the ladies and other more valiant spirits. Mattocks and spades are ready. The country offers all assistance, and we shall soon have a line made, and then to work. While these skirmishes were ongoing, the commissioners with the army were doing their best to keep the besieging forces supplied with provisions and money.

> Writing to the House of Lords on 2 January 1646, they stated that they had used their best efforts to reduce Newark and Belvoir, and find very ready compliance by the answers received to their letters and don't doubt that their actions will be suitable. The counties adjacent are very supportive in this service, and the officers and soldiers vigilant and full of courage. General David Leslie has asked for the provision of a weekly maintenance for the Scots' Army as follows: 3,600 foot, at 4*d* per day for seven days, £420; officers of foot of eight regiments, £500; 4,000 horsemen, at 1*s* 6*d* per day, £300; 2,100 officers of the horse, £1,860; officers with the staff and train of artillery, £300; in all, the weekly sum of £5,280. The Committee of Parliament replied that they would provide £10,000 for twenty-eight days, a third in money and two-thirds in provisions; whereupon General Leslie wrote, 'it will not amount to the half of what we need to [sic] subsist, and is impossible for me to condescend to it.' The committee declared they could not provide more, and in a dispatch to the House of Commons stated, 'We on the place know too well provisions in these counties to be exhausted.' They urged the house to 'finish this service speedily.'

When, on 17 January, the Army of the Solemn League and Covenant mustered on Markham Moor near Newark, the College of Justice Horse Troop under John Cockburn, serving under Lieutenant-General Leslie as part of the force besieging Newark comprised sixty-nine men and officers. David Leslie's regiment numbered ten troops – 554 rank and file, ten sick and two absent; Leven's regiment – eight troops – 535 rank and file, and four sick. Major-General John Middleton's regiment listed seven troops – 348 rank and file; Sir James Ramsay's horse eight troops – 417 rank and file, six sick. The Scots' Army comprised in total nine regiments of foot, ten of horse, two companies of dragoons and thirteen independent troops of horse.

The deplorable condition of the county is clearly illustrated by a petition of the inhabitants on the north side of the Trent, presented in January, setting out that the cost to the county over the last three years amounted to over a million pounds. The petitioners declared that the charge of the army was already £261,189 7*s* 2*d* though all the bills had not yet been brought in, and they went on to state 'this part of the county is still charged with an assessment of £2,506 weekly, besides … free quarter for all officers and listed soldiers, and for all men, women, and boys depending on or shadowing themselves under that army, and worst of all, the tyranny and evils incident to free quarter in the best governed armies. If that £2,500 with the charge of free quarter were to continue, it cannot be less in our opinion than £5,000 weekly, which must be borne by only half of the county, caused by untenanted grounds and places visited with the plague.' It was pointed out that the people could not carry on like this for much longer and that unless some way could immediately be thought of for maintaining the troops, the siege

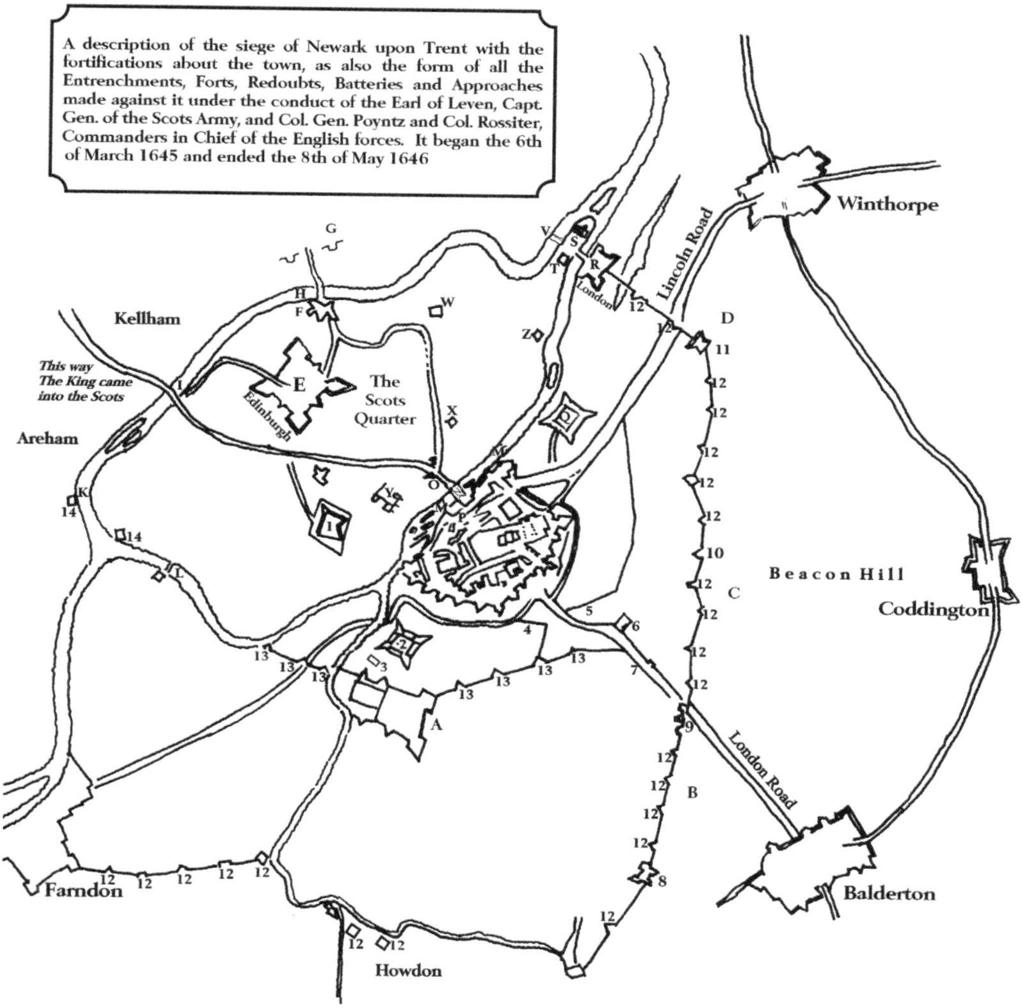

A– Col. Gen. Poyntz' quarter in the field. B– Col. Rossiter's quarter in the field. C– Col. Theophilus Gray's quarters. D– Col. Henry Gray's quarters. E– The Scots' quarters. F– A Sconce formerly kept by the Newarkers. G– Two works made by the Scots. H– The place where Muscombe Bridge stood. I– The place where Kelham Bridge stood - now a bridge of boats. K– A ford in the river staked over. L– The dam made over the river by Gen. Poyntz. M– Two dams made by the Newarkers to hold up the water. N– The bridge over the Trent fortified with an iron turnpike. O– An outwork kept by the Newarkers. P– The Castle of Newark. Q– The King's Sconce. R– Col. Gray's Sconce. S– An old work of the Newarkers. T– A Redoubt of the Scots with a breastwork passing over the corner of the island. V– Two bridges made with boats over the river. W– A Redoubt of the Scots. X– Another redoubt of theirs. Y– Three works of the Scots. Z– A flanked redoubt of the Scots by the Red Lodge. 1– A work of the Scots palisaded about. 2– The Queen's Sconce. 3– A Redoubt of Gen. Poyntz. 4– Gen. Poyntz' Approach. 5– Col. Rossiter's Approach. 6- Col. Rossiter's Battery. 7– The approaches and works made in Balderton Lane from the first line. 8– Rossiter's Sconce upon the first line. 9– Crawford's Sconce upon the first line. 10– Gray's fort. 11– Moll's Horn works. 12– The Redoubts Bulwarks upon the line of circumvalation. 13– The Redoubts and Bulwarks upon the second line of circumvalation. 14– Two works of the Scots near the ford at Areham.

would have to be raised. Parliament decided to meet the difficulty by requesting a reduction of the Scots Army to 2,000 horse and 1,000 dragoons. This was in February, the same month a bitter complaint was made by the Scots about the non-payment of their troops, then 4,136 horse and 2,836 foot. In a letter to the peers they say, 'The foot soldiers have not received eighteen-pennyworth of provisions since our coming to Newark, and when the Quartermaster-General, who has been sent a second time to represent the necessities of the army, returned, there was not £10 worth of provisions in the magazine for the whole army.'

The outcome was that the harassed population was daily deserting the county, consequently increasing the evil for those who remained. General Leslie, who had succeeded Leven in command, indignantly repudiated the suggestion that his men had been guilty of ill conduct and secured the signatures of forty-six gentlemen and freeholders to a certificate confirming the good character and discipline of the army, but the parliamentary committee fully endorsed the account of the miserable state of the wasted county which the petitioners had drawn.

In February parliament ordered £15,000 per month to be paid for the upkeep of the Scots, and Leslie ordered to all under his command not to presume, on pain of death, to offer the least wrong or violence to the persons or goods of the habitants.

Grave complaints were made from the villages that, in their dilemma, the Scots had inflicted harsh treatment on the inhabitants. There had been similar complaints of outrages previously committed in Yorkshire, which caused the English Commissioners to write to General Leslie on the subject, stating that these things so concerned the public service against Newark, and the good relations of both kingdoms, 'that we desire a speedy redress.' General Leslie, in a letter dated from East Bridgford, 23 January 1646, promised that if anything came to his knowledge the offenders would be punished. A pamphlet was issued, containing two letters from Lieutenant-General Leslie to the Scottish Commissioners in London, together with the voluntary service of various well affected gentry in Nottinghamshire, with their names inscribed, concerning the carriage of the Scots Army in these parts. A letter from General Leslie dated from Kelham, 25 February 1645, stated that he was grieved to hear so many false reports regarding the behaviour of the army, yet it was of some comfort to him that the gentry of Nottinghamshire, where the main army was quartered, had been pleased to write of them in a better light. He said, 'I have likewise thought fit to acquaint your Lordships that I have received discharges from several villages where the army quarters, and you may rest assured that everything will be done that lies in my power for easing the country. I wish that the bridge was made over the river quickly so that we might join with the forces on the other side to block up the town on all parts.' The certificate attached stated that the burdens had been equally and regularly laid upon them, and acknowledged with thankfulness the readiness of General Leslie to ease them, 'and so to order and regulate the army and to do his best endeavours to preserve them.' The writers said,

'We are sorry that our poverty and weakness cannot answer your merits and nobleness', and concluded, 'We shall ever pray for the increase of your honour and happiness in the manifestation we have now.' The document was dated from Southwell, 3 February 1646, and forty-seven signatures were appended to the certificate. General Leslie added that he had issued a proclamation, commanding all officers and soldiers not to presume, on pain of death, to offer the least wrong or violence, and inviting any who shall receive any wrong or injury to make their appearance freely at headquarters to exhibit their complaints. Meanwhile, 'the siege of Newark went slowly on, every inch of ground being disputed by the besieged.'[114] The Earl of Rutland, in a letter dated Lincoln, 3 March, wrote that 'their whole army on the south side of the Trent were drawn together: the farthermost foot quarters about a mile from the town; others at Farringdon, Houghton, and Balderton, so to Trent again at Winthorp.' That evening about 300 horse and foot of the garrison faced them, but would not advance from under the cover of their own cannon. The Scots Army was drawn up on the north side of the Trent, and the soldiers were all full of courage, and very few sick amongst them. He concluded by saying that 'he hoped shortly to give the Lords a good account of the place.'

On 5 March 1645–6, Colonel Rossiter stated that while he was at Lieutenant-General Leslie's quarters, the enemy sallied out of Newark with all the horse and foot they could possibly muster – about 1,000 foot and 400 horse – and fell on the Scots guard on the island with the intention to capture their great fortified camp which the Scots called 'Edinburgh', made to stop the enemy from grazing any cattle on the island. Muscomb Bridge having being broken down by ice which had covered the bridge in January, the Scots could not reinforce their own men other than very slowly by boat, about six at a time, so that the enemy overpowered their horse – being only four small troops – and made them retreat towards Muscomb Bridge with some loss. Then the enemy attempted to take the work itself, but were beaten off with some loss. A handful of Scots – about 150 horse and 200 foot – held their trenches at push of pike until sufficient troops were ferried across to force the Royalists back into the town. As soon as the Lieutenant-General received the alarm, he and the rest of his company hastened with all speed over the river, where he commanded the horse to rally, led them himself to the work, took some foot from there plus some other foot which had crossed the river, and marched to confront the enemy, who retreated after some small skirmishing, into the town. On the Scots' side a captain, two lieutenants, and eight soldiers were killed, and fifteen or twenty soldiers wounded. The Royalists had left some dead on the place, and had one captain and various others slain and wounded. It was decided to make a bridge from Winthorpe side at the very point of the island to Muskham, which would not only serve as communication between the Scots and Colonel Grey, but also as an access from both sides into the island. Lieutenant-General Leslie would guard one end of the bridge, and Colonel Grey the other. The dispatch concludes: 'If your Lordship please to hasten down the pinnace,[115] it may be of good use while the bridge is making.' A letter from one of the parliament commissioners at Lincoln, dated 7 March, states:

> The enclosed dispatch from Col. Rossiter will show what the Newarkers lately attempted with a great deal of resolution, coming up to the works even to push of pike; and if the Scots had not been stout and resolute foot (they who knew them say they are the best men in the army, and the oldest soldiers being the Lord Sinclair's regiment), if it had transpired that any other regiment had been there instead, it is feared matters would scarcely have gone so well, they were so overpowered with numbers. Now all men may see (that which some have not heretofore believed) that Newark is a considerable garrison to the king, as they can spare such a large number for a sally and yet be able to man the town and works besides. The truth is that it happened very fortunately, that the success proved so well, having no greater strength, we had not half so many men as they had, and yet most of the Scots' commanders, also Poyntz, and with him several of his chief officers, and Col. Rossiter and many of his chief officers were at the same time in the Isle, onto which no one can get into or out of except by boats, and then no more than ten or twelve at a time; so if our forces the Newarkers tried to surprise had been routed, our men (amongst whom were so many great officers) would have been in a pinfold, yet the enemy did not show enough courage to take their opportunity to the utmost, but through a pannick fear, supposing our men to be of greater number, greater than they really were, their terrour being the greater in seeing our men come over and still increase as fast as they could, by that weak means so that they imagined that the whole body of the Scots' army was coming upon them. Col. Gray was there with Col. Rossiter, who said that he never did see them do better service. Their Highland foot charged with the Scots' horse, and gave fire and wheeled amongst our horse very nimbly and actively, and so galled the enemy exceedingly. The line is now begun, and all our materials are now in readiness for a siege, and the next week we shall lay it. [But] the associated forces are so ill paid, both their horse and foot, that unless some speedy course be taken to send them money we shall not be able to keep them together, for where the army lies those areas cannot furnish them with necessary provisions without being paid, and if they pay for what they take, all provisions will be brought into their quarters, both from Boston and this town; but if they should grow unruly and take provisions by force, they will be starved or forced to rise, which we have endeavoured all we can possibly to prevent; but how the £2,000 we brought down with us being disbursed, if present pay is not forthcoming, I fear for the consequences; two months' pay would, I am sure, relieve both them and all these parts from that oppressing tyrannical garrison. There has recently been great contestation in Newark between Governor Bellasis, the king's Commissioners

> and the officers and soldiers, for pay and provisions. The Governor told the Commissioners that his soldiers wanted [were without] monies, but they [the commissioners] professed there was none; but he might issue to them what quantities of provisions he saw fit. Bellasis replied that soldiers must and should have monies whilst any one of them had a farthing, and that regarding the provisions in the magazine the greatest part no dog would eat, and so demanded they bring out better, or he and his soldiers would rifle their houses and take the provisions they had stored for themselves, and leave them the rotten stuff in the magazine to feed on; and he also told them that they were not to expect that he and his soldiers would fight to save them and their town unless these matters are resolved, and finally for his part he knew very well how to make honourable and good conditions for himself, his officers, and soldiers, and would leave them and the townsmen to shift for themselves if they did not take care of the soldiers; and so they broke up in a great heat and discontent.

A letter of 18 March declared that the pinnace did arrive, and speaks of the progress of the fortifications. 'One of the bridges across the Trent against Winthorpe was ready three days ago. The Trent there divides, and the other bridge will be finished in a day or two. We have brought a Pinnace Musket within half a mile of Newark, in which are two guns, and which will hold forty musketeers. The cannon from York have come to Winthorpe. One strong fort has been made to secure the bridge, and another is in preparation near the enemy's great sconce. Culverins and mortar pieces have been sent to Balderton and Farringdon. The great mortar piece is to see service on Wednesday at Nottingham. We shall lose no time or pass up any opportunity to reduce Newark.'

The Parliamentarians had constructed lines running around the walls to the south and east of Newark, 'about a cannon distant', consisting of a chain of small square earthwork forts 180–230m apart, linked by a curtain rampart and trench. As effective musket range was 230–360m, this arrangement ensured that each camp could count on effective support from its neighbours if attacked, and enabled the whole line between them to be swept with musketry. Farther back, the villages of Stoke, Balderton, Coddington, and Winthorpe, were all fortified to form an outer girdle of defences not only against any breakthrough by the garrison, but also against an attempt to relieve the town from without. Meanwhile the Scots had secured their hold on the island by building their great fortified camp, nostalgically named Fort Edinburgh. These formidable works housed an army, which by March consisted of 7,000 Scots, and about 9,000 English troops drawn from Lincolnshire, Nottinghamshire, Derbyshire, Yorkshire, and the Eastern Association counties. By mid-March, Newark was completely surrounded and all access cut off to the outside world, while the Scottish and Parliamentarian armies maintained communication by bridges of boats across the River Trent north of the town.

Towards the end of the month, the besiegers held a day of prayer to seek a blessing on their designs.[116] The text was Deut. xxiii. 14 and in his dedication to 'the Commissioners from the Parliament of England, residing with the forces before Newark,' the author says, 'This sermon was preached by your appointment, and is drawn forth to public view by your importunity.' Another preacher on the same occasion was Robert Ram, who also published his discourse that a soldier follows a lawful and honourable calling: 'none were so fit to be soldiers as good Christians and godly men, especially in God's battles. The highest powers under God call on us to arm ourselves at this time against the enemies of Church and State. By the highest powers I mean the Parliament, which, according to the constitution of our Government here in England, has the most sovereign powers over us ... Religion, law, liberty, and whatever is dear to us, now call on us to take up arms; these are mightily invaded, and unless we stand forth manfully, we shall be spoiled forever.' The preacher then exhorted the commanders and common soldiers to behave with soberness, chastity, and holiness; and concluded, 'I beseech you then let every one of us put these things in practice, which, if we do, I dare promise that Newark will soon be ours, and we shall suddenly see our desires upon all our enemies.'

The commissioners met the Committee of the Parliament of Scotland, and agreed to send a summons into Newark,[117] demanding the surrender of the town, promising honourable and fair conditions; and pointing out that while they could use force to obtain what they want, they would rather achieve this by treaty, the parliament having 16,000 horse and foot before Newark, their soldiers being men of experience, united and in health and courage. 'This', they added, 'is not mentioned as if we trusted in the arm of flesh (God the Lord of Hosts has shown that we fight his battels), but to show you the vast costs which will be caused by the continuing of this siege (for which your estates must answer), and so that you do not tempt the Almighty further by continuing to hold out. Though you might not recognise your own coming ruin, though others might share your opinion, still, should that wealthy town be sacked, and others perish with you that see their own misery and wish to avoid it?' The letter asks for an answer within three days and was directed to 'the Governor of the town and garrison of Newark, the gentlemen there, and the Mayor, aldermen, and burgesses of the town.' Lord Bellasis forwarded a spirited reply, in which he referred to the paper 'putting the gentlemen and Corporation on equal terms with me (though the joyning us together was with the intention to divide us),' and said, 'I am neither to be struck into apostacy by the mention of fair conditions in a misty notion, nor frightened into dishonour by your running diversion upon the fate of Chester,' in regard to which 'I hope this garrison shall never be the transcript of their calamity.' He concluded: 'You may do well to use your fortune modestly, and do not think that God Almighty applauds your cause by reason of your victories, or that he has not a blessing in store for ours. Whereas you emphasise the expense of the siege and the pressure on the countrey in supporting your charge there, being caused by yourselves that is of no concern to me; yet in order to ease them, if you will grant a pass to some gentlemen to go to the king and return, I may find out his Majesty's pleasure, whether he will wind up the business in general, or leave me to steer my own course; then I shall know what to decide; otherwise, I desire you to note that, when I received my commission for the government of this place, I annexed my life as a label to my trust.' The commissioners, in forwarding these documents, say, 'Colonel Poyntz wishes to suddenly turn the course of the river Trent which runs close under Newark, and will in a little time turn the river Smite into a new channel, so that their mills will not work and so that no water hinders the approaches on the north side of the Trent. The field officers have viewed the most convenient places for forts to shoot either into the town, or sconces, which are in preparation, and will soon be finished. We shall lose no time to make a good end of this service.'

Poyntz and Rossiter closed their approaches before Newark, then turned the river course, which perplexed the besieged to find the courses of both Rivers Trent and Smite diverted. 'In regard to the turning of the Trent, they made no works of moment to defend themselves on that side of the town. As we [the besiegers] close in our approaches, we raise forts to safeguard the places. We have raised a fort to cut off all communication between the Queen's fort and the town; we have another fort raised at Balderton, another on Beacon Hill.'

Poyntz's damming the rivers was to stop the town mills producing corn and gun-powder and force the townsfolk to rely on wells for their drinking water. During April, the besiegers' siege lines advanced to within musket shot of the defences. On the island, the Scots captured a Royalist work called Sandhills sconce on which they mounted artillery to bombard Newark Castle. Although supplies were running low and plague had broken out in the town, Bellasis refused to surrender.

The Leicester forces have marched to assist at the siege. 'The enemy in Newark begins to be more anxious, not least because our mortarpiece has begun to play upon them, although at first causing more fright than actual execution, because the gunners could not find their range.'

General Leven, who some time ago went to Scotland, now returned to the Scots' Army, but because the country was unable to quarter the Scots horse and there was little for them to do here, 1,000 have been sent back to Yorkshire. 'We believe something will shortly be effected for the speedy reducing of Newark.'

To meet the urgent demands for money, a Mint had been set up in Newark. Royalist noblemen and gentlemen freely gave their flagons and drinking cups to be fashioned into lozenge-shaped coin; half-crowns, shillings, ninepences, and six-pences. Mrs Markham says that on some of them can still be seen the pattern of the cup or salver from which they were hastily cut. This money is called siege money or 'money of necessity.' The coins bore a Royal crown between C.R., and the value in Roman numerals; and on the reverse 'OBS. (obsidium, siege), Newark,' and the year 1645 or 1646, in which they were coined. They would doubtless all be struck in 1646, for, at this time, the year did not alter its date until March 25.[118]

While the Scots and Parliamentarians made preparations to storm Newark, events elsewhere were moving to bring the Civil War to an end. In July 1645, Cardinal Mazarin of France had appointed a young agent, Jean de Montreuil, as his envoy to negotiate with the Scottish Commissioners resident in London. Mazarin hoped to influence a resolution of the Civil War that was favourable to French interests and was anxious to help Charles, increase the power of France's old ally Scotland, and at the same time keep England weak. Encouraged by Montreuil, the Scots discussed the possibility of a separate peace treaty with the king. Early in 1646, Montreuil acted as an intermediary in secret negotiations to prepare for the king's surrender to the Scots rather than to parliament.

On 27 April, with the New Model Army closing in on Oxford, King Charles fled from the Royalist capital in disguise, having cropped his hair and beard, and with only two companions, passed through fourteen enemy garrisons and made his way to the camp of the Scottish Army before Newark. He arrived at the Scottish headquarters at Southwell on 5 May 1646 and surrendered himself to Lieutenant-General David Leslie, who was acting commander of the Covenanter army while Lord Leven was at Newcastle.

Leslie was anxious to convey the king to Newcastle, being a secure garrison and closer to Scotland, but did not wish to leave himself open to accusations of deserting his Parliamentarian Allies, so he urged the king to order the immediate surrender of Newark on reasonable terms. Although Lord Bellasis is said to have wept when he received the order, he had no choice but to obey. Newark surrendered on 6 May 1646 and Bellasis marched out with his depleted garrison. On 8 May, the Scots broke camp and marched north, with the king in semi-captivity.

Montrose Disbands

A MONTH EARLIER IN the Scottish highlands, the Marquis of Huntly, to whom the siege of Inverness had been entrusted by Montrose, had retired from the task with disgrace, in defiance of his commander's entreaties,[119] leaving Montrose resolved to attempt it himself, though by no means backed by a sufficient force. He set fire to the outskirts of the town and detachments of his army pillaged all Lord Lovat's country, killing the country people and burning their habitations. From the Green of Inverness to the Guisachan, in the top of Strathglass, it is narrated on the authority of an eyewitness[120] that not a horse, cow, sheep or fowl was left in that extended sweep of country.

Intelligence was brought to Montrose that General Middleton had arrived at Aberdeen with a force of 600 horse and 800 foot. He now renewed his entreaties to Huntly to join him immediately that they might either reduce Inverness or march jointly upon Aberdeen and attack Middleton; Huntly, however, refused to accede to Montrose's request. This refusal exasperated Montrose to such a degree that he resolved to have recourse to force to compel compliance, as he could no longer endure to see the authority of the sovereign, whose deputy he was, thus trampled upon and despised. As he had already brought over to his side the Earl of Seaforth, who had induced the heads of some of the principal clans to form a confederation for obtaining a national peace, he was fully in a condition to have reduced Huntly to obedience. Montrose, having got a new commission, sent a copy of it to Huntly, and as governor and general of the royal forces charged him to come without delay, with his whole force to Inverness, and there receive further orders. Huntly appears to have made preparations for complying with this order, but Middleton's sudden advance on Inverness induced him to alter his purpose.

Wishart relates rather an incredible story respecting an alleged piece of treachery on the part of Lord Lewis Gordon on this occasion. He states that, as Montrose had no reliance on Huntly, and as he began now to think it high time to look more carefully to his own safety, lest Huntly's malice might at last carry him the length even to betray him, he sent three troops of horse to the fords of the Spey to watch the motions of the enemy, with orders, if they approached, to send him immediate intimation of their movements. This body, it is said, occupied the most convenient stations, and watched with very great diligence for some time, till Lord Lewis, who then kept the castle of Rothes, having contrived his scheme of villainy, assured the officers who commanded the horse that the enemy was very far distant and had no intention to pass the river; he therefore advised them to cease watching, and having invited them to the castle where they were sumptuously entertained by him, plied with wine and spirits, and detained till such time as Lord Middleton had crossed the Spey with a large army of horse and foot and penetrated far into Moray, he dismissed his guests with these jeering remarks – 'Go, return to your General Montrose, who will now have better work than he had at Selkirk.' Gordon of Ruthven, however, contradicts this very improbable story, and attributes Middleton's unmolested crossing of the Spey to the negligence of the troops who guarded the passage; asserting that Lord Lewis knew nothing of it till Mortimer, one of the captains in command of the troops appeared at Rothes to tell him that Middleton was on the other side of the Spey on his way to Inverness. Moreover such a statement carries its own condemnation upon the face of it, for even supposing that Montrose's officers had acted the stupid part imputed to them, they would certainly not have forgotten their duty so far as to order their men to abandon their posts.

It was in the month of May 1646 that General Middleton left Aberdeen at the head of his army, on his way to Inverness. He left in Aberdeen a regiment of horse and one of foot, for the protection of the town, under the command of Lieutenant-Colonel Montgomery. Middleton made a rapid march, and arrived in the neighbourhood of Inverness on 9 May, driving before him the few troops of horse which Montrose had stationed on the Spey to watch his motions. The trumpets of his advance picquets sounding at Petty, a village about a league off (4.8km), first warned Montrose of Middleton's approach, and he drew his troops together, and took up a position some distance from the town just as his pursuers entered it. Middleton's superiority in cavalry induced him to retreat across the River Ness to the other side. His memoirs state that the enemy attacked his rear, but being gallantly received, were forced to retire – the losses being inconsiderable and nearly equal on both sides. The Covenanters' version was that Middleton dispatched two regiments of cavalry after him, who attacked his rear, cut off some of his men and captured two pieces of cannon and part of his baggage. Montrose continued his retreat by Kinmylies and Beauly into Ross-shire, where he was pursued by Middleton, hoping to bring him to an engagement in the low ground; but Montrose avoided contact, dreading their superiority in horse. As Seaforth's men, who had joined Montrose at Inverness under their chief, began to desert in great numbers, and he could not depend on the surrounding population, he made the circuit of Loch Ness and marched through Strathglass and Stratherrick[121] to the banks of the Spey. Middleton, after the earlier skirmish, had meanwhile entered Inverness, to the great joy of the inhabitants, refreshed his troops, and set out next morning in pursuit of the retreating army. He marched through the parish of Kirkhill, under the guidance of Sir James Fraser of Brea, who was governor of the castle of Inverness, and commanded there during the siege. The members of Lord Lovat's family being greatly dispersed during these troubles, it was Sir James Fraser of Brea who exerted an oppressive authority over the family.

The two armies continued in sight of each other for two days, having the Beauly between them. On the fourth day, Montrose broke up his camp and set it on fire. Sir James Fraser of Brea, who had the rank of colonel, entertained Middleton at Lovat, and then conducted him across the ferry of Beauly to Channory, in Ross, where Middleton laid siege to the castle of the Earl of Seaforth, which he took after four days. He behaved with great politeness towards the Countess of Seaforth, who was in the castle, and restored it to her after taking away the ammunition it contained.

Colonel Montgomery, Middleton's second in command, had been beating up Royalist positions at Kintore during the night with a party of horse, but was repulsed by Lord Lewis Gordon with some loss, and forced to retire to Aberdeen. The absence of Middleton from Aberdeen afforded Huntly an opportunity to attack the town and he appeared at the gates of Aberdeen at noon the following day (the 14th) with 1,500 highland foot and 600 horse, storming it in three different places. The garrison defended themselves with courage, and twice repulsed the assailants, in which contest part of the town was set on fire; but a fresh reinforcement having entered the town under Lord Aboyne, the attack was renewed, and Montgomery and his horse were forced to retire down to the edge of the River Dee, which they crossed by swimming. Colonel William Forbes, Captain Lockhart, son of Sir James Lockhart of Lee, and three captains of foot, besides a number of privates, were killed on the side of the Covenant; Huntly lost only about twenty men.

Although the city of Aberdeen had done nothing to incur Huntly's displeasure, he allowed his highlanders to pillage it. About twenty officers were taken prisoner, among whom were Colonels Urry, Barclay, and David Veighton; as well as Sir William Forbes of Craigievar, and other country gentlemen.

As Huntly's force was considerably reduced when the highlanders who accompanied his force returned home with the booty they collected in Aberdeen, and, apprehensive of the imminent return of Middleton, he stayed only a short time in Aberdeen. Marching up the north bank of the Dee, he encamped in Cromar; but the sudden appearance of Middleton, who had heard of Huntly's advance on Aberdeen and had retraced his steps and re-crossed the Spey, made him retire into Mar. Middleton, after pursuing him for a short distance, returned to Aberdeen, which he found had suffered severely from Huntly's visit.

After an ineffectual attempt by Montrose to obtain an interview with Huntly at the Bog of Gight, where he had moved his forces to on Middleton's return to Aberdeen, Montrose resolved to make a tour through the highlands, hoping, by his personal presence, or the promise of suitable rewards, to encourage the clans to rise up for their sovereign; but with the determination, in case of refusal, to enforce obedience to his commands. This resolution was not taken by Montrose without the concurrence of some of his best friends, who promised to aid him by every means in their power, in carrying it into effect. In the pursuit of this plan, Montrose was just about to set out on his journey, when, on the last day of May, a messenger arrived with a letter from the king, requesting him to disband his forces and retire to France, where he would receive 'further directions'.

Ever since the disastrous Battle of Naseby, fought on 14 June 1644 between the English Royalists and Parliamentarian forces, the campaign in England on the part of the king 'presented little more than the last and feeble struggles of an expiring party'. Granted, thanks to the recall to Scotland of David Leslie's horse, which had travelled as far as Nottingham on their way to Hereford, the king had been able to drive the Parliamentarian infantry back from the siege of Hereford; however, the surrender of Bristol to parliament on 10 September, and the defeat of the Royalists at Chester on the 23rd of the same month, completed the ruin of the king's affairs. Having shut himself up in Oxford for the last time in November, Charles, after his secret treaty with the Catholics of Ireland was discovered, had tried to negotiate with the English parliament in the hope that if he could gain either the Presbyterians or independents to his side, he would be able to get the upper hand of both. That negotiation having failed, another was instigated through the medium of Montreuil, the French envoy, with the Scots Army before Newark, the leaders of which offered an asylum to the king on certain conditions. At length Charles, undetermined as to the course he should pursue, on hearing of the approach of the Parliamentarian army under Fairfax, had left Oxford at midnight on 27 April 1646 in the disguise of a servant, accompanied by Mr Ashburnham and Dr Hudson, a clergyman. After traversing the neighbouring country, he arrived at Southwell on 5 May, where he was introduced by Montreuil to the Earl of Leven, and the officers of his army staff. The arrival of the king seemed to surprise the officers very much, although it is supposed that they had been made aware of his coming by Hudson, who had preceded him, and they treated him with becoming respect, the commander tendering his bare sword upon his knee; but when Charles, who had retained Leven's sword, indicated his intention to take the command of the army by giving orders to the guard, that crafty veteran had unhesitatingly declared: 'I am the older soldier, Sire, your majesty had better leave that office to me.' The king was, in fact, now a prisoner. As soon as the intelligence reached the capital that the king had retired to the Scots camp, the two parliamentary factions united in accusing the Scots of perfidy and sent a body of 5,000 horse to watch their motions; but the Scots, desiring to avoid hostilities, raised their camp and hastily retired to Newcastle, carrying the king along with them.

On his arrival at Newcastle, the king was waited on by the Earls of Lanark and Callander, and by Lord Balmerino, who paid their respects to him. As Callander was understood to be favourably inclined to the king, Lanark and Balmerino wished to get rid of him, and so persuaded his majesty to send Callander back to Edinburgh with a letter, which they had induced his majesty to write to the Committee of Estates expressing his desire to comply with the wishes of the Scots parliament, and containing instructions to them to order Montrose, Huntly, and Sir Alexander Macdonald to disband their forces. And it was also at the desire of these two noblemen that the king wrote the letter to Montrose already referred to.

After Montrose had read this letter, he was both surprised and concerned. All his schemes for accomplishing the object of his ambition were dashed in an instant. He was suddenly placed in one of the most painful and difficult situations conceivable. He had no doubt that the letter had been extorted from the king, yet he considered that it would be neither prudent nor safe to risk the responsibility of disobeying the king's orders. Besides, were he to attempt to act contrary to these instructions, he might by his own actions compromise the king's safety, as his enemies would find no difficulty in convincing the army that Montrose was acting according to private instructions from the king himself. On the other hand, by instantly disbanding his army, Montrose would be leaving the Royalists and those friends who had shared his dangers to the mercy of their enemies. In this dilemma, he determined to convene a general meeting of all the principal Royalists, to consult as to how he should act – a resolution which showed good sense, and a just feeling, towards those whom he had convinced to risk their lives and fortunes in the cause of the king. Despite the many slights put upon him by the Marquis of Huntly, Montrose, anxious to preserve a good understanding with him, sent Sir John Hurry and Sir John Tunes to invite him to attend the proposed meeting, and, so that there might be no appearance of dictation on the part of Montrose, the time and place of meeting was left to Huntly's own choice. But this nobleman answered that he himself had received orders similar to those sent to Montrose, which he was resolved to obey immediately, and so declined to attend any meeting on the subject.

Placed in this position, Montrose considered that his best course of action would be to keep his army together until he should receive another communication from the king in answer to a letter which he sent by a messenger of his own, in which he begged his majesty to acquaint him with the real state of affairs, whether he considered himself safe in the hands of the Covenanters, and if Montrose could be of any farther service to him. He also begged to be informed by the king if he was determined to persevere in his resolution to disband an army which had fought so bravely in his defence, and this at a time when his enemies in both kingdoms were still under arms; and if so, he wished to be instructed by his majesty as to the course he should pursue, for the protection and security of the lives and fortunes of those brave men who had encountered so many dangers and had spent their blood in his defence, as he, Montrose, could not endure the idea of leaving such loyal subjects to the mercy of their enemies. The king returned an answer to this letter, by the former messenger, Ker, in which he assured Montrose that he no less esteemed his willingness to lay down arms at his command, 'for a gallant and real expression' of his zeal and affection to his service than any of his former actions; but he hoped that Montrose had not such a mean opinion of him that for any particular or worldly respects he would suffer Montrose to be ruined – that his only reason for sending Montrose out of the country was that he might return with greater glory and, in the meantime, to have as honourable an employment as the king could confer upon him, that Ker would tell him the care he had of all Montrose's friends, and his own, to whom, although he could not promise such conditions as he would have wished, yet they would be such, all things considered, as were most fit for them to accept. 'Wherefore,' continued his majesty, 'I renew my former directions, of laying down arms, unto you, desiring you to let Huntly, Crawford, Airlie, Seaforth, and Ogilvy, know that want of time hath made me now omit to reiterate my former commands unto you, intending that this shall serve for all; assuring them, and all the rest of my friends, that, whensoever God shall enable me, they shall reap the fruits of their loyalty and affection to my service.'

These conditions, which consisted of several articles, and in the drawing up of which the king probably had no concern, were far from satisfactory to Montrose, who refused to accede to them. He even refused to treat with the Covenanters, and sent back the messenger to the king to notify him that as he had acted under his majesty's commission, he would admit of no conditions for laying down his arms or disbanding his army, which did not come directly from the king himself; but that if his majesty imposed conditions upon him, he would accept of them with the most implicit submission. The king, who had no alternative but to adopt these conditions as his own, put his name to them and sent back the messenger with them, with fresh instructions to Montrose to disband his army forthwith under the pain of high treason. Besides Ker, the king dispatched another trusty messenger to Montrose with a private letter urging him to accept the conditions offered, as in the event of his refusal to break up his army, his majesty might be placed 'in a very bad condition,' such as he would rather leave Montrose to guess at than seek himself to express. From this expression, it would appear that Charles already began to entertain some apprehensions about his personal safety. These commands of the king were too peremptory to be withstood any longer, and as Montrose had been informed that several of the leading Royalists, particularly the Marquis of Huntly, Lord Aboyne, and the Earl of Seaforth, were negotiating with the estates on their own behalf, and that Huntly and Aboyne had even offered to compel Montrose to lay down his arms in compliance with the orders of the king, he immediately resolved to disband his army.

As Middleton had been entrusted by the Committee of Estates with ample powers to negotiate with the Royalists, and to see the conditions offered to Montrose implemented by him in case of acceptance, a cessation of arms was agreed upon between Montrose and Middleton; and in order to discuss the conditions, a conference was held between them on 22 July, on a meadow near the River Isla in Angus, where they 'conferred for the space of two hours, there being none near them but one man for each of them to hold his horse.' The conditions agreed upon were that, with the exception of Montrose himself, the Earl of Crawford, Sir Alexander Macdonald, and Sir John Hurry, all those who had taken up arms against the Covenanters would be pardoned on making their submission, and that Montrose, Crawford, Hurry, and Graham of Gorthy should transport themselves beyond seas, before the last day of August in a ship to be provided by the estates. This arrangement was ratified by the Committee of Estates, but the Committee of the Kirk exclaimed against it, and petitioned the Committee of Estates not to sanction it.

Prior to disbanding his army, Montrose arranged its rendezvous at Rattray, in the neighbourhood of Coupar-Angus. There, on 30 July, he discharged his men, after addressing them with feeling and animation.

> Giving them due praise for their faithful services and good behaviour, telling them his orders, and bidding them farewell, an event as sorrowful to the whole army as to himself; and, despite his greatest efforts to raise their flagging spirits and encourage them with the prospect of a speedy and desirable peace, and assuring

> them that by this action he contributed to the kings safety and interest, as much as he had previously done by his military efforts; they still concluded that on that day a full stop was being put to the king's authority, convinced the orders had been extorted from the king or granted by him only to avoid a more immediate evil and, on however favourable conditions their own safety might be provided for, they lamented their fate, and would rather have undergone the greatest fatigue and hardship than be obliged to remain inactive and idle spectators of the miseries befalling their sovereign. They also expressed concern for the unworthy and disgraceful opinion which foreign nations could not fail to have of the Scots, as universally dipped in rebellion, and guilty of defection from the best of kings; and sorrow at the thought of being separated from their general, who was now obliged to enter into a kind of banishment, to the irreparable loss of the king, the country, themselves, and all good men, at a time when they never had greater need of his services: And falling on their knees, with tears in their eyes, they begged him that, seeing the king's safety and interest required his immediate departure from the kingdom, he would take them with him to whatever corner of the world he would retire, expressing their readiness to live, fight, and, if it so please God, to die under his command. And not a few of them had privately determined, though at the evident risk of their lives and fortunes, to follow him without his knowledge, and even against his inclination, and 'to offer him their service in a foreign land, which they could no longer offer him in their own distressed native country.

Upon the dissolution of Montrose's army, the Scots officers and soldiers retired to their homes, and the troops marched west into Argyle, from where they embarked for their own country, being accompanied there by the Earl of Crawford, who from there went to Spain.

Yet a remnant of Montrose's followers kept the garrison of Redcastle, in Ross, for the king. To reduce it, a troop of Strachan's horse were ordered out of Inverness, where Sir James Fraser of Brea was now the appointed governor. Their leader, Captain McLean, approaching near enough to hold converse with the besieged, was shot upon the spot; which so irritated the soldiers that they set fire to the castle and reduced it to ashes. They then carried the captain's body to Kirkhill, where they buried him, determined, as they said, he should not lie with 'the recreant McKenzies'. A stone was erected over his remains in the church yard with the inscription 'Here lies one of David's worthies.'

Montrose, alone with the few friends who were to follow him abroad, took up his abode at his seat of Old Montrose, to await the arrival of the vessel due to convey them to the continent. The day fixed for Montrose's departure was 1 September, and he waited with impatience for the arrival of the expected vessel; but as the month of August was fast expiring without such vessel making its appearance, or any apparent preparation for the voyage, Montrose's friends applied to the

Committee of Estates for a prorogation of the day set for his departure, but they could obtain no satisfactory answer.

At last, on the final day of August, a vessel for the reception of the marquis entered Montrose harbour, in which he proposed immediately to embark, but he was told by the shipmaster, 'a violent and rigid Covenanter', that he meant to careen his vessel before going to sea, a task which would take a few days. In the course of conversation, the shipmaster bluntly stated to his intended passengers that he had received express instructions to land them at certain ports. The behaviour of the captain, added to the information he had communicated and the fact that several English ships of war had been seen for several days off the coast, as if watching his embarkation and departure, created a strong suspicion in Montrose's mind that a plan had been laid for capturing him, and induced him to consult his own safety and that of his friends by seeking another way of leaving the kingdom. The anxiety of Montrose and his followers was speedily relieved by the arrival of intelligence that a small vessel had been found in the neighbouring harbour of Stonehaven; and that the master had been engaged [on being promised a handsome fee], to be in readiness on an appointed day, to sail with such as should appear.

Accordingly, after sending off Sir John Hurry, John Drummond of Balloch, Graham of Corthy, Dr Wishart, and a few other friends by land to Stonehaven, on 3 September 1646, he himself left the harbour of Montrose in a small boat, disguised as the servant of James Wood, the clergyman who accompanied him; and the same evening went safely on board the vessel, into which his friends had embarked, and setting sail with a fair wind, arrived in a few days at Bergen, in Norway, where he received a friendly welcome from Thomas Gray, a Scotsman, the Governor of Bergen.

***

Whatever transactions that took place between the Scots and English concerning the disbanding of the Scottish Army and the delivery of the king to the English parliament, while the Scots are not free from blame for having betrayed their king after he had cast himself upon their loyalty and mercy, the king himself was only playing a game and that placing himself in the hands of the Scots was his last desperate move; neither would he have had the least hesitation in deceiving, and even destroying, his protectors. In September 1646, an agreement was reached between the Scots commissioners and the English parliament that the Scots Army should be disbanded, on the latter paying £400,000 as payment in full of the arrears of pay due to the army for its services. There was no mention then made of the delivery of the king, and the evidence on both sides would indicate that the one transaction was quite independent of the other. That fanaticism and self-interest had steeled the breasts of the Covenanters against the more generous impulses of loyalty and compassion may be granted; but more than this cannot be legitimately inferred from any proof of history.

Fraser's Horse in Northumberland – Regimental Crimes

BETWEEN JANUARY AND MAY 1646 the actions of Fraser's horse had done much to exacerbate Scottish – English relations. The regiment had apparently previously departed from Scotland very poorly provided with horse. For a week the troopers stole horses in the Northumberland parishes of Chillingham and Newton, some 20 miles south of the Scottish border, attacking any owner who tried to recover his beast. From there the regiment proceeded into the West Riding of Yorkshire, seizing money in Ripley, Derbyshire, 20–30 miles west of Newark. By 30 January it had reached Tickhill, Doncaster, 30 miles north of Newark at the southern tip of the riding. On that day Lieutenant-Colonel Monro[122] addressed letters to the constables of Sheffield, Rotherham and Darnall, all within 15 miles to the west, demanding a total of £1,507 12*s* per week for the maintenance of the regimental staff and three companies. If the inhabitants did not pay, they would be quartered upon. Information on these payments is hard to find, but it is known that on 9 February Rotherham provided the £485 6*s* assessed for the support of Captain Muir's company. Rotherham also had to quarter the entire regiment of 400 men and horse on the 23rd. Meanwhile the officers had established two zones between Rotherham and Doncaster to provide for the regiment's weekly maintenance. To the south of the River Don the officers cessed a group of twenty-five parishes, centred on Maltby (including the headquarters at Tickhill). There, figures exist for two weeks of the cess. In the first week the parishes provided £4,545 9*s*, and in the second they gave £3,653 7*s*. The group of thirty parishes north of the river stretched from Wentworth to Bentley and were assessed £3,798 9*s* per week. Unfortunately there is no information about the promptness of payment or about the subsequent increase or decrease of demands by the officers. The regiment remained quartered in the area until early May, when it retired further north after the fall of Newark.

As well as monetary exactions, indiscipline was another grievance the English had against the regiment. The first material on the regiment's crimes concerns the trial of reformado officers at Thirsk. Lieutenant-Colonel Monro was in command of a special regimental guard of these men. In April, Lieutenant-General Leslie convened a court martial at Tickhill to try the prisoners. Colonel Fraser served on the panel of judges. Monro, however, was unable to produce several of the prisoners. In a fit of anger, Leslie had him arrested. On 21 April, Fraser held his own court martial with officers of the regiment at Laughton En Le Morthen (6 miles from Tickhill and 30 miles north-west of Newark) to try eight offenders. The court acquitted three men of rape and two of assault. One trooper was sentenced to death for assault and robbery. Another accused of assault had his case delayed. The eighth man, a corporal, stood charged of bigamy, but failed to appear. Two weeks later the English Commissioners at Balderton, Nottinghamshire, condemned Fraser's council of war as a mockery of justice. They claimed that no witnesses had been called, although they had appeared and waited at other times for appointed courts, which did not sit. The commissioners insisted upon another trial of the offenders, because justice was not done. It is unlikely that such a trial took place. For one thing, the regimental officers had already shown little respect for English wishes by illegally cessing parishes for their support. Furthermore, the regiment departed the area for the North Riding or the north-eastern counties after 7 May (the time the rest of the Scottish Army also set out northward with King Charles). The regiment had until then possessed an excellent service record; however, its relations with English civilians failed to gain it the reputation of being 'Godly'.

From 1 August until 1 November 1646, Fraser's were north of York again, free quartered and billeted at Cleveland.

Newark – The Final Days

While Newark was so bravely holding out, around the 8 or 10 April, the king sent word to Lord Bellasis, the Governor of Newark, of his intention to come to the Scots, and in regard to Newark left a latitude to him. 'Seeing himself besieged and without hope of relief, he treated.' While the terms were under discussion, his majesty reached Kelham. Major-General Poyntz wrote on 5 May to the speaker announcing the king's arrival that day at the Scots' quarters, and saying he had 'posted away his Secretary' to assure him that his majesty was safely secured at Kelham. He goes on to say, 'Our process in the Treaty was in great forwardness, but we now rather expect his Majesty's commands for a surrender than the prosecution of a parley.' Poyntz was right in this. As soon as the king was in the Scots' camp he was induced to send terms of surrender to the garrison. These terms were worse than had been previously submitted, and were by no means satisfactory to Lord Bellasis, and the valiant men associated with him. His lordship sent a letter requesting that they might still keep the town for him, for they retained a hope that before their store could be spent, some last minute change or other would come to his majesty's advantage and relief, but his majesty wished him to deliver up the town that night at which he was 'troubled'.

His majesty continuing his command, they, as obedient loyal subjects and to their great grief, laid down their arms, and the garrison marched out a day before the appointed time, so great was the sickness raging in its ranks and amongst the inhabitants. 'Newark', wrote an eyewitness, 'had become a miserable stinking infected town.' With Bellasis went Lords Deincourt and Lexington, with 1,500–1,800 men. They left behind the great gun known as 'Sweet Lips', as well as eleven other cannon, two mortars, a number of drakes and a large store of match, powder, muskets and other arms and armour.[123] Colonel Hutchinson and his regiment occupied the town and orders were at once issued to the inhabitants of the surrounding villages to come in with shovels on the following Monday and throw down the fortifications which surrounded it. Within a week these works had been rendered untenable and some of them levelled to the ground. The normal trade of the countryside soon began to flow into the marketplace once more, but all that summer the plague was still rife and filling the churchyards of the neighbouring villages with its victims. A Mrs Hutchinson claimed that the plague raged so badly that it 'almost desolated' Newark.[124] In the answer of the commons to the Scots' Commissioners' Papers of 20 November and their letter of 24 October 1645, the commons asserted that the kingdom of Scotland had no right of joint exercise of interest in disposing the person of the king while in the kingdom of England. They stated that, 'if the king were duly in Scotland, we should not claim any joint interest in disposing of his person there.' The lengthy argument on this and related matters ran to many pages, the only local references being within the reply of the Scots Commissioners, in which they stated that the quarters in which they had stayed during the siege being exhausted, and the service for which they came south being completed, they were marching into Yorkshire, and 'the king, as he came to them of his own accord, was along with them voluntarily'; adding that 'their keeping and preserving the king was without the least thought of hindering his voluntary return to his Parliament.' The commons replied that their committee earnestly pressed them that the king might return to Southwell, and not go to Kelham, 'where the body of your army lay, to cajole or disturb your soldiers,' but could not obtain consent thereto. The next day they complained again without effect, and the following day (Thursday, 7 May), the Scots Army marched off and took the king with it. The commons concluded by expressing the hope that there will be 'a sweet and brotherly agreement between the nations.'

The Reverend John Shaw, vicar of Rotherham wrote: 'I was with the six commissioners for Newark. General Leslie did not deliver the king to the English commissioners, or to the Parliament, at which all people wondered. They marched away, leaving the siege with a swifter march than ordinary, carrying the king with them to Newcastle. Lord Bellasis yielded up the town to the commissioners with whom I then was and the forts and works of Newark were demolished.'

Shaw concluded that the Newark garrison appeared very dissatisfied at the king placing himself in the hands of the Scots, and when 800 of them had marched out with Lord Bellasis, they would not nominate any other garrison to go to for the further service of the king, but like the rest who came out, about 1,000 or so, they went to their own homes.

Northumberland and Newcastle had been in the hands of the Scots since the siege of Newcastle in 1644. By this time, the county was in a pitiable state from their depredations. A Royalist writes: 'We have a regiment lately come in from Scotland ... They are very oppressing to our country, going up and down, burning towns, as the soldiers phrase it, receiving £3, £4, £5 and more, according to the bigness and littleness of the towns, and where they quarter at night, they demand, as I am told by a preacher, who is their own countryman and who regrets their actions, for a captain 12s., for a lieutenant 6s., ensign 4s., and for common soldiers 2d. a man, which they levy before their departure from their quarters. Their usual march is 5 or 6 miles a day, and not directly forwards neither ... The committee is about to write to the general to let him know about this [sic] and hopes to get relief from him, or else the county will be undone.' Minutes from the Gateshead parish accounts tell the same story: March 1645–46, 'Pd to Captain Grey, a fine which the Committee laid upon the Town and for his and his mens charges when they came about the fine; £11 15s. 0d.' March 1645–46, 'Pd to the Skotts to redeem the great new gate which they had taken away and carried to their leaguer[camp]; which gate did hang at the entering into the Town fields 1s. 2d.' June 1646, 'Pd to men for assisting us to drive the Fell and watching the beasts when they were pinded (but James Towers of Newcastle procuring assistance of the Skotts came violently and took them away by force) his beasts being, in number 79, also there was at that time 90 of another man's 9s. 3d.'

Charles I entered Newcastle about five o'clock in the afternoon of Wednesday, 13 May. By order of Sir John Lumsden, the governor, the road was lined from Gateshead to his residence with musketeers and pikemen. Charles's immediate escort consisted of 300 horse or less. An eyewitness gives an interesting and minute account of the scene: 'Some that attended his Majesty rid before all bare [headed]. Then his Majesty marched with the General and some other Scottish officers, several of whom also that were near the king, rid bare. None went out of Newcastle to meet his Majesty, neither the Scottish Lords that were in the town, nor the Deputy-Mayor; nor any other. His Majesty was not received in triumph (as some would have had it to be done), nor did they in any solemn manner take notice of his Majesty. The king rid in a sad coloured plain suit, and alighted at the General's quarters.[125] No guns were discharged, either by land, or by water, by way of triumph. There was no acclamation by shooting muskets, sounding trumpets or beating drums, and yet there was a good store of both Kettle-drums and trumpets in Newcastle; yet were they so far from any public way of triumph, that they did not sound or beat as much as when one troop of Scottish Horse marched into Newcastle.' Another eyewitness describes Charles as being 'very silent, without bells ringing, or bagpipes playing, or Mayor and Aldermen, not as at Doncaster.' A single shout only was raised as Charles entered the court gates; a demonstration that at once drew from Leven a proclamation forbidding Charles's adherents to have access to him. Among those who entered the town with Charles, who were denied his presence by this order, were Major Gilbert Errington of Denton and Lieutenant Colonel Carr.

Very particular precautions were taken both by Leven and the town's authorities to secure the king. His escort having withdrawn after his arrival at the court, he was left in the charge of the mayor. A guard of musketeers was mounted, and 'inhabitants of trust' were appointed to act as sentries round the king's residence. Leven also ordered 'that some of the ancient men of the Inhabitants of the Town should constantly sit in every passage to examine and take notice what persons came in or out,' and 'Proclamation was made by beat of Drum and sound of Trumpet, that although His Majesty was come thither, All persons should yield obedience to the Ordinances of Parliament.' No Scotsman could enter the town without a pass from the estates, nor any Englishman without the sanction of the parliament, the English commissioners, or the deputy-mayor. Charles was in fact a prisoner. His letters to the queen on 20, 28 May and 3 June expressed his indignation at this unlooked-for treatment. He seemed 'melancholy, and very gray with cares,' and a careful observer of his appearance noted that 'The hair of His Majesties face is not shaven (as some have writ), but cut round both on the chin, and upper lip also, his lock is cut off and his head rounded.'

Anderson Place, the residence of Sir Francis Liddell, was assigned to Charles by order of Leven and the commissioners. It had, until recently, been the residence of the Governor, Sir John Lumsden. Since it is also spoken of as being Leven's quarters, it is clear that it was utilised as the official hostelry for the high guests whom those stirring times called to Newcastle.

In the midst of these exciting events, a curious circumstance is recorded by the *Weekly Account*. 'His Majesty was told that a young woman at Morpeth, which gave out that she was the Princess which married with the Prince of Orange, she was sent for to Newcastle, examined, and found a counterfeit; yet she had some retinue. This trade she took up (as she said) to get money. She was whipped and sent going.'

The Scots detained the king until 1647 as a pledge for the arrears that they claimed. By their account, the sum amounted to near two million, as they had received little regular pay since entering England. After many discussions it was agreed that in lieu of all demands, they should receive £400,000, half to be paid immediately; but at the same time the king should be delivered up to parliament.

Throughout January 1647, the interest of both kingdoms was centred on Newcastle, and the arrival there of the money which was to take both Charles and the town out of the hands of the Scots. On 16 December, thirty-six carts containing £200,000 had set out under convoy from London. On 3 January, the money reached York. Here, the task of counting the money began the morning after its arrival. By the 8th, barely £50,000 of it had been 'told,' and a week more was needed to complete the task. Arrangements regarding the payment of the money to the Scots had already been made. Five days after the money had been told at York, £100,000 was to be paid over at Topcliffe, near Northallerton. Meanwhile, the evacuation of Newcastle by the Scots was underway. The first £100,000, paid at Topcliffe on the 21st, reached Newcastle on the 24th, 'and now,' writes a correspondent on the 28th, 'is dividing amongst them, each one reaching out for his share.'

The Scots had appointed their headquarters at Morpeth, the roads had been prepared for their progress as far as Berwick, and a small force of only 500 remained in Newcastle, when on Saturday the 30th, Skippon[4] arrived. The Scots withdrew quietly at about three o'clock that afternoon – 'a friendly and brotherly parting,' as Leven had enjoined – parading all their cavalry through the centre of the town and before the king's residence before leaving it to the English garrison that had arrived about two o'clock.[126]

Montreuil however relates: 'The English officers had considerable trouble, with blows and threats, to prevent the women of the town from following the Scottish troops and throwing stones at them while they were leaving it.' Skippon took the Scots sick in Newcastle under his care. The Scots left behind twenty guns that had formerly belonged to the Earl of Newcastle.

On 27 December 1646, the Scottish Estates had given instruction to their commissioners at Newcastle: 'You must provide ships to transport the provisions of victual to Scotland. For which purpose you are warranted to give order for pressing Scottish ships, and if the wind serve not before the removal of the garrison from Newcastle or Tynemouth, assurance must be given for their passage and safe convoy.'

Fraser's regiment remained quartered in England until the beginning of February 1647, when it returned to Scotland as part of the Scots horse which had left Yorkshire on 25 January. Stockton and Hartlepool too were abandoned on 30 January.

It was written of the Scots departure: 'most of them go very willingly, especially those who are considerable, though indeed some are discontented. General Leven carries himself most excellently in the managing thereof. The Scots officers behave themselves very inoffensively. As for the common soldiers, they have such warm quarter, that [I believe] they go away very unwillingly, considering the season and the cold climate through which they march.'

A Scot wrote of the march itself (written 11 February):

> We went from Newcastle to Morpeth where we stayed till our artillery (which was brought up by English) came to us: from hence we intend to Alnwick, and so to Northam, and there we shall soon be over the River Tweed; we have ten days allowed for our march, but General Leven hopes to finish it in five. When we get to Scotland, we do not know the rendezvous point, some think it will be near Edinburgh where we shall disband, all but 5,000 foot and 1,800 horse which shall be employed against Montrose, Kilketto and the rest of that barbarous crew, who still hold some small mountain garrisons, which we shall soon reduce and then we shall be able to assist our poor brethren in Ireland. Out of Scotland we hear of the great preparations of our friends to welcome us home, expressing much cheerfulness to hear of our daily motion towards them. I had almost forgot one very remarkable particular, how General Leven executed one of his soldiers for murder,

> which gave great content to the country people; who came to our assistance, by throwing down the hedges and making the ways easier for our march, rejoicing to see such harmony at the farewell, being glad that the work is so well ended; all the more because many wicked people would have rejoiced at our being divided, and laid a foundation for more misery by a second War.

Once the king had been handed over to parliament on 3 February, a second £100,000 was paid to the army.

The NMA & Reduction of the Scots Armies

An act of 5 February 1647 had ordered a general disbanding of the regiments on foot in England and Scotland, the infantry on 9 February 1647 and the cavalry on 10 February. The 'new modelled forces', which it was proposed to keep on foot, in accordance with an order of the estates of 29 January, consisted of seven regiments of infantry – 6,000 men; fifteen unregimented troops of cavalry – 1,200 men; and two companies of dragoons, being about 200 men; a total of 7,400 rank and file. Leven was appointed Lord General, David Leslie Lieutenant-General, and John Middleton Major-General. The 'new model' regiments were formed as follows:

INFANTRY – Two highland and one lowland formed exclusively from units in Scotland. The remaining four regiments – each of six companies and 800 rank and file – were to be formed of drafts from regiments returning from England.

CAVALRY – 1,200 troopers were to comprise 560 from Scottish units and 460 from regiments returning from England.

DRAGOONS – Two companies each of 100 men taken entirely from units in Scotland.

INFANTRY (SEVEN REGIMENTS)

COLONEL	LIEUTENANT-COLONEL	MAJOR
General Sir Alexander Hamilton's regiment.		
Sr Alexr. Hamilton	John Home	James Innes
Major General Jas Holburn's regiment[1]		
Major General Holburn	John Innes	Meldrum
Colonel Colin Pitscottie's regiment[1]		
Colin Pitscottie	John Rough	John Towers
Colonel Walter Scott's regiment[1]		
Walter Scott	John Hadden	Blair

Colonel William Stewart's regiment[1]

William Stewart	David Wemys	Agnew

Marquis of Argyll's highland regiment[12]
Campbell of Ardkinglas's highland regiment[2]

CAVALRY (FIFTEEN TROOPS)

Colonel Robert Montgomerie's[2], Colonel Lockhart's[2], Colonel Mungo Murray's[2], Colonel James Mercer of Aldie's[2], Colonel Keith of Ludquharn's[2], Colonel Harry Barclay's[2], Major David Barclay's[2], Sir John Browne's[1], Lieutenant-Colonel Thomas Craig of Riccarton's[1], Colonel Hugh Fraser of Kinneries'[1], Lieutenant-Colonel Strachan of Thornton's[1], Lieutenant-Colonel Gilbert Kerr's[1], (staff:) Earl of Leven's[1], Lieutenant-General David Leslie's[1], Major-General John Middleton's[1].

DRAGOONS

Colonel Patrick Blair's[2]
Major William Sharp[2]

While the negotiations for handing over the king had been pending, Charles, who appears to have been fully aware of them, contemplated escaping from the Scots Army, and putting himself at the head of such forces as the Marquis of Huntly could raise in the north. Further to this scheme, around the middle of December, Charles had sent Robert Leslie, brother of General David Leslie, with letters and a private commission to Huntly, by which he was informed of his majesty's intentions and prompted to levy what forces he could, and have them ready to take the field upon the king's arrival in the north. On receipt of his majesty's commands, Huntly began to raise forces, and having collected them at Banff, fortified the town and awaited the king's arrival. But Charles was prevented from putting his plan into execution by its premature discovery, and was from then on guarded much more strictly.

After the delivery of the king to the English, the Scots Army had returned to Scotland, Leven's forces crossing the Tweed at Kelso on 11 February and the horse, including Fraser's, disbanded thereafter. By a later charge of arms received from the army upon its returning from England and its disbanding, listed among other items was, from Colonel Fraser's Regiment: ninety-seven pairs of pistols and twenty-four old muskets. The regiments already in Scotland had been disbanded on the 9th. Hugh Fraser now found himself in command of a troop of some eighty NMA horse, formed from units returned from England, but from which units is unconfirmed. This number (for all troops of horse) was to be further reduced to seventy-five men on 5 March. The army was thus remodelled and reduced to 6,000 foot and

1 Formed from regiments not in Scotland on 29 January 1647.

2 Formed from regiments in Scotland on 29 January 1647.

1,200 horse; a force considered sufficient both to keep the Royalists in awe and to reduce the Marquis of Huntly and Sir Alexander Macdonald (Kolkitto), who were still at the head of some men. The dispersal, therefore, of the forces under these two commanders became the immediate object of the parliament. An attempt had been made in January, by a division of the Covenanting army in Aberdeenshire, under the command of a Major Bickerton, to surprise Huntly at Banff, but which had been obliged to retire with loss; and Huntly continued to remain in his position until April when, on the approach of General David Leslie with a considerable force, he fled with a few friends to the mountains of Lochaber for shelter. Leslie proceeded to reduce the castles belonging to the marquis, starting with that of Strathbogie, sending its commander, the laird of Newton-Gordon, to Edinburgh. This was followed by the castle of Lesmore and then the Bog of Gight, or Gordon Castle, the commander of which, James Gordon of Letterfurie, and his brother Thomas Gordon of Clastirim, and other gentlemen of the same clan, were also sent to Edinburgh as prisoners. Leslie next took the isle of Lochtanner, in Aboyne, which had been fortified by Huntly. Quarter was given to all the men who garrisoned those places, except the Irish and deserters, who were hanged immediately on their capture.

Leslie then marched into Badenoch, where he captured the castle of Ruthven. From there he proceeded into Lochaber, and took the fortress of Inverlochy. Huntly disbanded his forces in Badenoch, retaining only a few as a bodyguard for himself and his son, 'showing them that he was resolved to live an outlaw till provident heaven should be pleased to change the king's fortune, upon whose commandments his life and fortune should always depend'. The Covenanting general marched south with some of his forces, leaving the rest camped in Strathallan under Middleton, while he himself took up headquarters in Dunblane, where he remained till mid May, when he was joined by the Marquis of Argyll, and ordered to advance into that nobleman's country to drive out Sir Alexander Macdonald. Accordingly, he set out on the 17th, and arrived at Inverary on the 21st. Sir Alexander Macdonald was in Kintyre with 1,400 foot and two troops of horse – enough to check Leslie – but he seems not to have been aware of his advance, and had taken no precautions to guard the passes leading into the peninsula, which might have been successfully defended by a handful of men against a considerable force. Having secured these difficult passes, Leslie advanced into Kintyre, and after skirmishing lasting the whole of the 25th, forced Macdonald to retire. After throwing 300 men into a fortress on the top of the hill of Dunaverty, and in which 'there was not a drop of water but what fell from the clouds,' Macdonald, on the following day, embarked his troops in boats provided for the occasion, and passed over into Islay.

Leslie immediately laid siege to the castle, which was well defended; but the assailants having taken a trench at the bottom of the hill which gave the garrison the command of water, and in the storming of which the besieged lost forty men, the latter craved a parley, in consequence of which Sir James Turner, Leslie's adjutant-general, was sent to confer with the garrison on the terms of surrender. Leslie would not grant 'any other conditions than that they should yield on discretion or mercy. And it seemed strange to me,' continues Sir James Turner, 'to hear the lieutenant-general's nice distinction, that they should yield themselves to the kingdom's mercy, and not to his. At length they did so, and after they had come out of the castle, they were put to the sword, every mother's son, except one young man, Macleod, whose life I begged to be sent to France, with 100 fellows which we had smoked out of a cave, as they do foxes, who were given to Captain Campbell, the chancellor's brother.' This atrocious act was perpetrated at the instigation of John Nave or Neaves, 'a bloody preacher,' (but, according to Woodrow, 'an excellent man') 'who would not be satisfied with less than the blood of the prisoners.' Turner's eyewitness account reads:

> Here it will be fit to make a stop, till this cruel action be canvassed. First, the lieutenant-general was two days irresolute what to do. The Marquis of Argyll was accused at his arraignment of this murder, and I was examined as a witness. I declared, which was true, that I never heard him advise the lieutenant-general to it. What he did in private I know not. Secondly, Argyll was but a colonel then, and he had no power to do it of himself. Thirdly, though he had advised him to it, it was no capital crime; for counsel is no command. Fourthly, I spoke several times to the lieutenant-general to save these men's lives, and he always assented to it, and I know he was unwilling to shed their blood. Fifthly, Mr John Nave (who was appointed by the commission of the Kirk to wait on him as his chaplain) never ceased to tempt him to that bloodshed, and threatened him with the curses, which befell Saul for sparing the Amalekites, for his theology taught him to compare the Dunaverty men with them. And I truly believe that this prevailed most with David Leslie, who looked upon Nave as the representative of the Kirk of Scotland.

The fact of Sir James and David Leslie's repugnance to shed the blood of those defenceless men is fully corroborated by Bishop Guthrie, on the authority of many persons who were present, who says that while the butchery was going on, and while Leslie, Argyll, and Neaves were walking over their ankles in blood, Leslie turned and addressed Neave: 'Now, Mr John, have you not once got your fill of blood?' Some of the victims were Irish, and some belonged to the clan Dougal or Coull, to the castle of whose chief, in Lorne, Colonel Robert Montgomerie proceeded to lay siege, while Leslie himself, with a part of his forces, left Kintyre for Islay in pursuit of Macdonald.

On landing in Islay, Leslie found that Macdonald had fled to Ireland, and had left Colkittoch, his father, in the castle of Dunniveg with a force of 200 men to defend the island against the superior power of Leslie. The result turned out as might have been anticipated. Although the garrison made a brave resistance, being without water, they found themselves unable to resist, and offered to capitulate on certain conditions. These were that the officers should be entitled to go where they pleased, and that the privates should be sent to France. These conditions were agreed to, and were punctually fulfilled. Old Colkittoch had, however, the misfortune not to be included in this capitulation, for, before the castle had surrendered, 'the old man, Colkittoch,' says Sir James Turner, 'coming foolishly out of the house, where he was governor, on some parole or other, to speak with his old friend, the captain of Dunstaffnage castle, was surprised, and made prisoner, not without some stain to the lieutenant-general's honour. He was afterwards hanged by a jury of Argyll's sheriff-depute, one George Campbell, from whose sentence few are said to 'have escaped that kind of death.'

Leaving Islay, Leslie 'boated over to Jura, a horrible isle'. Turner continues:

> [It was] a habitation fit for deer and wild beasts; and so from isle to isle, till he came to Mull, which is one of the best of the Hebrides. Here Maclaine saved his lands, with the loss of his reputation, if he ever had any. He gave up his strong castles to Leslie, gave his eldest son for hostage of his fidelity, and – in an act of unchristian baseness in the lowest degree – he delivered up fourteen prettie Irishmen, who had been all along faithful to him, to the lieutenant-general, who immediately hanged them all. It was not well done to demand them from Maclaine, but inexcusablie ill done by him to betray them. Here I cannot forget one Donald Campbell, fleshed in blood from his very infancie, who with all imaginable violence insisted that the whole clan Maclaine should be put to the edge of the sword; nor could he be commanded to give up his bloody purpose by the lieutenant-general and two major-generals; and only with some difficulty was he commanded to silence by his chief, the Marquis of Argyll. For my part, I said nothing, for I did not care if he had succeeded in his wishes, the delivery of the Irish had so irritated me against that whole clan and name.

While Leslie was subduing the Hebrides, Middleton pursued Huntly through Glenmoriston, Badenoch, and other places. Huntly was at length captured in Strathdon by Lieutenant-Colonel Menzies in December 1647. Having received intelligence of the location the marquis had retreated to, Menzies had come to Dalnabo with three troops of horse around midnight, and entered the house just as Huntly was going to bed. The marquis was attended by only ten gentlemen and servants as a sort of bodyguard, who despite the great disparity of numbers, made a brave attempt to protect the marquis, during which six of them were killed and the rest mortally wounded, among whom was John Grant, the landlord. On hearing that the marquis had been taken prisoner, all his vassals in the neighbourhood, to the tune of 400–500, with Grant of Carron at their head, flew to arms to rescue him. Lieutenant-Colonel Menzies carried the marquis to the castle of Blairfindie, in Glenlivet, about 4 miles from Dalnabo, where Huntly received a notice from Grant and his party that they had solemnly sworn either to rescue him or die to a man, and they requested him to give them such orders to carry their plan into effect as he might judge proper. But the marquis dissuaded his people from the attempt, and returned the answer that, worn out with grief and fatigue as he was, he could no longer live in hills and dens, and hoped that his enemies would not drive things to the worst; but, if such was the will of heaven, he could not outlive the sad fate he foresaw his royal master was likely to undergo; and be things as they would, he did not doubt that the just providence of God would restore the fortune of the royal family, and his own along with it.

Besides the gentlemen and servants about Huntly's person, there were some Irish who were quartered in the offices about Dalnabo. These were carried prisoners by Menzies to Strathbogie, where Middleton was residing, who ordered them all to be shot. In consequence of an order from the Committee of Estates at Edinburgh, Menzies carried the marquis under a strong horse guard to Leith, where, after being kept two days, he was delivered to the magistrates, and incarcerated in the city jail. The committee had previously debated the question whether the marquis should be immediately executed or reprieved till the meeting of parliament, but although the Argyll faction, notwithstanding the Marquis of Argyll withdrew before the vote was taken, and the committee of the church did everything in their power to procure the immediate execution of the marquis, his life was spared till the meeting of the parliament by a majority of one vote. The Earl of Aboyne and Lord Lewis Gordon had the good fortune to escape to the continent. The first went to France, where he shortly thereafter died; the second took refuge in Holland. A reward of £1,000 sterling had been promised to any person who should apprehend Huntly, which sum was duly paid to Menzies by the Committee of Estates.

There appears to be no doubt that Argyll was highly gratified at the capture of Huntly. It is related by Spalding, that taking advantage of Huntly's situation, Argyll bought up all the comprisings on his lands, and that he caused summon at the market-cross of Aberdeen by sound of trumpet. All of Huntly's wadsetters and creditors were to appear at Edinburgh in the month of March following Huntly's imprisonment, to produce their securities before the lords of session, with certification that if they did not appear, their securities were to be declared null and void. Some of Huntly's creditors sold their claims to Argyll, and having thus bought up all the rights, he could obtain upon Huntly's estate at a small or nominal value, under the pretence that he was acting for the benefit of his nephew Lord Gordon, he granted bonds for the amount, which, according to Spalding, he never paid. In this way Argyll acquired possession of the marquis's estates, which he continued to enjoy for the next twelve years until the restoration of Charles II in 1660.

When the king, who was then a prisoner in Carisbrook Castle, heard of the capture of Huntly, he wrote a letter to the Earl of Lanark in London, urging him to do all in his power in behalf of the marquis. The earl appears, however, to have paid no attention to this letter.

Shortly before the capture of the Marquis of Huntly, John Gordon of Innermarkie, Gordon, younger of Newton-Gordon, and the laird of Harthill, three of his chief friends, had been taken prisoner by Major-General Middleton and sent to Edinburgh, where they were imprisoned. The two latter were condemned to die by the Committee of Estates, and although their friends procured a remission of the sentence from the king, they were both beheaded at the market-cross of Edinburgh.

It was about this time, on or before 1648, that Colonel Hugh Fraser married for a second time, to a Jean Gray by whom he had a daughter, Katherine.

The Duke of Hamilton

While the hopes of the Royalists, both in England and Scotland, seemed to be almost extinguished, a ray of light showed itself on the political horizon, but any expectations were destined to be dashed. The Duke of Hamilton, who had recently formed an association to release the king from captivity, persuaded the parliament, which met in March 1648, to appoint a committee of danger, and to agree to a levy of 40,000 men. The bulk of the English population, with the exception of the army, had grown dissatisfied with the state of matters and their eyes now turned towards Scotland – news of the Scots' levy giving them hope that they would be able, with the aid of the Scots auxiliaries, to throw off the military yoke and restore the king on conditions favourable to liberty. But Hamilton, thwarted by Argyll and his party, could not take advantage of the favourable disposition of the English people, and instead of raising 40,000 men, he found that, after over three months' labour, he could at the most only bring 15,000 men into the field, and that was only after s everal insurrections in England in favour of the king had been suppressed.

It was Hamilton's misfortune that he had neither the capacity to imagine nor the resolution to execute bold and decisive measures equal to the emergency of the times. Like the king, he tried to act the part of the cunning politician, but was wholly unfit for the role. Had he been able to separate Leslie and his nephew from the party of Argyll, by placing the planning of military action in their hands, he may have succeeded in raising a force able to cope with the parliamentary army of England; but he succumbed, after both these generals had joined the Kirk in its remonstrance to the parliament that nothing should be done without the consent of the committee of the general assembly, to having himself appointed commander-in-chief of the army, a step which disgusted these hardy veterans.

He failed in an attempt to reconcile the Marquis of Argyll, who did everything to foil Hamilton's designs. Argyll went to Fife and induced the gentry there not only to oppose the levies, but to make ready to rise on the other side when called upon. He was less successful in Stirlingshire – very few of the gentlemen of that county agreeing with his views – but in Dumbartonshire he met with complete success. After attending a meeting with Lord Chancellor Loudon, the Earls of Cassilis and Eglinton, and David Dick and other ministers, at Eglinton's house on 29 May, Argyll went home to raise his own people.

The only noteworthy instance of opposition to the levy took place in Ayrshire, where a body of armed insurgents, numbering 800 horse and 1,200 foot according to one writer, or 500 horse and 2,000 foot according to another, headed by several ministers, assembled at Mauchline. They were defeated and dispersed on 10 June by Middleton, who had been appointed lieutenant-general of horse, with the loss of eighty men.

It is likely only a few men were raised in the highlands for Hamilton's army while, understandably, not a single man was raised in Argyleshire and scarcely any in the adjoining part of Inverness-shire where Argyll's influence extended. The Earl of Sutherland, who had been appointed a colonel of foot in his own division, declined the office, and Lord Reay was so disgusted with 'Duke Hamilton's failure' that he took ship at Thurso to Norway, where he was appointed Governor of Bergen, and received the colonelcy of a regiment from the King of Denmark, whom he had formerly served. The only person who could have aided the royal cause in the north was the Marquis of Huntly, but Hamilton, who could have easily obtained an order from the parliament for his freedom from prison, allowed him to remain there, contenting himself with obtaining a warrant for changing the marquis's place of incarceration from the jail to Edinburgh Castle.

Due to his many difficulties in collecting troops and equipment for his army, the duke could not begin his march until 8 July, when he set out towards the borders. His force – about 10,000 foot and 4,000 horse – was composed of raw, undisciplined levies, and he had not one field-piece. He entered England by the western border, where he was met by Sir Marmaduke Langdale with 4,000 cavaliers, all devoted to the king. At this time Lambert, the parliamentary general, had invested Carlisle, and Hamilton was persuaded by the English Royalists to march upon Carlisle and force Lambert to raise the siege. That general, who had orders from Cromwell not to engage the Scots till he could join him, accordingly withdrew, and Carlisle was delivered up next day to Hamilton by the English Royalists, who also put him in possession of Berwick.

This mismanaged and unfortunate expedition ended a month later when Sir Marmaduke Langdale was defeated by Cromwell at Preston on 17 August, and on entering the town after the defeat, was mortified to find that his Scots Allies had abandoned it. Langdale, having now no alternative but flight, disbanded his infantry, and along with his cavalry and Hamilton, who had remained in the town, swam across the Ribble.

The Scots Army retired overnight towards Wigan, where it was joined by the duke next morning, but so weakened as to be quite unable to resist the victorious troops of Cromwell, who pressed hard upon them. The foot, under Baillie, continued to retreat during the day, but were overtaken at Warrington and surrendered. About 3,000 capitulated. More than 6,000 had already been captured by the country people, and the few who could escape joined Munro and returned to Scotland. The prisoners were sold as slaves, and sent to the plantations.

The duke, abandoning Baillie, carried off the whole cavalry; but he had not gone far when his rear was attacked by the parliamentary army. Middleton made a gallant defence, and was taken prisoner; but the duke escaped, and fled to Uttoxeter, followed by his horse, where he surrendered to General Lambert, who sent him prisoner to Windsor. The Earl of Callander, having made his escape, went to Holland, disgusted at the duke's conduct.

As soon as the news of the defeat reached Scotland, the western Covenanters began to stir, and a party of them, under Robert Montgomery, son of the Earl of Eglinton, attacked a troop of Lanark's horse quartered in Ayrshire, killed some and routed the rest. The Committee of Estates, concerned that a spirit of insurrection would speedily spread, immediately ordered out all fensible men in the kingdom to put down the rising in the west. A difference of opinion arose, however, in the choice of a commander – The Earl of Lanark and the Earl Marischal were proposed by their respective friends. Lanark's chief opponent was the Earl of Roxburgh, who, (says Wishart), 'in a grave and modest speech, earnestly entreated him, for the sake of their dear sovereign and their distressed country, not to insist in demanding that dignity, which was extremely unseasonable and ill-judged at that time'. Roxburgh's plea had no effect on Lanark, who, on a vote being taken, had a majority, and was apparently so anxious to obtain the command that he actually voted for himself. He even had the imprudence to announce that he would not allow any other person to command in his brother's absence. This rash behaviour so incensed Roxburgh and his friends, who justly feared the ruin of the king's affairs, that they immediately withdrew altogether from public affairs.

As soon as Lanark had been appointed, he set about raising the new levy with great energy, sending circulars to every part of Scotland, calling on all classes to join him. These had the desired effect. The people beyond the Forth, and even the men of Fife, obeyed the call. The Earl of Seaforth raised 4,000 men in the Western Islands and Ross-shire, and the Earl of Morton brought 1,200 men from the Orkneys. With the exception of Argyll, there were few places in Scotland from which considerable bodies of men might not have been expected.

Before the defeat of Hamilton's army, Lanark had raised three regiments of horse, which, with the re-enforcements arriving daily from different parts of the kingdom, were enough to have put down the insurrection in the west; but instead of marching west, Lanark, to the surprise of everyone, marched towards the eastern borders to meet Sir George Munro, who was retreating towards Berwick before Cromwell's army. The people of the west, relieved from the prospect of a visit, assembled in great numbers, and taking advantage of Lanark's absence, a body of 6,000 men, headed by the chancellor, the Earl of Eglinton, and some ministers, advanced on the capital, which they entered without opposition, the magistrates and ministers of the city welcoming their approach by going out to meet them. Bishop Wishart described this body as 'a confused rabble, composed of farmers, cow herds, shepherds, cobblers, and such like mob, without arms, and without courage,' and says that when they arrived in Edinburgh, 'they were provided with arms, which, as they were unaccustomed to, were rather a burden and encumbrance than of any use,' that 'they were mounted on horses, or jades rather, which had been long used to the drudgery of labour, equipped with pack saddles and halters, in place of saddles and bridles.' This body was however soon put into proper order by the Earl of Leven, who was invested with the chief command, and by David Leslie, as his lieutenant-general, and presented a rather redoubtable appearance, as on Lanark's return from the south, he did not undertake to engage it, though his force was some 4,000 or 5,000 horse and as many foot, many of whom were veterans who had served in Ireland under Munro.

In declining to attack Leslie, Lanark acted against the advice of Munro and his other officers. According to Wishart, Lanark's advanced guard, arriving at Musselburgh, encountered some of Leslie's outposts defending the bridge over the Esk, and Lanark's troops, though inferior in number, immediately put them in great disorder and killed some of them without sustaining any loss. This success was reported to Lanark, and it was put to him that by following up immediately, while the enemy remained in the state of alarm which the outpost skirmish had thrown them into, he might obtain a bloodless victory and take possession of Edinburgh and Leith before sunset.

Instead, leading his army along the base of the Pentland hills, Lanark proceeded to Linlithgow, which he entered on the evening of 11 September, where he almost surprised the Earl of Cassillis, who, at the head of 800 horse from Carrick and Galloway, had taken up his quarters there for the night; but a notice having been sent to him of the Earl of Lanark's approach by some friend, he fled precipitately to Queensferry, leaving the supper which was cooking for him and his men on the fire, which meal was greedily devoured by Lanark's troops.

Ever since Lanark's march to the borders to meet Munro, Argyll had been busily employed raising men in his own territory to assist the insurgents, but it had been so depopulated by the ravages of Montrose and Macdonald that he could scarcely raise 300 men. With these and 400 more, which he had collected in the Lennox and west Stirlingshire, he advanced to Stirling, entering it on 12

September at 11.00 a.m. After assigning the troops their different posts in the town and making arrangements with the magistrates for their support, Argyll went to dine with the Earl of Mar at his residence in the town, but while the dinner was serving up, Argyll, to his horror, heard that a party of Lanark's forces had entered Stirling. This was the advanced guard, commanded by Sir George Munro, who, hearing that Argyll occupied the town when only 2 miles from it, had, without the knowledge of Lanark, who was behind with the main body of the army, pushed forward and entered the town before Argyll's men were aware of his approach. Argyll, as formerly, having a great regard for his personal safety, immediately mounted his horse, galloped across Stirling Bridge, and never looked back until he reached north Queensferry, where he immediately crossed the Firth in a small boat and proceeded to Edinburgh. Nearly 200 of Argyll's men were either killed or drowned, and the remainder were taken prisoner.

A negotiation for peace ensued between the two parties, and on 15 September a treaty entered into by which the Hamilton party agreed to refer all civil matters in dispute to a parliament to be held before 10 January, and all ecclesiastical affairs to an assembly of the Kirk. It was also stipulated that both armies should be disbanded before 29 September, or at the latest 5 October, in order that the adherents of the king should not be disturbed; and that all prisoners taken in Scotland should be released. Munro, believing that the king's affairs would be irretrievably ruined by this compromise, objected to the treaty, and would have stood out had he been backed by the other officers; but very few supported his views. He therefore addressed the troops who had accompanied him from Ireland in St Ninian's Church, and offered to lead back to Ireland those that were inclined to serve under their old commander, Major-General Robert Munro. Later, having received intelligence at Glasgow that the general had been taken prisoner and sent to London, he disbanded the troops who had followed him, and retired to Holland.

According to the treaty the two armies were disbanded on the appointed day, and the 'Whigamores,' as the insurgents from the west were called, immediately returned home to cut down their corn, which was ready for the sickle. Argyll's men, who had been taken prisoners at Stirling, were freed and conducted home to their own country by one of Argyll's officers.

The Marquis of Argyll, Loudon the chancellor, the Earls of Cassilis and Eglinton, and others now met at Edinburgh, and formed a body under the title of the Committee of Estates. Having arranged matters in such a way as to secure their own influence, they summoned a parliament to meet on 4 January. Meanwhile, Oliver Cromwell, who, after the pursuit of Munro, had laid siege to Berwick, was waited upon by Argyll, Lord Elcho, and Sir Charles Erskine, to compliment him upon his success at Preston. After making Ludovick Leslie deliver up Berwick to him, they invited him and Lambert to Edinburgh. Cromwell took up his residence in the House of Lady Home in the Canongate, where he received frequent visits from Argyll, Loudon, the Earl of Lothian, Lords Arbuthnot, Elcho, and Burleigh, and the most noted of the ministers. It is said that during these conferences, Cromwell communicated to his visitors his intentions with respect to the king, and obtained their consent.

In the meantime the Independents were doing their best to persuade the English parliament to try the king for high treason. Having been defeated in this by the Presbyterians, they convinced Fairfax to order Hammond, Governor of the Isle of Wight, to attend him at Windsor, and to send Colonel Euro with orders to seize the king at Newport, where he was conferring with the commissioners, and imprison him again in Carisbrook Castle; but Hammond refused to allow Euro to interfere without an order from the parliament, Euro leaving the island without having attempted to fulfil his instructions. Hammond then left the island with the commissioners, and handed Charles into the custody of a Major Rowe (who had only six months before been charged with a plot on the king's life, and who had escaped trial because only one witness had attested the fact before the grand jury).

It appears that the king was aware of the danger of his situation, and on the morning of 28 November, when the commissioners left the island, he gave vent to his feelings in a strain of the most pathetic emotions, which drew tears from his attendants. He addressed the commissioners; 'My lords, I believe we shall scarce ever see each other again, but God's will be done! I have made my peace with him, and shall undergo without fear whatever he may suffer men to do to me. My lords, you cannot but know, that in my fall and ruin you see your own, and that also [of those] near you. I pray God send you better friends than I have found. I am fully informed of the carriage of those who plot against me and mine; but nothing affects me so much as the feeling I have of the sufferings of my subjects, and the mischief that hangs over my three kingdoms, drawn upon them by those who, upon pretences of good, violently pursue their own interests and ends'. As soon as the commissioners and Hammond had left the island, Fairfax sent a troop of horse and a company of foot under the command of Lieutenant-Colonel Cobbett to seize the king, who was told of the approach of this body and of its purpose next morning by a person in disguise; but although urged by the Duke of Richmond, the Earl of Lindsay, and Colonel Coke to make his escape, which he could easily have done, he did not, considering himself bound in honour to remain. Consequently Charles was taken prisoner by Cobbett, and transported to Hurst Castle.

The rest of this tragedy is well known. After the (purified) House of Commons had passed a vote declaring that it was high treason for the king to levy war against the parliament and kingdom of England, his majesty was brought to trial before a tribunal erected *pro re nata* by the house, called 'the high court of justice', which judged him 'a tyrant, traitor, murderer, and public and implacable enemy to the Commonwealth of England … to be put to death by the severing of his head from his body,' sentence to be carried out in front of Whitehall on 30 January 1649.

On the day of his execution, he dressed with special care, telling his servant, combing his hair: 'Prithee, though it be not too long upon my shoulders, take the same pains with it as you were wont to do: I am to be a bridegroom today and must be trimmed.' He added: 'Let me have a shirt on more than ordinary [thickness], by reason the season is so sharp as probably may make me shake, which some observers may imagine proceeds from fear. I fear not death. It is not terrible to me. I bless my God I am prepared.' He was kept waiting four hours, between ten and two, before being taken to the scaffold. There, he 'looked very earnestly upon the block and asked if it could be no higher'; but this was refused. After his last speech and his profession of faith, he handed his 'George' [garter] to Bishop Juxon to give to the Prince of Wales, with the word 'Remember'. To Colonel Hacker, in charge of the guard, he said 'Take care that they do not put me in pain'. Then, to Juxon: 'I go from a corruptible to an incorruptible crown, where no disturbance can be, no disturbance at all.' Then, looking again at the block: 'Is it fast?' 'It is fast, sir.' To the headsman, Gregory Brandon: 'Strike when I put my arms out this way' (stretching them). Then 'immediately stooping down, he laid his head on the block'. But his hair came loose, and Brandon put it back again; the king, thinking he was going to strike, said 'Stay for the sign.' Brandon: 'Yes I will, as it please Your Majesty.' Then the king gave the sign. Philip Henry, a student, testified: 'At the instant when the blow was given there was such a dismal groan among the thousands of people that were in sight of it (as it were with **ONE CONSENT**) as he had never heard before; and desired he might never hear the like again, nor see such a cause of it.' Then, 'immediately after the stroke was struck … according to order, one troop [began] marching from Charing Cross towards King Street, purposely to disperse and scatter the people'. Nevertheless, many crowded round the scaffold to 'dip their handkerchiefs' in the king's blood and were 'admitted for moneys'. The soldiers sold pieces of the blood-stained scaffold boarding, from a shilling to half a crown each, 'according to the quality of the persons that sought them'. Payment was also charged to see Charles in his coffin at St James's Palace, 'by which means the soldiers got store of moneys, insomuch as one was heard to say, 'I would we could have two or three such majesties to behead, if we could but make such use of them''.[127]

The Duke of Hamilton, who by his incapacity had ruined the king's affairs when on the point of being retrieved, was not destined to survive his royal master by very long. In violation of the articles of his capitulation, he was brought to trial, and although he pleaded that he acted under the orders of the Scottish parliament and was not amenable to an English tribunal, he was, under the pretence that he was Earl of Cambridge in England, sentenced to be beheaded, which fate he suffered on 9 March.

The Marquis of Huntly had languished in prison since December 1647, and during the life of the king the Scottish parliament had not ventured to put him to the block; but now that both the king and Hamilton were out of the way, they felt no such restraint, and accordingly, on 16 March the parliament ordained the marquis to be beheaded at the market-cross of Edinburgh, on the 22nd of that month. As he lay under sentence of ecclesiastical excommunication, one of the 'bloody ministers,' says the author of the history of the family of Gordon, 'asked him, when brought up to the scaffold, if he desired to be absolved from the sentence'; to which the marquis replied, 'that as he was not accustomed to give ear to false prophets, he did not wish to be troubled by him.' And thereupon turning 'towards the people, he told them that he was going to die for having employed some years of his life in the service of the king his master; that he was sorry he was not the first of his majesty's subjects who had suffered for his cause, so glorious in itself that it sweetened to him all the bitterness of death.' He then declared that he had charity to forgive those who had voted for his death, although he could not admit that he had done anything contrary to the laws. After throwing off his doublet, he offered up a prayer, and then embracing some friends around him, he submitted his neck, without any symptoms of emotion, to the fatal instrument.

10. Charles II

BY 1649 MATTERS HAD assumed a different complexion. The issue of conflict between Charles I and parliament, and Charles' subsequent beheading, created a revulsion of feeling among many who had up until then vigorously opposed the policy of the Crown in Scottish ecclesiastical matters.

In Edinburgh, on 5 February 1649, Charles II was proclaimed King of Great Britain, France and Ireland. It was decided by him and his friends, all still in exile, that Montrose should make a second attempt to recover the kingdom. Charles had declined the humiliating terms offered to him by the states, and it was in conjunction with the plans of Montrose, that a rising took place in the north under Thomas Mackenzie of Pluscardine – brother to the Earl of Seaforth, then in exile with the king.

On Sunday 22 February, Pluscardine, Sir Thomas Urquhart of Cromarty, and Colonel John Munro of Lemlair, with some Mackenzies, Mackays and others got to a head, having mustered 700 horse and foot for this service, and as one body crossed over the Ferry Kessock and rendezvoused at Markinsch in full view of Inverness. At about nine in the morning Colonel Hugh Fraser, who had until then been living in his home at Kinmylies, joined them with his retinue, and so they marched forward towards Kill Baine, and crossed the ford above the Isle of Inverness. The water level of the river was very low, which they took to be a good omen in support of their cause. They drew up in a battalion above the town at Aldniskiach, from where they directed a trumpet and two single horsemen very martially with a message to the garrison to surrender. Major Murray, the depute governor under Colonel Sir James Fraser of Brea, who was himself away in southern parts, had been hurrying about to secure the ports and put the fort in a fensible posture. The whole town was in confusion, not knowing whose side to declare themselves for.

First, the major had set about the business of making secure the Castle Street gate to the south, where the besiegers lay, and, while busy ordering the construction of palisades, a timber beam fell and struck him on his brow, sorely wounding him, and raising his passion and temper; a bad start to his preparations. Next, his soldiers started to mutiny in the streets, just as he was returning from the port. A Sergeant John McKenzie, a pretty man, having a sword in his hand, obviated[128] the major, who, drawing his pistol, shot him dead through the heart, and the sergeant fell instantly back onto a dunghill midden and expired gasping. The major cried out, 'Take thow that for heading a mutiny'. One Lieutenant Eneas M'Kdonell was another of the mutineers who narrowly escaped the major's fingers, having got someone to apologise for him, being the colonel's foster brother, and bearing his livery. The major, stepping down the street, then met Lieutenant William Forbes, who told him that the magistrates had decided amongst themselves to dispose of him, and were not to be trusted, and therefore he should look to himself and escape. On the east side of the Court of Guard stood a Captain Cransdown on horseback, with his troop drawn up in the street, who called out to him in a loud voice; 'Major Murray, instantly horse and begone, else yow are betrayed.' Instantly the troop all rode away in haste out of the east street, leaving the town a prey to the invaders. The magistrates had the Castle Port opened, making it patent to those outside that they were welcome as loyal persons. The magistrates having declared themselves for the Royalist cause, the garrison was allowed to depart, and may have taken refuge in the stronghold of Lovat.

West of Bunchrive, two ministers encountered a lieutenant out of the Inverness garrison with 100 men out on a party for deficiency in Urquhart, who immediately upon receiving the report of the taking of Inverness, returned to Lovat and stayed in that garrison until his master the colonel returned.

Another lieutenant with a further 100 men had been quartering in Strathspey – their absence from the town having further weakened the garrison. So the disloyal walls and fortifications, fort and ramparts of Inverness were demolished and levelled to the ground. 'I doubt not but your honour has heard of the in taking of Inverness by the Lairds of Cromarty, Pluscardine, Lemlair, Colonel Fraser, and their adherents, and the flocking of men of all sorts to them.'[129] On the 26th a council of war was held in Inverness, where the Royalists framed certain enactments in terms of which they took the customs and excise of the six northern counties into their own hands. However, on hearing that General Leslie had been sent against them, they retired to the mountains of Ross-shire. Leslie made terms of surrender with all the leaders except Pluscardine, who would not listen to any accommodation and who, on Leslie's return south, immediately descended from his mountain fastness and re-took the castle of Chanonry.

There was another insurrection in the north of Scotland on 3 May, Cross Day. Lieutenant-General Middleton having escaped from Berwick into these parts, the Lord Reay and the Mackenzies mustered 1,500 men and coming over via Kessock and Beauly, crossed the bridge of Ness on the Lord's Day at the time of Divine Service, and caused great alarm to the people of Inverness, disrupting God's worship in the town as, instead of bells to ring people in to service, all that was heard was the noise of pipes, drums, pots, pans, kettles, and spits in the streets, to provide this force with victuals in every house and in their quarters. This rude rascality would eat no meat at their tables until the landlord laid down a shilling Scots upon his trencher that sat, terming this ARGID CAGGING (chewing money), which every soldier got; so insolent they were. And here they failed in their conduct by a rupture among themselves. Some were for giving the ordering of the battalions to Colonel Hugh Fraser, and the whole command to him as an expert soldier; others gave it to the Lord Reay and Captain Thomas McKenzie of Pluscardine, and this latter was carried by the majority vote. On Monday, at about ten o'clock, they marched from Inverness, well appointed and furnished with ammunition, money, all manner of arms, provision in abundance, nothing wanting that might encourage men in a good cause. Forward the army went, and advanced through Murray, crossed the River Spey, and encamped at Balvany Castle, where Donald Lord Reay had the ordering of the camp. After a consultation, Captain Thomas McKenzie and other officers, with a party of their men, were sent off southwards to meet Middleton, and the Gordon joined with them. In the meantime, 'these green heads, inexpert, shaking off all care and fear, lay at their leisure eating and drinking, and rose up to play; like laish, a people that were at quiet and secure, ready to be smote with the edge of the Sword.' Unnoticed, at about dawn, Colonel Kerr and Lieutenant-Colonel Strachan,[5] with only two troops of horse, surprised this great number, attacked them in their camp and trod them underfoot, without meeting any manly resistance. Four hundred were reportedly killed on the spot, 1,000 made captives, and all disgraced to a man. The Lord Reay and twenty of his officers made no attempt either to resist or to escape; they were taken prisoner and sent to the castle of the Bogg. This crowd of captives, like cows in a fold, were kept in a little bottom with a guard about them. This may be called hard fate and misluck, but was a disastrous defeat, the ground having been so advantageous to them, with hedges and ditches that 100 men could have defied 500, yet in a trice, they were all basely baffled and taken almost sleeping. As soon as could be arranged, a party of twenty horse and three companies of foot were ordered to convey this captive army back over the Spey and through Murray to Inverness, where these same men who in their former march would hardly eat their meat without money now had to beg and, like dogs, lap the water which was brought them in tubs and other vessels in the open street. From there, they were conducted over the bridge of Ness and every man dismissed armless and harmless to his own home.

This defeat in the north dispirited all others in the south and west who supported the king's cause. All but Pluscardine submitted to the authority of David Leslie and retired to their homes. Pluscardine, meanwhile, took to the hills but was to be hunted down, captured and imprisoned.

Sir James Fraser of Brea, brother of Lovat, Tutor of Lovat and Governor of Inverness (born 1610), died at Lovat a month later on 12 June 1649.[130] His body was conveyed from there to Kirkhill 'in great state and magnificence, no less than thirteen trumpets sounding at his funeral,' all the forces having joined to bury him with military honours.

***

Our history is on the verge of drawing to a close. Several of the main characters have shuffled off their mortal coils. Before another passing, perhaps some clarification is required as to the medical beliefs of the time, which were somewhat different from those of today:

> If you would get rid of the ague,[132] go by night alone to a crossroads, and just as the clock is striking midnight turn round three times and drive a large nail into the ground up to the head. Walk backwards from the nail before the clock has finished the twelfth stroke. The ague will leave you, but will go to the person next to step on the nail.[133]

People faced epidemic diseases, such as the plague, which struck quickly and unexpectedly, often dramatically reducing town and village populations; and endemic diseases, such as common colds and measles.

The Chinese had been using plants for medicinal purposes for 4,500 years and some of these had been brought to Europe. Many domestic plants, such as foxglove and marshmallow, were also used to cure illnesses, as were rock salt, violet, beet root, camomile flowers, fennel seed, linseed, cinnamon, cardamom seed, saffron, cochineal, cowslip flowers, liquorice, sweet almonds, absinthe, extracts of thistles, rue, mint and angelica, melon seeds, manna, slippery elm, black cherry water, extracts of flower of lime, lily of the valley, gentian root, nutmeg, and cloves.

It was understood and universally adopted by physicians that there were four bodily fluids or 'humours', with the following characteristics and qualities:

HUMOUR	QUALITIES	ELEMENT	CHARACTERISTIC
Black bile	Cold & dry	Earth	Melancholy
Blood	Hot & moist	Air	Sanguine
Yellow bile	Hot & dry	Fire	Choleric
Phlegm	Cold & moist	Water	Phlegmatic

The belief was that diseases were caused by an excess of a particular humour and were treated with remedies that displayed opposing qualities to reduce this excess. Therefore bloodletting and purging were popular, as they would remove excess amounts of the offending humours. Any analysis was further complicated by the association of the humours with the seasons, and with the effects of astrology – another important factor to be considered when treating illness. All living things were considered linked to the whole of the natural world, including the planets and stars visible in the night sky. Each part of the human body was ruled by, and shared, characteristics of the planets and stars. Plant ingredients for recipes were often picked at certain times of the year, or at a specific time of day or night, to preserve the potency of the characteristic they displayed.

Many metals, gems, or precious stones were considered valid ingredients of recipes. Some were used because they were associated with an astrological sign and believed to possess a similar characteristic or quality.

Doctors also believed in the power of powders made from strange ingredients such as horn from the unicorn or rhinoceros, and bezoar[134] stone, (claimed to be the tears of a stag, turned to stone). Live worms, fox lungs, spiders' webs, and the skulls of executed criminals were also highly sought after ingredients. The *Pharmacopoeia*[135] contained such ingredients, most quite inert, including the bone from the heart of a stag, elephant tusk, mummy taken from the tomb, frog spawn, crayfish eyes, penis of a bull, flesh of vipers, nest of swallows, oil of foxes, powdered elephant tooth, fat of a marine horse – the hippopotamus – and dried hippo testicles; all very reminiscent of the witch's brew.

Remedies included boys' urine dropped into the ears or, mixed with rosewater, dropped into the eyes or in a gargle. Adult urine for gout, wild boar urine in honey or mulled vinegar helped epilepsy, or dropped into the ears helped pain and deafness. There were many more repulsive things, mostly only used for plasters, ointments and oils.

Human skull preferably from a person who had suffered a violent death, when powdered, was a cure for epilepsy. Moss from a human skull applied outwardly cleansed wounds and cured gangrene and the itch; and in a clyster (an enema administered using a syringe with a rectal nozzle and plunger, generally administered by apothecaries or servants) loosened the belly.

Health care was provided by physicians, surgeon-barbers, druggists, midwives, clergy, ladies of manor houses, or by peddlers selling their wares.

Countless household and medical recipe books existed with ladies up and down the country keeping prescription books, usually mixed with cooking recipes.[135] Women's' knowledge of therapeutics was, however, not altogether approved of. Thomas Sydenham complained that, 'Nowadays every house has its old woman practiced in an art that she never learned to the killing of mankind'. His advice was that patients abstain from animal food and fermented liquors; keep indoors, but not to keep always in bed. 'When the symptoms are departing, purge the patient with some mild laxative, accommodated to his age and strength. By treatment thus simple and natural, this ailment is dispelled without either trouble or danger. Otherwise, we over treat the patient and the sick man dies of his doctor.'[136] Physicians, writing the same prescription on different occasions, were known to produce medicine varying in scent, taste, colour, strength etc. according to the quality of ingredients, or how cleanly or accurately it was made, while apothecaries altered prescriptions, omitting items, and censured the practice of physicians who kept their prescriptions short.

William Vaughan in his writings[137] argued that 'they who observe a good diet do not need artificial physic.'[138] He warned that all purgations have poisonous effects, and their frequent use is dangerous and aging. He gave recipes for purgatives for phlegm, choler and melancholy, and a list of things to take into account in purgations – its quality, time of year, climate, age of the patient, his habits, the disease, the strength of the sick person, and the position of the moon. He gave recipes for glisters [suppositories], e.g. honey, wheat meal, fresh butter – 'make your glister into a long form, dip it in oil, and use it' – and he included the smoking of tobacco, used then for medicinal purposes as a purgative, but warned of the dangers if its use for this purpose and detailed the effects of the 'abuse' of tobacco. He recommended: 'Cane tobacco well dried, and taken in a clean pipe fasting, in a moist morning, during the spring and autumn, cures megrim [migraine?], toothache,' etc.

He believed that 'a vomit is the expulsion of bad humours (contained in the stomach) upwards. It is accounted the most wholesome kind of Physic: for that which a purgation leaves behind, a vomit roots out.' He provided recipes for emetics, suggesting that, if they fail to work in an hour, 'stick your left middle finger in your mouth'.

Clearly a strong emphasis was placed on purges of various sorts and strengths. These included: hyssop, called the 'holy herb' because of its cleansing properties, used as a cleansing agent causing bowel movements. There were two types of cathartic herbs. Laxative cathartics (the milder form); and purgative cathartics (the stronger). Hyssop was a purgative cathartic herb, which cleared the colon of intestinal mucus and could be used to alleviate gas.

Antimony, a metal that caused vomiting, sweating, and purging of the bowels.

Antidotus Magna Matthioli adversus Venena et Pestem, containing more than 130 ingredients including Theriaca and Mithridates each of which were blunderbuss prescriptions in their own right.

Pilulae ex duobus colocynth, a drastic purgative made up of oil of cloves and syrup of purging thorn and condemned thus: 'Surely the College know not what they do, else they would never invent such pills as this.' 'In truth tis pity. But they should have the just reward and be forced to take it themselves: they [the purgatives] being not only too strong but also of a base gnawing nature.' It was known as de Laune's pill and was administered to Charles II.

The last listed was scammony. Culpeper described it: 'it is a desperate purge, hurtful to the body by reason of its heat, windiness, corroding or gnawing and violence of working. I would advise my countrymen to let it alone. It will gnaw their bodies as fast as doctors gnaw their purses.'

With this fresh insight into the practices of healthcare of the period, our history can continue.

The Mystery of Fraser's End

Colonel Hugh Fraser, living in pretty grandeur at Kinmylies, in what was formerly one of Lord Lovat's houses, but now his own heritage, found himself indisposed, and, being now in the autumn and fall of the leaf, a proper time for phisick, he resolved and set himself for it to take his purge, and with good government, but with what medicine or drug it was, what dose or weight, whence he had it or by whose direction we shall never know; but within less than an hour after the taking of it, he fell in a high distemper and rage, could hardly suffer any near him, no, not his beloved spouse, raved in a high degree, all he spoke was high Dutch[139] or Slavonick, knew few or none. The ministers of Inverness, Mr John Annand and Mr William Fraser coming to see him and to pray over him, he had little sense to consider what was said; he was found somewhat composed at singing of psalms, six or eight men about him, holding him fast by arms and feet, yet could hardly fix him or keep him in bed or chair: he slept none, was drunk much, and impatient after it. It was terrible and astonishing to behold so dismal a sight, and his sad, disconsolate family: nothing heard or seen but dejected faces, mourning eyes, weeping lamentation and woe. The third day he calmed a little. He was heard to say to William Wardlaw, 'stay by me, and pray to God for me.' That night (30 September) about one o'clock in the morning, he expired, without having the opportunity of seeing Charles II return to Scotland as would happen that summer coming. Hugh was interred in the Lord Lovat's aisle at Kirkhill on 6 October 1649. All the forces of horse and foot stationed at Inverness, accompanied by all the numerous neighbourhood and relations, made him a parade from his house at Kinmylies to Lord Lovat's chapel at Kirkhill, where he was buried with military honours – a splendid, solemn funeral, with very noble conduct.

The 1650s

The following March, James Graham, Marquis of Montrose reached Orkney with a force of 1,200 continental mercenaries, where he was to be joined by Lord Eythin[140] with an additional force. In early April of that year, Major-General John Urry travelled from Orkney to Caithness, to be quickly followed by Montrose, before moving further south to Carbisdale. On 16 April General Leslie was ordered north with an army to oppose Montrose, Strachan was sent north to take command of troops already there and at Inverness he mustered five troops of horse and advanced to Ross. On the 25th Leslie's army rendezvoused at Brechin and, after a council of war, a final advance was made, resulting in the Battle of Carbisdale in which one Covenanter was reportedly drowned while some 400–500 Royalists were killed [including] 200 drowned, and 450 captured. The news of this blow to their cause had other Royalist sympathisers flee Caithness back to Orkney and from there to the continent, while the less fortunate James Graham, Marquis of Montrose, soldier, poet and one of the most romantic figures in British history, was left wandering in the hills with a hue and cry out against him. So hungry that he was reduced to eating his gloves, he finally took refuge at Ardvreck Castle, home of Neil MacLeod of Assynt, but, tempted by the substantial reward to be earned for him, Macleod surrendered Montrose to the authorities. Macleod got his money but at the cost of his name, rank in Scottish nostrils ever since.

Montrose's captors moved him south by Inverness and Dundee, preceded by a herald who proclaimed, 'here comes James Graham, a traitor to his country'. Mounted on a carthorse, he reached Edinburgh on a cold Saturday afternoon in May, in the presence of a huge crowd. At the Water gate he was met by the hangman, transferred to the hangman's cart and tied to the seat, to be taken through the streets to the Tollbooth prison. Argyll was watching from a house on the route and the two men's eyes are said to have met for a moment as the cart trundled by. Far from stoning and reviling the prisoner, as had been hoped, the watching crowds were silent, and observers sensed an air of reluctant admiration and sympathy. The cart reached the Tollbooth prison about seven o'clock in the evening. Montrose spent the Sunday in his cell, pestered by Presbyterian ministers, who renewed their assault on Monday, when he was taken to the parliament to hear the death sentence.

On Tuesday morning Montrose rose for the last time on earth and made himself ready. Carefully combing out his long hair, he was reproached by one of the Puritan divines for paying so much attention to his appearance at such a time. 'My head is still my own,' Montrose replied. 'Tonight, when it will be yours, treat it as you please'. At two in the afternoon he was taken on foot along the High Street to the Mercat Cross, where a gallows 30ft high had been erected on a platform. The condemned man was dressed in his finest scarlet and lace, with white gloves, silk stockings, ribboned shoes and his hat in his hand. He was 37 years old and, according to one observer, he looked more like a bridegroom than a criminal. Another saw in him a gallantry that 'braced the crowd'. He was not allowed to address the spectators, for fear of what he might say. He gave the hangman some money, his arms were pinioned behind him and he climbed the ladder. His last words were reported as 'God have mercy on this afflicted land!' Tears were running down the hangman's face as he pushed him off.

The body was left hanging for three hours and was then cut down and dismembered for the limbs to be sent for public display in Stirling, Aberdeen, Perth and Glasgow. The head was cut off and fixed on a spike on the Tollbooth, where it would remain rotting for eleven years, when Argyll's head would take its place. The rest of the carcass was buried in a box on the Burgh-Moor, from where it would be rescued after the restoration of Charles II and given honourable interment in the High Kirk of St Giles.[141]

Regardless of the discouraging start at Carbisdale, Charles II landed at Garmouth on 24 June 1650, in response to which there was a general rising of loyalists north and south, amongst whom a Captain Alexander Fraser, the young Lovat's uncle, came north with a lieutenant-colonel's commission to raise the Frasers in the interests of the king. The place of rendezvous was at Tomnahurich, near Inverness, where this Colonel Fraser mustered 800 of his clan in full armour, their other officers being – Hugh Fraser of Struy, Major; Thomas Fraser of Beaufort, the late lord's brother, first Captain; Hugh Fraser of Foyers, second Captain; Alexander Fraser of Phoineas, third Captain; William Fraser, Reelick's brother, and Alexander Fraser, younger of Clunavachy, Captain-Lieutenants; Andrew Fraser of Leys, Ensign; and Alexander Fraser, a son of Phopachy, Quarter-Master.

Late the following month, Leslie with 15,000 foot and horse was behind the Leith-Edinburgh Castle line, Berwick and East Lothian completely stripped of food and fodder. On the 29th, Charles was received into the Scots Army. After a little over a month of manouvring and minor skirmishes, and Cromwell having retreated from his previously held positions to Dunbar, Leslie descended Doon Hill on 2 September in preparation for doing battle the following day. He was taken completely by surprise by Cromwell launching his English forces in an all-out attack on the unprepared Scots at 4.00 a.m. on the 3rd, Leslie losing some 4,000 dead and as many as 10,000 captured, only 4,000, mainly horse, escaping to Edinburgh.

The Scottish forces in disarray, new levies were sought with which to raise a further army, but English advances were relentless. While Cromwell had, on occasion, to fall back, he occupied Glasgow in October, and while some Covenanters deserted to the Royalists after the treaty of Strathbogie on 4 November, many more Royalists submitted, disbanded or went over to Cromwell.

1650 rolled into 1651, and Charles was crowned at Scone. Cromwell's campaign in Scotland continued, despite Cromwell himself having to retire to Edinburgh due to an illness, from February to June; at the end of which month, the Scots Army was encamped at Torwood. Of the clan Fraser troops raised in the north, a Lieutenant Donald Fraser and a Lieutenant Schivez, who were trained soldiers under Colonel Fraser in Ireland, were appointed to exercise the men in military drill every day by turns. At the end of April 1651, the Frasers thus commanded and marshalled, marched through the streets of Inverness, and from there through Badenoch and Appin to Stirling, where they arrived at the king's camp on 6 May. Having veteran officers at their head, they were exercised every day, and 'never was a Prince more delighted with his men than king Charles was with his highlanders,' while each corps strove to excel the others. For the next few months they lay encamped around Stirling and the Torwood, until they ate or destroyed all the provisions in the district.

On 17 July, Lambert crossed the Forth with a force of 4,000–5,000 men, capturing north Queensferry fortalice on the Inverkeithing peninsula. A few days later, on the 20th, he engaged the Scots at the Battle of Inverkeithing, inflicting losses amounting to a half of their 4,000 force.

Cromwell's 14,000 strong army in Fife took Perth on 1 August, while the king's army marched off into England via Carlisle to arrive at Worcester on 22 August. By the time the English Army under Cromwell confronted them on 3 September it numbered 31,000 against the Scots' 13,000. The 'Glorious Defeat' at Worcester cost the Scots a further 2,000 killed and 10,000 captured, Leslie escaping north with his cavalry but he and his forces being captured outside Manchester. The rest of the year, into 1652, saw only occupation, defeat and surrender on the part of the Scots, until Monk's Highland campaign began in June '52, followed, from August to October, by Argyll finally submitting to the English. England, Scotland and Ireland subsequently evolved from being the commonwealth it had declared itself as in 1649 onwards, to being – after the dissolution of the rump parliament in April 1653[142] – a protectorate under Oliver Cromwell, Lord Protector for life, supported in subsequent years by the rule of the major-generals.

After Oliver Cromwell's death in September 1658, his third son and the new Lord Protector, Richard Cromwell, was unable to control the army and resigned in May 1659. After a chaotic short revival of the Commonwealth, the monarchy was restored in May 1660.

Epilogue: How the Scots & Fraser's Dragoons Won the War

THERE IS AN ARGUMENT to be made that the first Civil War was won for parliament – in turn enabling Britain, or England, to become the cradle of western democracy – thanks to the hand that the Scottish Army of the Covenant played in affairs martial from January 1644 onwards. The overwhelming size of the Scottish force – some 21,000 troops, not including the additional 6,000 under the Earl of Callendar – was significantly larger than any other army fielded in Britain throughout the period. In addition to its sheer force of numbers, the quality of its troops was, once again, significantly superior to those raised further south, in that the men were better practiced in and accustomed to warfare than their English brethren. This may have been due to an accident of history, as Scotland had been accustomed to contributing such a large proportion of her impoverished population to the ranks of European armies over the preceding decades, and had received in return, upon making her clarion call, a tidal wave of troops and field officers, all well schooled and versed in the latest technologies of warfare, experienced and battle hardened, and perhaps capable of fighting with more fire in their bellies than their counterparts south of the border, those English who, however committed to their cause – of whichever persuasion – were still, at the end of the day, Englishmen somewhat reluctantly fighting fellow Englishmen.

Thanks to the Scots' utter defeat after 1651 at the hands of Cromwell's by then more organised army, it was the English, as victors and conquerors, who wrote the histories of the preceding decade. In a time when the history makers were so evidently partisan (on all sides), it is hardly surprising that little or no credit was to be given to the Scots' contribution to parliament's successes during the principal periods of the Civil War. This is exemplified by the fact that the wars are now known as the English Civil War when, at the time, they were referred to as the Great Civil War, and Scotland certainly contributed, and lost, more men per head of population than the rest of Britain did.

The evidence for the above expostulation is widespread and substantial.

During the campaigns in northern England, it is undeniable that there were insufficient forces available within the English armies to surround and successfully besiege the city of York. It may be a petty and primitive argument simply to rely upon a head count; however, having besieged York and having drawn off to Marston Moor to await Prince Rupert's forces when news of his imminent arrival reached the Allied besieging forces, the battle which followed was the largest conflict on English soil since the Wars of the Roses, and was the deciding factor in the eventual outcome of the war. It was a victory for the forces of parliament, won only by the skin of its teeth. It was a victory hinging upon the actions of the Scots, time after time, throughout the battle.

While parliament's left wing experienced success and made major advances, its right wing, placed upon far harder territory to make gains, was routed by the opposing Royalist forces, and it fell to the Scots, forming the battle, or centre, to hold its ground against subsequent and repeated charges by the victorious Royalist horse of that wing. The Battle of Marston Moor was won due to the centre holding out until, in the nick of time, parliament's left wing swept across the battlefield to drive off the Royalist forces and save the day. The central battle, which held out long enough for the rescuers to arrive, was comprised of Scottish infantrymen. The left wing of parliament was only able to make its initial successful advances against Rupert's cavalry and musket through the success of the Scots – Fraser's dragoons – in driving an opposing force of Royalist redcoat musketeers out of the cross ditch which would effectively have secured that flank of the battlefield for whoever held it, followed shortly thereafter by the same dragoons advancing to successfully clear the ditch of Royalist infantry and thereby allow the Scots cavalry and Cromwell's ironsides to sweep across and drive Rupert's horse from the field. This statement raises another point. Cromwell's self-aggrandising assertion that 'we drove all before us'; that 'they were as stubble to our swords', clashes with the reports of him receiving some small injury to his neck and leaving the field while his horse vacillated; it denies the eyewitness statements that, rather than Cromwell's indomitable ironsides led by the great man himself dealing a crushing and decisive blow to Rupert's cavalry, it was once again the Scots – this time the Scottish cavalry under David Leslie – which rallied the irresolute ironsides and, together, charged the prince's horse until the Royalist horse fled the field. Only by this decisive action on the part of the Scots in commanding the actions of parliament's left wing were those same forces then able to cross the field of battle just in time to engage in one last fray against those Royalist forces making their final charge against the unconquerable Scottish infantry battle.

There is little doubt that this huge battle was won, on so many counts, by the resolute, spirited and timeous actions of the Scots. Had Rupert won the day, on the other hand, Manchester's and Fairfax's armies would have withdrawn south while the Scots would, in all probability, have had to retreat north, so as not to have been caught with a large, victorious and highly spirited Royalist army between them and their own country. Probably outnumbered by Rupert, having suffered greater casualties in fleeing the field of battle, demoralised by defeat, the Scots would have moved first to Newcastle, but then probably continued across the border to ensure that the Royalists in their own country were dealt with comprehensively, rather than continue what would be seen as further hazardous adventure in England. Manchester and Fairfax too, would be demoralised and, having doubtless lost substantial casualties on being routed by Rupert, would not be in a hurry to face a force larger than their own, which controlled the whole of the north of England. The morale boost to Royalists in the south by this alternate scenario cannot be underestimated, as the democratic leanings of the English Parliamentarian armies would ensure that the common soldiery would want their views represented, which may well be that further war against their sovereign would be much longer than previously anticipated, entailing further and considerable hardships for troops who were already more and more commonly behind in their pay, and a war seen as, quite possibly, ultimately futile. This state of affairs may have existed had Marston Moor not gone parliament's way.

Shortly after the resounding success at Marston Moor and York however, the English broadsheets were already complaining that the Scots had not yet taken Newcastle, forgetting that this was a hitherto unconquerable stronghold of the north; never before taken by siege, until Callander's and Leslie's combined assault forces took the town for the first time in its history.

After Newcastle, Carlisle – the English reporting of which siege was once again critical of the Scots, suggesting that David Leslie was deliberately prolonging affairs purely to exact greater quantities of disbursement from their English parliamentary paymasters, despite the ultimately successful outcome of the Scots' actions and despite the Scots never, by all accounts, receiving the major portion of their pay from parliament. Next, Hereford, during which siege the Scots horse had to travel back to Scotland in order to address their own domestic affairs in the shape of the Marquis of Montrose, who had been so badly mauling the Scottish parliament's militia troops.

The actions of Montrose north of the border and in particular his successes, illustrate two further points. First, that as far as the Scottish parliament went, it had clearly sent the flower of its forces south to participate in the main theatre of war within Britain, retaining, somewhat unfortunately, the least experienced troops with the poorest quality of incompetent, politically motivated and in-fighting leadership to defend the Scottish homeland. Second, his successes highlight the total inability of the Scots gentry to present a united front against a common enemy, when division erupted through their all-pervasive and over-riding personal interests, fear of losing power and influence through being seen to have supported the 'wrong' side in the nation's conflict, the irresistible opportunity to profit from the troubles by waging private wars on neighbours for gain, to settle old scores etc. all serving to undermine the possibility of dealing in any way effectively with the threat posed by Montrose and his undeniably insignificant forces. This indecisiveness and lack of any cohesive policy bore stark contrast to the process of gathering together, funding, clothing and equipping the Army of the Covenant, so ably demonstrated by the leadership provided by the Scottish Presbyterian Kirk.

Twenty-first-century minds may find it difficult to relate to the religious and military balance of the times, over a third of a millennium ago. Bearing in mind that history is a place where the imposition of present day values can blind you to what that place may have been like, rather reluctantly, I would suggest as a current comparison Afghan fighters, fighting sometimes with a spiritual fervour, frequently driven on by their clerics' or mullahs' fanatical religious urgings, to acts of almost foolhardy bravery or of unforgivable horror; all this intolerance spewed out under the guise of being done in the name of God.

Similarly, by a fanatical, powerful and influential body of clerics and ministers accompanying the Army of the Covenant, committed to engaging in its religious instruction and supervision, the soldiers of Scotland were also the 'Soldiers of God' in the eyes of the Kirk, doing God's bidding, even to the extent of committing what were clearly considered even by the customs of the time and doubtless by some, at least, of the soldiery as well as the soldiers' commanders, inhuman atrocities. These acts were committed in the name of extreme Old Testament Christian teachings spouted by rabid clerics in their efforts to compel the troops to do their bidding – the horrendous aftermath of Philiphaugh being a clear case in point, while sadly not in any way a solitary instance of the practice of slaughtering, without conscience or compassion, not just any Irish combatants without quarter, but everyone attached to them – women and children, even newborn and, as yet, unborn babies.

After Philiphaugh and Hereford, the Scots once again played a major role in the investment of Newark and, of course, it was to Leven and his Scots army that Charles submitted his person in 1646, ending the siege and effectively concluding that part of the Civil War.

Perversely, it was only with this final downfall of Charles that things became unstuck for the Scots. With the disbanding of the army in favour of the New Model, and with the changed political complexion in the country, the Scots never recovered that level of commitment and impetus exhibited in previous years, while Cromwell over the same period had started to, and continued to, live up to the martial image he had created for himself, outmanoeuvring and outfighting the now floundering Scottish.

It must have been a bitter lesson to those Scots who survived all three civil wars, to see the tremendous achievements and successes gained by the flower of Scotland, capped by the king's person placing himself within the body of the army of Scotland, only to see all of these gains slip like sand through their fingers, assimilated by a politically and militarily ascendant Cromwell as he proceeded to crush Scotland under his heel, turning what was once a dream of universal Presbyterianism into just a deeply regrettable misadventure.

Amongst other points, minor yet worthy of note in this history, is evidence of senior and commanding officers absenting themselves from their units for what must have been lengthy periods of time. While the Scots Army was in the middle of besieging Carlisle, albeit at a leisurely pace and with reports of large quantities of alcohol being consumed upon both sides, Colonel Hugh Fraser had, at some point, left his regiment under the command of Lieutenant-Colonel Crawford, travelled north to Inverness, married his first wife Christian Baillie sometime in April 1645, had then boarded ship at Inverness in May due for London, reportedly observing Montrose's victory at the Battle of Auldearn from the ship's deck upon the following day when the ship drew into the river mouth at Nairn to take on fresh water for the trip south. Similarly, at sometime in 1648, when he was in command of one of the NMA troops of horse, Fraser was once again able to marry – his second wife, Jean Gray.

It is a huge disappointment to me that vast tracts of the history of the regiment of Fraser's dragoons remain undiscovered. Where and with whom did Fraser serve on the continent? What actions did he participate in there and did he achieve the fortune he returned home with through great deeds of valour or through succumbing to the corrupt practices which seemed rife across Europe at the time? Where and with whom did the four 'complete companies' that the regiment was formed around, serve in the continental wars? What were the details of the poor behaviour they were charged with on leaving Scotland and re-entering England? What happened to Hugh's first wife? How did he meet and marry his second wife? What was the true background to his hideous death by poisoning? From what existing units was his NMA horse troop formed – were they, or any of his officers at least, carried over from the original regiment? The list of unanswered questions may go on, but a line has to be drawn under the history somewhere, and it has taken thirty years of (albeit intermittent) research to get this far. I can go no further.

End Tables

Undernoted are tables identifying examples of the acquisitions of the regiment of Fraser's dragoons which, combined, help to make up a picture of how the regiment was supplied, equipped and paid.

ARMES & AMMUNITION RECEIVED, COLONEL FRASER HIS REGIMENT (LBs weight)[143]

1644		POWDER	MATCH	BALL
27th January	By Quartermaster James Achesone	27	27	27
30th	Captain Alex Fergusone	50	50	50
6th February	Malcolm Smith, Quartermaster	50	50	50
8th	David Simpsone, Quartermaster	100	100	100
12th	David Kennedy	50	50	50
13th	Captain David Lumsdane	100	100	100
19th	James Somervill	50	50	50
20th	Captain Jon Forrester	100	100	100
6th March	Quartermaster Achesone	100	200	100
8th	Captain David Lumsdane	24	24	24
12th	Thomas Urquhart, Scrivener	50	50	50
19th	Captain Lumsdane	48	50	
22nd	Captain Forrester		100	
25th	Colonel Fraser himself	200	100	

By Col. Fraser the receipt wt ye commanded men		100	100	
27th	By Lieutenant Alex Hamilton		100	
2nd April	Quartermaster Somervill		100	
11th	Captain Michael Bruce	100	100	
15th	Jon Evermor		100	
23d	Major Monro		100	
1st May	Captain Forrester		100	
9th	Cornet Andro Ker	100	100	100
13th	Wm. Borthwick	100	100	100
25th	Sergeant Andro Stenhous	100	50	100
3d June	Colonel Fraser	100	100	100
9th	Quartermaster James Achesone	100	100	100
29th	Lieutenant Hamilton	100	100	100
31st	Lieutenant Hamilton		50	
6th July	Quartermaster Alex Fraser	50	100	100
27th	Sergeant Rot. Stephenson	100	50	100
–	Captain Michael Bruce		150	
17th August	Cornet Wm. Elphinstone	100	100	100
27th	Lieutenant Hamilton	200	200	200
19th September	Colonel Fraser	400	100	
31st October	Cornet Andro Ker		100	
2nd November	Sergeant David Simsone		100	
14th	Lieutenant Colonel Crawfurd	200	400	200
30th December	Captain David Lumsdane	200	400	200

1645		POWDER	MATCH	BALL
23rd January	Sergeant Thomas Fergusone	400	400	400
2nd March	Andro M'Heart	200	300	100
27th	Robert Phillip	100	100	
3rd April	Roger Gordoune	100	200	100
13th	Sergeant George Thompsone	100	100	100
21st	Thomas Urquhart	100	200	100
22nd	Thomas Urquhart	300	400	100
29th	Thomas Urquhart	200	200	
8th May	Andro Urquhart	200	200	200
23rd June	Sergeant William Peibles		100	
3rd July	Corporal Jon Huntar		100	
9th	Thomas Scott		100	
19th	Corporal Jon Veech		100	
20th	Quartermaster Wm. Gillespie		100	
27th	James Bailzie	100	200	100
2nd August	James Bailzie	100	100	100
6th	Captain Andro Monro	100	100	
11th	James Bailzie	100	100	100
21st	Cornet Wm. Borthwick		20	
1st September	Cornet Wm. Borthwick	20	30	20

1646		POWDER	MATCH	BALL
31st March	Quartermaster Tweedie	40	40	40
10th May	Sergeant Maxwell	50	50	50
		5009	7191	4111[144]

ARMES DELIVERED TO COLONEL FRASER HIS REGIMENT

1644		MUSKET	BANDOLIER	SWORD
27th January	Captain David Lumsdane	30	30	24

30th	Captain Alex Fergusone	80	80	80
19th February	Captain Forrester	20	20	
4th April	Captain Forrester	32	32	
31st October	Cornet Andro Ker	60		
10th December	Lt. Col. Crawfurd	40	40	
30th	Captain Lumsdane	40		

1645		MUSKET	BANDOLIER	SWORD
8th March	Lt. Col. Crawfurd	60		
19th	Lt. Col. Crawfurd	60		
30th April	Major Jon Monro	60	60	

1646		MUSKET	BANDOLIER	SWORD
29th October	Colonel Hugh Fraser	30		
		512	262	104

MONEYS PAID TO COLONEL HEW FRASER HIS REGIMENT OF DRAGOUNNERS

1644		LSD
23rd November	Imprimis, paid to William Borthwick ensigne in cloth & other furniture to him	0011 01 0^{6} [145]
9th December	Item, paid to Lt. Col. Hew Crawfurd for ½ a month's pay to officers & 13s. 4d. to each soldier of the Regt.	0644 01 06[146]
30th	Item, paid to Capt. Dvd. Lumsdane for the use of the Master of the Regt.– £10 Sterling	0010 00 00

1645		
1st May	Item, paid to Major Jon Monro by bill of exch. on the Ld. Mayor of York, six hundred LB Sterling	0600 00 00

2nd	Item paid to Thomas Urquhart Regt. QM, ½ a month's pay to officers & whole months pay to soldiers of the Regt.	1429 02 06
17th July	Item, paid to Wm. Lindsay servitour to Lt. Col. Crawfurd for his master's use to accompte 20 LB Sterling	0020 00 00
18th	Item, paid to Col. for ½ months meins to officers and 10s to each dragouner of the regt.	0521 10 00[147]
1st October	Item, paid for routmaster Thomas Hamilton in Dalhousie's Regt. for use of commanded men of this regt.	0012 13 04

COLONEL FRASER'S REGIMENT OF DRAGOONS

1645/6		
10th January	Paid to said Col. in part payment of his English months pay to sd. Regt per order & his receipt eleven thou. fourscore	£11,080 00 00[148]
18th June	Paid to Jon Bruntoun hurt soldier for his pnt subpley & subsistence per order & receipt one hundred pounds	0100 00 00

COLONEL HEW FRASER HIS REGIMENT OF HORSE

1646/7		
22nd January	Paid to Cornet Colhoune for ½ months pay to the officers of the commanded party & 20/- to each of the 32 troupers	0067 05 00
	Paid for 1/3d part of 1 weeks assessment for the use of the commanded party from 14 – 22 January.	0007 08 00
11th February	Pd to Lt. Col. John Monro to accompt of Regt.	0402 01 10 ½
23rd	Paid to Lt. Col. Monro for the use of the regt.	0002 05 00
21st March?	Paid to David Baillie QM for the use of the minister p receipt.	0001 17 06
29th April	Paid to Col. H. Fraser for so much he wanted in Jan.	0013 10 00

20th February	Paid to Commanded party by assessment in County of Nottingham from 11 December '45 – 22 January.	16460138 08 00
21st March	Paid by Co. of Yorkshire in free quarter billetinge or otherwise from 27 January to 1 March.	1359 03 04[149]
4th July	Paid to Mr Fergus Alexander Minister to accompt per order..	0020 00 00
	Suma Lateris two thou. eleven pounds seventeen shillings eightpence half-penny stert	2011 17 08 ½

MONEY PAID TO COLONEL. FRASERS REGIMENT.

1646		
2nd August	Paid to Cornet Borthwick conforme to his receipt.This article to be discompted out of the 1st money due to the Regt conforme to act of Committee.	0044 18 02 ½

TO COLONEL FRASERS REGIMENT

Paid to sd. Regt in free quarter & billeting first as dragouners then as horsemen (by and above the billet money pd to them the time they lay before Newark already discharged in former accompte) from 20 Jan 1644 to 1 Aug 1646, 25,886 13 03.[150]

Paid to sd. Regt in free quarter and billetinge in Cliveland from 1 August to 1 November 1646 03,489 17 04.

References

Acts Vol vi part I

Barratt (2002)

Bellasis

Bowles, Manifest Truths (London 1646)

William Brockbank, Sovereign Remedies, A Critical Depreciation Of The 17th-Century London Pharmacopoeia

Buchannan, Truth Its Manifests, Edin. 1645

Calendar State Papers

Carlisle Letters Vol. 20, pp. 113–114

Stanley D. M. Carpenter, *Military Leadership in the British Civil Wars, 1642–1651*,

(Margaret Cavendish, 1667)

Richard Cavendish, Execution of Montrose

Chamberlains accounts

Bod. Clarendon MS, 1805

E. Furgol, *A Regimental History of the Covenanting Armies* (Edinburgh, John Donald, 1990)

Clive Holmes, *The Eastern Association in the English Civil War*

English Heritage Battlefield Report

S. R. Gardiner, History of the Commonwealth and Protectorate, 1903

Historical Collections, Vol. V

History of the Mackenzies

Historylearningsite.co.uk

William Godwin, History of the Commonwealth

Kenyon, J. and Ohlmeyer, J. (editors), *The Civil Wars: a Military History of England, Scotland and Ireland 1638–1660* (Oxford 1998)

Mackenzie, History of the Frasers

Memoirs of Montrose

Moderate Intelligencer, May 7–14.

MSS of Frasers

Steve Murdoch and Tim Wales, James King, Lord Eythin, Oxford DNB, 2004

National Archives Scotland

Newman (1981)

Parliamentary History

Paul Rollinson, *The Civil War in Hereford*
Perfect Diurnall, Dec. 8–15, Dec. 15–22, Jan. 5–12
Perfect Occurrences, Dec. 12–19.
Rushworth
Somerville, Memorie Vol. II
Spalding, History of the Troubles in Scotland
David Stevenson, *The Scottish Revolution 1637–44* (Newton Abbott 1973)
C.S. Terry, *The Army of the Covenant, 1917* (Scottish History Society)
C.S. Terry, *Historical Essays: The Siege of Newcastle-upon-Tyne by the Scots in 1644* (28/9/1898)
M.S. Anderson, *War and Society in Europe of the Old Regime 1618–1789*
C.V. Wedgwood, *The King's Peace, 1637–41* (London, 1955)
Cha. Wenham, T*he Great & Close Siege of York*
Wikipedia
Lucy Worsley, Cavalier (2007)

Endnotes

i Charter of Resignation by Hugh, Lord Fraser of Loweit [Fraser of Lovat], in favour of William Fraser, his brother german, of lands of the two Gowissachanis [Guisachan, Kiltarlity pa.] and Fregaye, in lordship of Loweit [Lovat, Kirkhill pa.] and sheriffdom of Innernes [Inverness] to be held in blenchfarm for yearly payment of a silver penny. 15/1/1541.

Culbokie was in Ross-shire near Dingwall. William Fraser of Guisachan (d 1544), brother of Hugh, Lord Fraser of Lovat, died in 1544 and was succeeded by his eldest son Hugh Fraser of Culbokie and Guisachan (d 1587), who inherited the lands of Culbokie from his uncle James Fraser. He was succeeded by his second son, Hugh Fraser, Colonel Hugh Fraser's father. A commentator referring to the transactions by which Hugh obtained possession of his brother's lands and later on of the Barony of Drumchardiny, says of the first transaction that 'a more cruel and barefaced impetration, sanctioned by relatives, cannot by quoted,' and of both that 'to Hugh's credit or discredit it has to be recorded of him that he disinherited his brother and circumvented his chief'. Hugh Fraser of Culbokie and Guisachan (d 1634) acquired the barony of Drumchardiny and was succeeded by his eldest son William Fraser of Culbokie (d 1669), who acquired the barony of Kingillie in 1637. He was Member of Parliament for Inverness in 1649, 1650 and 1651 and died in 1669. He was succeeded by his eldest son, Hugh Fraser of Culbokie (d 1678) who was subsequently outlawed and lost the estates of Drumchardiny, Kingillie and Culbokie. Following the death of Hugh Fraser in 1678 his eldest son William (d c 1759), nominally of Culbokie and Guisachan, succeeded him and managed to regain Guisachan. This William Fraser (d c 1759) was succeeded by his son William Fraser of Culbokie. The latter was succeeded by his grandson, William Fraser of Culbokie, who sold Guisachan but continued to be known as 'Culbokie'.

In 1624 Simon Lord Lovat married, as his third wife, Dame Katherine Rose (1581–1658) of the Kilravock family, a match disapproved of by his friends, involving as it did a large burden upon the estate for a period of thirty years. During the years subsequent to his third marriage, Lord Simon lived principally at Bunchrew. He had left the administration of the estate to his eldest son by his first wife, Hugh, Master of Lovat [later 7th Lord], who had in 1614 married Isobel Wemyss (1598–1636), daughter of Sir John Wemyss, by whom he had a large family, living in the ancient residence of Lovat. Lord Simon also spent time in Inverness, where he had a mansion. He had built the castle of Dalcross as well as a residence at Bunchrew. To liquidate the great expense incurred for these and other purposes, he placed heavy mortgages on his lands. Lord Simon died at Bunchrew in April 1633 and was buried at Wardlaw.

Hugh Fraser 7th Lord Lovat (1591–1645), had the misfortune of inheriting a patrimony, great in area, but so encumbered with mortgages and other debts as to considerably reduce its value. Lord Lovat, finding himself in financial straits, solicited the assistance of his kinsmen.

We find him in 1633 leaving his affairs in the Aird district in the hands of Thomas Fraser of Struy, his heritable baillie, and taking up residence with his household at Meickle Garth, in Stratherrick. In the summer of 1634 he and his family and retainers are in residence at Dalcross. Judging by his establishment, his lordship did not suffer from stringency in money matters.

Mr James Fraser of Phopachy (d 1639), was Master of the Household – Fear an Tighe, as he was called – 'Mr Patrick Fraser, his cheefe gentleman; James Tarras, chaplain; David Carr, musitian; Jo. Reed Stuart; groomes, pantry boyes, cooks, all countrymen; and the principal families each a sone in his Court, to educate, polish and accomplish them,' &c.

The minister of Wardlaw [Rev. James Fraser, grandson of Mr James Fraser of Phopachy] comments on the domestic expenditure of Lord Lovat's household: 'The expenditure of this family extravagent – seven bolls malt, seven bolls meale, one boll floure, every week; 70 black cowes in the year, besides venison, fish, pullet, kid, lamb, duck, and mallart, etc., with all the presents and lists unaccountable; the wines in great quantities yearly from France, with sugar and all manner of spices, that it is incredible how any house could spend this store and provision yearly. For my own part, I have been amused, yea amased, in reading my grandfather's books of accounts, where he sets down the exact particulars of the vast spending of this noble family; and many would consider it very rant.'

On 11 May 1634, Hugh Lord Lovat has a business transaction with James Glendinning, who had been master of the household with Lord Simon, his father, and not improbably managed to feather his own nest comfortably under the lax rule of that amiable employer. Glendinning was Lovat's creditor, or had advanced a sum of 1,000 merks, and for this the latter pledged the town and lands of Kinmylies, in the regality of Spiny, the annual amount payable by Glendinning being sixteen bolls victual, in name of ferme or rent.

During 1636 Hugh Fraser 7th Lord Lovat (1591–1645) sustained a domestic affliction [this was the death of his wife], which so depressed his spirits that he took little or no practical interest in the affairs of his extensive property during the remainder of his years. Isabel Wemyss, Lady Lovat, passed away after a short illness, in the forty-eighth year of her age, and after twenty-two years of wedded bliss. Four years later, his oldest son, Simon, Master of Lovat, died in his twentieth year. Hugh,

Lord Lovat's second son, succeeded to the heirship; the administration of the estate having for some time been controlled by his lordship's half-brother, Sir James Fraser of Brea (1612–1649).

Contract between Hugh, Lord Fraser of Lovat, with consent of Hugh, Master of Lovat, and of James Fraser of Brey [Braes], brother of said Lord Fraser, and Thomas Fraser of Struy with consent of Hugh Fraser, his eldest son and apparent heir, and of Marie Lindesay [Lindsay], spouse of said Hugh, and of Thomas Fraser, eldest son of said Thomas by the deceased Elizabeth Dunbar, his second spouse, on the one part, and Major Hugh Fraser, brother german of William Fraser of Culbokie [Kilbokie], on the other, whereby the first party dispone to said Major Hugh the towns and lands of Fanellane [Fanellan], Ardellane, Teaknok and Cullachie, in lordship of Lovat [Kirkhill pa.] and sheriffdom of Innernes [Inverness], to be held in feufarm for yearly payment to said Hugh, Lord Fraser of Lovat, of 20 merks Scots. 1640.

Discharge by Mr William Fraser, minister of Convent and Kiltarlatie [Convinth and Kiltarlity], to Lieutenant-Colonel Hugh Fraser of Fanellan, for (1) £3 4*s* Scots and (2) 16*s* as silver duty of the parsonage teinds of (1) Fanellan and (2) Kiltarlatie, for the year 1640. 16/3/1641.

In June 1640 Hugh Fraser had a charter from Lord Lovat signed at castle Downie of the lands of Fanellan etc. to him, his heirs etc. By another charter dated at Lovat in July, Fraser, now of Fanellan, was named as Lovat's 'Consanguineius' and acquired the lands of Kiltarlity. In March 1642 he was also to obtain the lands of Kinneries from Thomas Chisholm of Kinneries.

Instrument of Sasine in favour of Major Hugh Fraser, brother of William Fraser of Culbokie [Kilbokie], of an annual rent of 400 merks Scots out of the lands of Easter and Wester Agais [Aigas, Kilmorack pa.] and Wester Eskidaill [Eskadale, Kiltarlity pa.] in lordship of Lovat and sheriffdom of Invernes [Inverness], following on precept, dated 26 June 1640, by Thomas Fraser of Struy with consent of Hugh Fraser, his eldest son and apparent heir, and Thomas Fraser, his eldest son by Elizabeth Dunbar, his second wife. Registered P.R.S. Inverness, 3 July 1640, vi, 319. 1/7/1640.

Discharge by Mr William Fraser, minister at Convent and Kiltarlatie [Convinth and Kiltarlity], to Lieutenant-Colonel Hugh Fraser of Famellane, of (1) three bolls two firlots three pecks beir and £3 4*s* and (2) fourteen pecks beir and 16*s*. out of the parsonage teinds of (1) Fannellan [Fanellan] and Cullach and (2) Kiltarlatie. 9/3/1642.

In April 1642, Hugh Master of Lovat (1624–1643), married Anna, daughter of General Leslie, later Earl of Leven, at Holyrood House. Although Lord Lovat was not in favour of his son accepting a lieutenant-Colonelcy in the army of Scotland, arranged by General Leslie, the master accepted the post and, while spending the winter in Edinburgh with his wife, suffered an illness from which he died in April 1643.

Ante-Nuptial Marriage Contract between Hugh, Lord Lovat, and Hugh, Master of Lovat, his son, with consent of Sir James Fraser of Bray [Braes], knight, brother of said Lord Lovat, and Dame Beatrix Weymes [Wemyss], his spouse, on the one part, and Alexander, Earl of Levin [Leven], Dame Agnes Rentoun [Renton], Countess of Levin, his spouse, and Lady Anna Leslie, their daughter, on the other, whereby Hugh, Master of Lovat, is to be infeft in the lands and barony of Lovat, lands of Bewfort [Beaufort], lands and barony of Bewlie [Beauly], and others, the said Anna to be infeft in liferent in lands of Eist Kynmyleis [Kinmylies] alias Brigend, Wester Kynmyleis, Bellaferrie [Ballifeary], Eister and Wester Abriachin [Abriachan], Kilwhynd, with the mill of Bught, and fishing of Ness called Freischet, in barony of Kinmyleis, and half the town and lands of Kiltarlatie [Kiltarlity] and fishing of Lyen alias Eff, and lands and maynes of Dalcroce [Dalcross], and in an annual rent of 2,000 merks Scots out of the lands and barony of Bewlie; her tocher being £20,000 Scots. Registered in B. of C. & S. 4 March 1643. NAS 1642.

Discharge by Mr William Fraser, minister of Conveth and Kiltarlatie [Convinth and Kiltarlity], to Colonel Hugh Fraser of Fanellan, for six bolls six pecks victual and £5 8*s* Scots in complete payment of his part of the said William's local stipend out of the parsonage teinds of the lands of Fanellan, Kineress [Kinerras], and Kiltarlatie. 21/4/1645.

Copy and Transcript of Contract between Hugh, Lord Fraser of Lovet [Lovat], with consent of Sir James Fraser of Bray [Braes], knight, his tutor, Alexander Fraser, Master of Lovet, his uncle and apparent heir, and David, Lord Elcho, donator of ward and marriage of the said Hugh, Lord Fraser, on one part, and Colonel Hugh Fraser of Kinneries [Kinnaries] on the other, whereby, for the sum of 53,000 merks Scots, the said Lord Lovet dispones to said colonel the lands of Eister Kinmylies alias Brigend, Wester Kinmylies, Bellaferie [Ballifeary], Eister and Wester Abriachan, with the mill of Bucht [Bught] and fishing of Ness called the Frie Schott, in barony of Kinmilies, half the town and lands of Kiltarlatie [Kiltarlity] in regality of Spynie and sheriffdom of Innernes [Inverness], with the parsonage and vicarage teinds thereof, to be held by double infeftment, the one of the said Lord Lovet, and the other from the said Lord Lovet of the Crown. 20/1/1647.

Ticket by William Law, clerk of Exchequer, on behalf of John, Earl of Craufurd Lyndsay [Crawford and Lindsay], High Treasurer of Scotland, acknowledging receipt from Mr Francis Hay of Balhoussie [Balhousie] WS, on behalf of Colonel Hugh Fraser of Kynnaries [Kinnaries], of £515 16*s* 4 1/2*d*, as the feu and other duties of the lands of Eister Kynmylies alias Brigend with the fishing-boats thereof, lands of Wester Kynmylies, Bellafarie [Ballifeary], Easter and Wester Obiriachains [Abriachan] with the mill of Bucht [Bught] and fishing of Nes [Ness] called the Frie Schot, and half the town and lands of Kiltarlatie [Kiltarlity], for which sum a discharge would be procured. Also a transcript of the above. 14/9/1647.

28a/ Copy Bond of Provision by Colonel Hugh Fraser of Kinneries [Kinnaries], to Anna Fraser, his daughter, at the desire of Christine Baillie, his spouse, of the sum of 5,000 merks Scots. 20/8/1647.

Bond by Colonel Hugh Fraser of Kinneries to Major David Lumsden, younger of Blanern 1647; papers relating to subsequent apprisings of Kinmylies, Ballaferrie, Mill of Bucht and others by Sir James Lumsden of Innergellie, 1657–9, and subsequent disposition of these to bailie Finlay Fraser, 1666, and by him to Hugh Fraser, son of Colonel Hugh, 1669. 1647–1669.

Execution of letters of horning raised at the instance of Alexander Fraser now of Kinneries [Kinnaries], only living son of the deceased Col. Hugh Fraser of Kinneries and the deceased Christine Baillie, his first wife, against Anna and Christian Fraser, daughters and heirs portioners of the deceased Hugh Fraser of Kinneries, son and heir of the said Col. Hugh Fraser, for various sums of money contained in bonds by the said Col. Hugh Fraser to his children. 5/6/1684

ii John Middleton, *c.*1608–74

John Middleton was the eldest son of Robert Middleton, laird of Caldhame, Kincardineshire. After enlisting as a pikeman in the regiment raised in 1632 by Sir John Hepburn for service in France, Middleton worked his way steadily up the ranks. He was a captain in the Covenanter army led by James Graham, Earl (later Marquis) of Montrose during the Bishops' Wars: Middleton led the successful attack on Brig of Dee outside Aberdeen in June 1639. On the outbreak of the English Civil War, he was commissioned a colonel in the Parliamentarian army. He served with Sir William Brereton in Cheshire during 1643 and became lieutenant-general of horse to Sir William Waller on the Oxford campaign of 1644. In 1645, Middleton returned to Scotland and joined the Army of the Covenant with the rank of major-general. He rode with Lieutenant-General David Leslie's cavalry detachment on the campaign against his former commander the Marquis of Montrose, whose forces had killed his father in his own house in 1645. Middleton was Leslie's second in command at the Battle of Philiphaugh (September 1645), which broke Montrose's power in Scotland. When Leslie returned to the war in England, Middleton stayed in Scotland. He was appointed commander-in-chief by the Committee of Estates in February 1646, campaigning against Royalists in the highlands and negotiating the final terms for Montrose's surrender in July 1646. Middleton supported the Engagement between Charles I and the Scots, and commanded the cavalry in the Duke of Hamilton's Engager army that invaded England in July 1648. The Engagers were defeated by Cromwell at the Battle of Preston (August 1648) and Middleton was taken prisoner. He is said to have broken his parole to return to Scotland, where he joined Sir Thomas Mackenzie of Pluscardine in an abortive Royalist uprising in the highlands during the spring of 1649. His support for Engagers and Royalists brought Middleton into conflict with the Presbyterians of the godly Kirk Party, and he was excommunicated in October 1650. Middleton was obliged to undergo a public penance in sackcloth at St Mary's Kirk in Dundee before he could take up his command in Charles II's Scots-Royalist army. This humiliation left him with an abiding hatred of Presbyterians, who equally disapproved of him because of his reputation for hard drinking and carousing. In September 1651, Middleton was Charles II's major-general at the Battle of Worcester. He was wounded during the fighting, then captured as he tried to escape back to Scotland and imprisoned in the Tower of London. Before he could be brought to trial for treason, Middleton succeeded in escaping from the tower and made his way to Paris, where he joined Charles in exile.

iii Robert Monro served in the Swedish Army, writing a famous history on his exploits – 'Monro, his expedition with the Worthy Scots Regiment called Mac-Keys'.

In 1642 he went to Ireland, nominally as second in command under Alexander Leslie, but in fact in chief command of the Scottish Army sent to put down the Catholic Irish rebels who had massacred Scottish settlers in Ulster during the Irish Rebellion of 1641. Monro's campaign in Ireland was largely confined to the northern province of Ulster. After taking and plundering Newry in April 1642, and ineffectually attempting to subdue Sir Phelim O'Neill, Monro succeeded in taking prisoner the Earl of Antrim at Dunluce Castle.

The arrival of Owen Roe O'Neill in Ireland strengthened the cause of the rebels, now organised in Confederate Ireland, and Monro, who was poorly supplied with provisions and war materials, showed little activity. Moreover, the English Civil War was now creating confusion among parties in Ireland, and the king was anxious to come to terms with the Catholic rebels, and to enlist them on his own behalf against the parliament. The Earl of Ormonde, Charles's lieutenant-general in Ireland, acting on the king's orders, signed a cessation of hostilities with the Catholic Confederates on 15 September 1643, and exerted himself to dispatch aid to Charles in England.

The conflict that took place in Ulster was particularly barbaric. Many of the raised troops were undisciplined and atrocity was being matched by atrocity. Monro's strategy was just as ruthless and no measure was spared in his campaign against O'Neil. The conflict led to thousands of innocent people being killed on both sides. While O'Neil waged a guerilla type offensive in Ulster, Monro, superior in numbers, systematically destroyed castles and villages throughout the land. Some accounts tell of him laying waste to Antrim and Down in what would now be called a 'scorched earth policy'.

Monro, holding his commission from the parliament of Scotland dominated by the Covenanters, did not recognise the armistice, and his troops accepted the Solemn League and Covenant, in which they were joined by many English soldiers who left Ormonde to join him. In April 1644 the English parliament entrusted Monro with the command of all the forces in Ulster, both English and Scots. He thereupon seized Belfast, made a raid into the Pale, and unsuccessfully attempted to gain possession of Dundalk and Drogheda. In response, the Irish confederates sent an armed expedition to Scotland to join the Scottish Royalists there under James Graham, 1st Marquis of Montrose.

Monro's force was weakened by the need to send troops to Scotland to withstand Montrose; clansmen were sent back under Monro's nephew, George Munro, 1st of Newmore. While Owen Roe O'Neill was strengthened by receiving supplies from the Papal Nuncio to Ireland, Giovanni Battista Rinuccini. On 5 June 1646 was fought the Battle of Benburb, on the Blackwater, where O'Neill routed Monro, inflicting over 2,000 dead on the Scottish force but allowing him to withdraw in safety to Carrickfergus.

In 1647 Ormonde was compelled to come to terms with the English parliament, who sent commissioners to Dublin in June of that year. The Scots under Monro refused to surrender Carrickfergus, Carrickfergus Castle and Belfast when ordered by the parliament to return to Scotland, and Monro was superseded by the appointment of George Monck to the chief command in Ireland. In September 1648 Carrickfergus was delivered over to Monck by treachery, and Monro was taken prisoner. He was committed to the Tower of London, where he remained a prisoner for five years. In 1654 he was permitted by Oliver Cromwell to reside in Ireland, where he had estates in right of his wife, who was the widow of Viscount Montgomery of Ardes. Monro continued to live quietly near Comber, County Down, for many years, and probably died there about 1680.

iv Philip Skippon started his military service early, serving in the palatinate under Sir Horace Vere. Skippon was wounded during the siege of Breda in 1625 and again at its recapture in 1637. He attained the rank of captain in the Dutch service, returned to England in 1639, and was recommended by the king to the Artillery Company for election as leader. After the attempted arrest of the five members of parliament in January, 1642, the House of Commons applied to the city for a guard, and Skippon was appointed to take command of the London Trained Bands, and to raise a guard for the defence of the parliament. By order of the commons, Skippon blockaded the tower, and tried to take possession of it by surprise, the attempt ending when the king removed Sir John Byron, the Royalist lieutenant of the tower, to York where the king then had his court. In 1642, when the king threatened London, and The London Trained Bands marched to Turnham Green, Skippon appeared at their head and went along with the soldiers, talking to them, sometimes to one company, and sometimes to another – the soldiers seemingly more taken with this than with any formal oration. Essex saw Skippon's value, and appointed him Sergeant Major-General of the army. When the New Model Army was formed, Skippon was appointed Sergeant Major-General to Fairfax, and he was instrumental in persuading the old generals of Essex's army to enrol in the new army, pledging his word to the men for good usage and constant pay, ending with the words '***I shall by the help of God be willing to live and die with you.***' At Naseby, he marshalled the foot of the parliamentary army and was dangerously wounded by a shot in his side towards the end of the fight, but declined to leave the field, telling Fairfax he would not leave the field as long as a man would stand. A physician was sent by the commons to attend him, and letters sent extending thanks from the speakers of both houses. Brought to London on a litter, at Islington 'a great Mastiff dog' ran out, savaged one of the horses and almost overturned the litter, which nearly killed him. In December 1645, he was appointed Governor of Bristol, and in 1646 he became Governor of Newark, commanding the convoy which carried parliament's £200,000 to the Scots at Newcastle in exchange for the king. In December, Skippon was to be recommended by Fairfax to be made Governor of Newcastle.

v Archibald Strachan, *d.*1652
Born at Musselburgh near Edinburgh to an obscure family, Archibald Strachan served in the army of the Earl of Essex as a captain of dragoons during the Civil War. His company was among those sent to join Sir William Waller's army on its advance into the west early in 1643 and he was promoted to the rank of major after the Battle of Lansdown in July. Strachan commanded Waller's regiment of dragoons in September 1643 and was praised by Waller for his courage during the attack on Basing House in November. After further service in parliament's armies in southern England, Strachan joined the Army of the Covenant and was a major in Sir John Brown's regiment of horse by May 1645. A radical in religion, he fiercely opposed the Engagement between Scotland and King Charles and joined Cromwell's army on the Preston campaign of 1648. Strachan accompanied Cromwell into Scotland and participated in the negotiations with the Whiggamores that resulted in the Treaty of Stirling in September 1648. In February 1649, Strachan's opposition to the Engagers secured him an appointment as lieutenant-colonel in Colonel Ker's Covenanter regiment, though Lieutenant-General David Leslie distrusted him because of his extreme religious views. Inspired by the biblical hero Gideon, Ker and Strachan believed that an elite force of godly warriors would always prevail over the hosts of the unrighteous. They routed the Royalist insurgents of Pluscardine's uprising at Balvenie in May 1649 and Strachan led Leslie's advance guard to win a decisive victory over the Marquis of Montrose at the Battle of Carbisdale in April 1650. The Scottish parliament rewarded him with £1,000 and a gold chain. The following July, Strachan was appointed colonel of a new cavalry regiment raised from funds contributed.

Notes

1 The Holy Roman Empire was a fragmented collection of largely independent states, such as the Austrian House of Habsburg which included Bohemia and Hungary and was a major European power ruling 8 million subjects. The empire also contained Bavaria, Electoral Saxony, the Margraviate of Brandenburg, the Palatinate, Hesse, the Archbishopric of Trier and Württemberg, containing a further 500,000 to 1 million inhabitants. The empire extended down to a considerable number of duchies, free cities, abbeys, bishoprics, and petty lords.
2 Wikipedia.
3 Montrose in his campaigns in Scotland was to suffer particularly from this phenomenon which, given the diminutive size of his forces at the best of times, meant a continual expenditure of his energy and resources on replenishing his army's numbers.
4 Historylearningsite.co.uk
5 M.S. Anderson, 'War and Society in Europe of the Old Regime 1618–1789'.

Chapter 1

6 Seventy English miles!
7 It was the second of the thirteen regiments of Scotch soldiers in the army of Gustavus Adophus.
8 The blue ribbon worn about the craig (neck) and down under his left arm was not adopted by the soldiery in the later campaign of 1644.
9 Breeches may have been threequarters one-eight i.e. 31.5 inches/80cm and the cloth of both coats and breeches first shrunk in cold water. Breeches were commonly cut 'full' – existing examples are interlined and padded, which must have been a consideration for riding.
10 History of the Troubles in Scotland, pp. 122–3
11 Terry xcvii.
12 8 ells = 5.62 sq.m. or, allowing for a 45 degree angle to the sides of a bivouac, a tent approx. 2m x 2m at its base.
13 It is not clear, however, whether the Scots used tents in the campaigns of 1644 and 1645.

14 Kenyon, J. and Ohlmeyer, J. (editors), The Civil Wars: a military history of England, Scotland and Ireland 1638–1660 (Oxford, 1998). David Stevenson, The Scottish Revolution 1637–44 (Newton Abbott, 1973). C.V. Wedgwood, The King's Peace 1637–41 (London, 1955).

15 Hugh's father married Catherine McKenzie of Gairloch around 1593, who bore him his heir and successor, William Fraser of Culbokie – born circa 1593 and married in 1622; John Fraser of Clunevackie, Alexander Fraser of Foyness, Colonel Hugh Fraser of Kinneries, Margaret and Agnes.

16 His wife Catherine survived him until 1667.

17 1624–1643.

18 Leslie gained fame as defender of Stralsund against Wallenstein, was with Gustavus Adolphus' army in Lutzen and was made field marshal in 1635. Two years later he was granted a pension for his services and the following year he received a request to return to Scotland to help his country. In October 1638 he reached Scotland with many other Scots officers who had been in the Swedish service.

19 Although Lord Lovat was not in favour of his son accepting a Lieutenant-Colonelcy in the army of Scotland arranged by General Leslie, the master accepted the post and, while spending the winter in Edinburgh with his wife, was to suffer an illness from which he would die the April following.

20 There are various and conflicting accounts of Fraser's rank about this time. While referred to as a major in the above tract, he is also described as lieutenant colonel as early as March 1642 (see end notes).

21 The number of companies later increased to seven during the siege of York, with an estimated sixty-four men in each, an estimated total of 448 men. Fraser's numbers are looked at in more detail in the end table footnotes.

22 It required a forked stand to hold its long barrel and the musketeer had to ignite powder in a touchhole with a hand-held burning wick, conditions which made the weapon very difficult to aim.

23 The matchlock musket and rest were virtually the only armaments of infantry from about 1550 to 1675. An English 1645 contract for the purchase of muskets still specified muskets with a barrel of 48" long, contrary to a belief that the barrels of muskets became shorter during the Civil War.

24 Approximately £1,333 7*s* Scots.

25 English sources refer to shoes and 'cockers' (gaiters), leaving officers to the expense of boots. This one item of clothing would differentiate dragoons from musketeers. There are no descriptions of dragoons wearing only shoes, and those worn would likely have been the 'close' type described by Randle Holme – a sort of 'brogan' for protection.

26 English currency was twelve times stronger than that in Scotland e.g. £12 Scots = £1 sterling and the Scots equivalent of the saddle prices would be: cavalry troopers – £9 12*s* and £9 18*s*; dragoons – £4 14*s*).

27 Sources cite a simple 'pad' (or 'pilch') saddle, i.e. without a tree, for easier mounting/dismounting, supplied with a crupper and martingale to restrict its movement. The great cavalry saddle was designed to withstand the shock of the charge. A simple unreinforced bridle and either a plain snaffle or curb bit; straps for equipment at the rear of the pad.

28 The Scots had buttoned coats and breeches, while there is no evidence that the English were similarly equipped, as not enough money was allowed for the suits. A pennyworth would buy only six hooks and eight buttons, but a lot more tape to bind and tie the coat. Tape or 'ribbon' ties were much cheaper, and any metal would have been better used in the manufacture of bronze cannon than 'dressing up a few coats'. The hooks and buttons were for breeches only.

29 Woodcuts show that even humble breeches had at least half a dozen buttons at the opening. 'Shambo' (chamois) or sheepskin pockets (2) are likely to have been fitted.

30 The idea of it being the custom in the north to dye shirts yellow or ochre using saffron seems to have been the preserve of 'the great', i.e. well to do.

31 Spurs were an item shown in every woodcut (English troops), but of the short rowel type, and without 'butterfly' leathers – probably unnecessary for the rank-and-file but 'de rigeur' for the officer, as silvered spurs were the height of fashion.

32 First described in 1618.

33 While any evidence points to English dragoon units being issued with flask and ball bag, or cartridges in a bag or box (or 'patron' – a metal-cased wooden cartridge box with drillings to accept ready-made cartridges) – an idea already 100 years old, Frasers were issued with bandoliers (see end tables).

34 Mattock – a tool like a pickaxe with one end of its blade flattened at right angles to its handle, used for loosening soil and cutting through roots.

35 Troubles in Scotland.

36 Oatmeal formed the mainstay of the Scottish diet. Wheat was not grown in much of Scotland and, unlike in England, bread was not a staple part of the diet. People would have porridge for breakfast and eat oat-cakes with most meals. The soldiers would therefore usually make a dough of oatmeal and water and bake this on hot stones from an open fire. Cavalry officers would carry a skillet for cooking oat-cakes. However, when the infantry soldiers were marching, or did not have access to fire or boiling water, they would moisten the oats with milk or water and knead it in their hands to provide a nourishing, if somewhat unappetising paste.

37 At 14.5 musket balls per pound of lead, this would equate to just over forty musket balls each (see end tables).

38 *According to Rushworth these officers (asterisked) already had experience of continental warfare.

39 Thomas Carlyle wrote TO DAVID LAING, 28 January 1846 (CARLYLE LETTERS, Vol 20: 113–114): 'kinsman, Skeldon Crawford, major of Lord Montgomerie's horse, 1642. Laing notes him as William Crawford of Nether Skeldon, Ayrshire (d. 1646), and does not differentiate between the two men. William Godwin, History of the Commonwealth'.

40 Historical tracts relate that there is still evidence to be seen of this sconce on the ground at Home Farm. The author has, however, been unsuccessful in finding any trace of this.

Chapter 2

41 David Leslie – this is the son of Lord Leven, not Major-General David Leslie, who had overall command of the Scots' horse.

42 Also known as Coria.

43 Who had been injured and captured at the Corbridge engagement.

44 In the days before smokeless gunpowder, musket units would create clouds of impenetrable smoke, potentially blinding them from observing their opponents movements, therefore wind strength and direction, as well as terrain, obstacles etc. had to be taken into account when arranging troop dispositions.

45 Possibly Lieutenant Colonel James Ballantyne of Leven's Lifeguard again.

46 Could this be Ballantyne again?

47 A merk was a Scottish silver coin. Originally the same word as a mark of silver, the merk was in circulation at the end of the sixteenth century and in the seventeenth century. It was originally valued at 13*s* 4*d* (exactly 2/3 of a pound Scots, or about one shilling in English coin), later raised to 14*s* Scots.

48 James King was the son of David King of Warbester in Orkney; his mother Mary was the daughter of Adam Stewart, an illegitimate son of James V of Scotland. King's military career began around 1609, when he joined the Swedish service. By 1630, he was lieutenant-colonel in a Scottish regiment in the Swedish Army commanded by Patrick Ruthven, and in 1636 he served as lieutenant-general in Alexander Leslie's army in Westphalia.

King retired from the Swedish service in 1639, receiving a Swedish knighthood and pension. He was unwilling to join the Covenanters in the Bishops' Wars against Charles I and became Charles' agent in raising money and forces from Europe in preparation for the Civil War in England. In March 1642, he was created Lord Eythin and was persuaded by the queen to take up a command in the Royalist army. Eythin accompanied the queen to Yorkshire in February 1643 and was appointed lieutenant-general and commander of infantry in the king's northern army. He acted as chief military adviser to the Marquis of Newcastle in the campaigns of 1643–4 against the Yorkshire Parliamentarians.

With the signing of the Solemn League and Covenant between parliament and the Scots, Eythin was placed in the invidious position of fighting against his fellow countrymen and his former commander Alexander Leslie, now Earl of Leven. Eythin held Newcastle-upon-Tyne against the Covenanters but his failure to prevent them from advancing south led to the expression of doubts regarding his loyalty.

Chapter 3

49 From the want of a proper commissariat arose the practice of quartering troops on the country, adopted in all parliament's armies from 1643 to 1651. The householder had to provide food and lodging for a number of soldiers at a fixed rate. In return, a ticket was given to him by the commissary or some other officer, specifying the number of soldiers quartered on him, the time they were maintained, and the amount due for their 'entertainment'. This was 'free quarter' which becomes so painfully familiar a phrase in the complaints of the country. It did not mean that food and lodging was provided gratis, but that payment for them was deferred. In the record office there are hundreds of such tickets receipted as paid by the treasurer of the Earl of Manchester's army. A sum was deducted from the soldiers' pay for this, usually about half the pay of the private, and one-third of the pay of the officers.

This method of maintaining the army led to complaints from the country. The burden imposed on the householder was very heavy; the prospect of repayment was doubtful and remote. The rates for entertainment of man and beast on the march were fixed. For the horse, threepence a night for grass and fourpence for hay: oats – fourpence a peck, pease and beans – sixpence a peck, barley and malt – sevenpence a peck. For a trooper, eightpence a day was allowed; for a dragoon, sevenpence; for a foot soldier, sixpence.

50 John Lilburne was one of the most prominent Levellers, known to his supporters as 'Free-born John', who campaigned for a radical change of England's political system.

Born in 1615 in Sunderland, one year younger than his brother Robert, who later became famous as one of the regicides who signed Charles I's death warrant, Lilburne was involved in printing and distributing unlicensed Puritan books and pamphlets, was arrested in 1637 and sentenced to be whipped, pilloried and sent to Fleet prison. Lilburne was stripped to the waist tied behind a cart, and, under a beating sun, marched the 2 miles from Fleet Bridge to New Palace Yard. Throughout the journey, the prisoner was lashed with a three-thonged knotted whip, receiving an estimated 500 lashes or 1,500 stripes to his back. Vivid descriptions from the period paint a painful picture of this tortured man:

his shoulders 'swelled almost as big as a penny loafe with the bruises of the knotted Cords' and 'the weales in his back, made by his cruel whipping, were bigger than Tobacco-pipes'.

He was in this condition when he reached New Palace Yard and after he refused to admit to any error, his head was clamped in the pillory. Weakened by his ordeal, still he spoke out. A crowd gathered to listen to him declare: 'Bishops derived their authority from the Pope, who was the Beast of Revelation, who was the Anti-Christ or the Devil', and he challenged them to deny it. In prison for three years and in poor health, Lilburne was freed in 1640 when Oliver Cromwell petitioned for his release.

When war broke out, Lilburne enlisted as a captain of foot and fought at Edgehill, then joined Manchester's Eastern Association army and became lieutenant-colonel of dragoons. He became friendly with Cromwell, serving with him in Lincolnshire and supporting him in his disputes with Manchester. After Marston Moor, Lilburne was to resign from the army after refusing to sign the Presbyterian Solemn League and Covenant, as required of officers in the New Model Army.

51 Manchester's army of the associated counties, commanded by Major-General Laurence Crawford, numbered 3,000 foot, consisting of three regiments, led by Colonels Russell, Montague, and Pickering, and thirty-eight troops of horse (about 2,280 men), under Lieutenant-General Oliver Cromwell.

52 The Yorkshire men also numbered about 3,000 men under Sir William Fairfax of Steeton with three colonels under him, John Bright of Badsworth, Needham, who fought at Selby, and Forbes, hero of Leeds Bridge. The horse comprised his own regiment of 500 men in five troops, plus some regiments composed chiefly of raw Lancashire recruits under Colonel John Lambert consisting of 2,200 sabres in fifty-three troops.

53 Leven's commissioners were the Earl of Lindsay and Sir Adam Hepburn.

Chapter 4

54 The Eastern Association in the English Civil War, by Clive Holmes.

55 Stanley D. M. Carpenter, Military Leadership in the British Civil Wars, 1642–1651.

56 A quarter of a mile north of the present road.

57 David Leslie, Lord Balgonie, was the cavalry commander shot in the shoulder at Corbridge when surprised by Sir Marmaduke Langdale.

58 At or near the line of the present road.

59 Rupert's diary, quoted in Barratt (2002), p.97.

60 Barratt p.149.

61 Barratt pp.84–5.

62 Quoted in Newman (1981), p.63.
63 In 1637, King commanded an army for the Landgrave of Hesse in an attempt to drive Imperial forces out of his territory. The following year, he joined forces with Charles Louis, the Elector Palatine, and his brother Prince Rupert against General Hatzfeld, but their army was defeated at the Battle of Vlotho in October 1638 and Rupert taken prisoner. King made an orderly withdrawal with the only part of the army not to be routed. He blamed the defeat squarely on Rupert's impetuosity. Recriminations over the Battle of Vlotho clearly still soured relations between Eythin and the prince six years later.
64 Bod. Clarendon MS, 1805.
65 Sir Hugh Cholmley, quoted in English Heritage Battlefield Report.
66 Bod. Clarendon MS.
67 This quote is of course referred to previously as having related specifically to the massacre of Newcastle's white-coats.
68 Margaret Cavendish (1667), p.48.
69 Sir John Hotham, 1st Baronet, of Scarborough, English Parliamentarian, belonged to a Yorkshire family, and fought in continental Europe during the early Thirty Years' War. In 1622 he was made baronet, and was Member of Parliament for Beverley in the five parliaments between 1625 and 1640, being High Sheriff of Yorkshire from 1634–35. In 1639 he was deprived by the king of his office of Governor of Hull, and joining the Parliamentary party, refused to pay ship-money. In January 1642 Hotham was ordered by the parliament to seize Hull, where there was a large store of munitions of war; this was at once carried out by his son John. Hotham took command of Hull and in April refused to admit Charles I to the town. Later he promised his prisoner, Lord Digby, that he would surrender it to the king, but when Charles appeared again he refused a second time and drove away the besiegers.

Meanwhile the younger Hotham was taking an active part in the vivil war in Yorkshire and Lincolnshire, but was soon at variance with other parliamentary leaders, especially with Lord Fairfax and his son Sir Thomas Fairfax, and complaints about his conduct and that of his troops were made by Oliver Cromwell and Colonel John Hutchinson. Soon both the Hothams were corresponding with the Earl of Newcastle, and the younger one was probably ready to betray Hull; these proceedings became known to parliament upon Newcastle's letters being captured at Marston Moor, and in June 1643 father and son were captured and taken to London. After a delay they were tried by court martial, found guilty and sentenced to death. The younger Hotham was beheaded on the 2 January 1645, and in spite of efforts made by the House of Lords and the Presbyterians to save him, the elder suffered the same fate the following day.
70 Soon Parliamentarian pamphlets would be circulating lists of crucifixes and other items indicative of poperty which were supposedly found amongst them.

71 Prince Rupert believed that Lord Eythin's (General King's) late arrival from York with Newcastle's white-coats and his lack of co-operation in marshalling the army was a factor in their defeat. After Marston Moor, Eythin advised Newcastle to escape abroad and accompanied him to Hamburg. He later learnt that Rupert had considered charging him with treason and wrote to the Prince in January 1645 protesting his innocence.

72 No cathedral in England suffered less from the Civil War than York Minster, and this immunity was due to the unceasing watchfulness of Sir Thomas Fairfax.

Chapter 5

73 Berm – this was a projection of the wall foundation at ground level and beyond the wall.

74 A work constructed beyond the main ditch of a fortress, and in front of the curtain between two bastions, intended to defend the curtain wall.

75 Shieldfield Fort stood on the east bank of the Pandon burn. The present Ridley villas in New Bridge Street mark its southern entrenchment. Thus it stood a little to the north of the line of the town wall at Carliol Tower from which it was distant about 550yd – a half-musket shot according to Lithgow.

76 This bridge of boats would be considerably to the east of the Ouseburn, and out of sight of the besieged by reason of the bend in the river, and also of the rising ground between Pandon and Ouseburn.

77 At Sandgate. Lithgow states Callendar placed two batteries here, one to intercept the besieged from his mines. He adds that they succeeded in beating down the top, face, and uppermost parts of the Carpenter's tower, probably immediately upon their being placed in position.

78 Palisade: A strong, long stake, one end of which is set firmly in the ground, and the other is sharpened, as a means of defence.

79 The Scottish artillery listed in 1644 ranged from 3 to 24 pounders.
Eight brass demi-cannon (24lb) requiring ten to twelve horse.
One brass demi-culverin (16lb) requiring eight horse. This could fire ten shots per hour at 2,100 paces.
Three brass quarter cannon (12lb).
Six iron demi-culverins (9–12lb). These could fire at an effective range of 320–380 paces.
Three iron field pieces (of the same calibre).
Eight petards.
Eight-eight frame guns (12lb). This lightweight leather-bound weapon, the invention of Sandy Hamilton, could be carried by one horse.

80 Scots foot regiments at the siege included: Angus; Aytouns; Clydedale; College of Justice /Sinclairs; Edinburgh; Fife; Galloway; Glencairns; Kyle & Carrick; Earl of Lanarks; Earl of Loudouns; East Lothian Regiment; Linlithgow & Tweeddale; Master of Cranstouns; Mearns & Aberdeen; Merse; Midlothian (part); Ministers; Niddries; Nithsdale & Annandale; Perthshire/Gask (part); Perthshire-Freelands; Stirlingshire; Strathearn; Teviotdale; Tweeddale; Viscount Kenmore's.

Chapter 6

81 Chamberlains accounts.

82 The Edinburgh Plague, first recorded in 1513, made several appearances over the years. Symptoms included swollen lymph glands, puss filled 'buboes' in the armpits and groin, and severe vomiting which could be so violent as to rupture the victims internal organs. Mortality rates were as high as 90 per cent in some outbreaks.

The worst (and last) outbreak in Edinburgh was that of 1645. It was recorded afterward that at its height, there were barely sixty men left able enough to defend the town.

The overcrowded state of Edinburgh's old town and the heavy infestation of rats made it very easy for the plague to spread. Fleas were the most common form of transmission and once infected the victims' chances of survival were very slim. Plague sufferers were confined to their homes and instructed to hang white sheets from the doors and windows; they would then be visited by the 'Plague Doctor', although 'treatment' was rarely a success.

The first plague doctor of Edinburgh died (of the plague) in June 1645 after only a short time in the job. A large salary was promised to the second plague doctor in Edinburgh, George Rae – a much more successful plague doctor, dressed in a truly frightening 'costume' designed to protect him from the plague as perceived at that time. He wore a large beaked mask, filled with sweet smelling herbs at the nose, along with a leather cloak. Although the plague was thought to be airborne, the leather happened to protect Rae from rat and flea bites – the real reason he survived the epidemic and was able to help so many sufferers. Rae would burst open the buboes of victims and sterilise the wound with a hot poker. Bear in mind however, that there were no anaesthetics available in Edinburgh at that time.

Edinburgh town council never intended to pay the large salary promised to Rae, as the doctor wasn't expected to survive. George Rae pursued Edinburgh's town council for the money for years afterwards but it is unlikely he was ever paid. In 2003 the entrance to a labyrinth of streets beneath Edinburgh was reopened, more than 350 years after it was sealed off during an outbreak of plague. Workmen have knocked through the floor of the city's council headquarters to expose the entrance to the redeveloped Mary King's Close. Local folklore says the narrow seventeenth-century staircase beneath the city chambers is where the council closed off 400 plague victims to die in 1645.

83 Paul Rollinson.

84 Harley Street in London is named after him.

85 The motto in gold letters on Stamford's azure banner read: FOR RELIGION. KING AND COUNTRY. Ma Puissance.

Chapter 7

86 Meaning 'left handed'.

87 He went on to have two sons and a daughter: Hugh of Kinneries, Alexander of Kinneries, John, named as 3rd lawful son in a legal transaction (and was by then dead), and Anna.

88 The author, having inspected the relative locations of both the site of the battle and the River Nairn, believes this to have been unlikely, if not impossible, although the passengers may have observed the government troops marching from the direction of Inverness towards where the battle was being fought, and heard the battle in progress.

Chapter 8

89 Spalding.

90 Lord Coupar's dragoons – described as consisting of 480 dragoons and officers in seven companies, but also as only sixty men, by Stephen Maggs.

91 Possibly one troop of sixty men, which might explain the lower number adopted by Stephen Maggs.

92 Lanark would personally capture Sir Robert Spottiswood, son of a former archbishop of St Andrews and a Royalist.

93 Major-General John Middleton was a colonel and lieutenant-general in the Parliamentarian armies from 1642. He spent close to £12,000 on raising his regiment, which included some Englishmen. Middleton and his regiment accompanied Leslie's cavalry strikeforce to Philiphaugh and his English troopers were widely praised for their role in the battle.

94 Montrose was never again to see MacDonald after he marched off to terrorise the west of Scotland again, before returning to Ireland, where he would be killed in a skirmish in 1647.

95 The Battle of Philiphaugh would take place a year to the day after Justice Mills and the sack of Aberdeen.

96 This description would correspond roughly with taking a route north round Manor Hill, to swing left down Corbylynn Road, but would mean that the second attack force would arrive to face the Royalists' front, they having had their left flank pushed back by Leslie, and conflicts with the description of the force being on the opposite side of the Etterick from Leslie's main force.

97 This direction for cavalry to retreat from the field would have been likely, whether the secondary Scots' force had advanced from round Manor Hill or Howden Hill.

98 A less likely route to flee if Leslie's secondary force had attacked from the north.

99 This is a list of forces so far discovered at Philiphaugh. (Compiled by Stephen Maggs)
Royalists: (800)
James Ogilvie, Earl of Airlie's Troop of Horse c60
Captain Blackadder's Troop of Horse c60
Captain Alexander Charteries of Amisfield's Troop of Horse c60
Major Nathanial Gordon's Troop of Horse c60
Captain John Mortimer's Troop of Horse c60
Lietenant-General Alexander Macdonnell's Regiment of Foot (very few as majority drawn off elsewhere)
Colonel Manus O'Cahan's Regiment of Foot c500
Covenanters: (3,400)
Colonel Harie Barcley's Regiment of Horse c40
Lord Coupar's Regiment of Infantry (a detachment of dragoons only?) c60?
Earl of Dalhousie's Regiment of Horse c320 or less – perhaps in reserve
Colonel Hew Frazer's Regiment of Dragoons c400
Lord Kirkcudbright's Regiment of Horse c600
Major-General David Leslie's Horse c550
The Earl of Leven's Regiment of Horse c550
Major-General John Middleton's Regiment of Horse c400
Lord Montgomerie's Regiment of Horse c470
John Hay, Master of Yester's Regiment of Foot (possibly not involved in the action).

100 This is impossible as Solway Flow (Moss) was fought over a hundred years before Philiphaugh, and Dunbar was yet to be fought, five years after Montrose's defeat, in 1650.

101 It also occurred on 16 December that the estates had ordered Montgomery's to Aberdeenshire with Eglinton's and Barclay's horse. This regiment was to gain a reinforcement of two companies of dragoons. Montgomery's men may not have been well supplied or paid then. From the Earl of Erroll's lands in Stannell, troopers took more than £20 of goods in plunder. In February 1646 troopers took at least £89 in grain and also stole clothing from Turriff. In March the

regiment took part in the relief of Inverness under Middleton, which Montrose had laid siege to, his Royalist forces plundering the surrounding area. The clan Fraser forts afforded safety for many as, besides Beauly, the Lovat Frasers controlled Wardlaw sconce, Culbokie's sconce (designed by Colonel Hugh Fraser), the Isle of Aigas and Little Struy. After Middleton lifted the siege in May, Sir James Fraser of Brea entertained him and his officers at Lovat Castle.

During Middleton's campaign in 1646, He delivered Chanonry Castle, whose Mackenzie garrison surrendered to Sir James Fraser of Brea, Tutor of Lovat (Brea garrisoned the castle with clan Fraser troops in spring 1647). Sometime afterward, Brea went south and Seaforth, one of Montrose's supporters, took the opportunity to press his Remonstrance on the Frasers by sending Roderick Mackenzie of Davochmaluag to meet with their leaders. The lairds of Struy, Culbokie (Hugh Fraser's elder brother), Belladrum Clunavackie, Foyers, Farraline, Reelich and Phoineas received Davochmaluag at Lovat Castle. After hearing his proposal for an alliance, Struy and Phoineas (the latter was governor of all the Fraser forts, captain of the Lovat garrison, musterer of the clan, and captain of its watch) spoke against it. Their opposition kept the Frasers in the Covenanter camp. Throughout 1646 and 1647 the Frasers maintained their garrisons. However, they suffered a reverse in 1647 when the Mackenzies recaptured Chanonry Castle from a Lieutenant Hugh Fraser, its commander. During the mid 1640s the allegiance of the Frasers to the Covenant played an important role in ensuring the safety of Inverness, an important garrison of the north.

Chapter 9

102 Clarendon.
103 Bellasis.
104 State Papers.
105 Sir Richard Willis, the ex-governor of Newark, made his peace with the king. Dugdale says (3 April 1646), 'This evening Sir Richard Willis first kissed ye King's hands since his coming to Oxford, after ye difference at Newark.'
106 Parliamentary pamphlet of the period.
107A large defensive ditch discovered later was found to be the southern corner of the Civil War structure, the king's sconce. The ditch measured 11m wide, increasing in width to 20m at the northern corner of the site. The excavations exposed the entire southern bastion of the king's sconce. The ditch probably had a very short life span. At the end of the Civil War the sconce was levelled and the local townsfolk once again forced to assist – this time in the demolition of the siegeworks. However, as an earthwork, king's sconce remained visible until the

nineteenth century when Baird's Maltings was constructed on the site between 1883 and 1900.

108 A structure projecting out from the main enclosure of a fortification, set into a straight (curtain) wall, allowing active defense against assaulting troops. It allows defenders of the fort to cover adjacent bastions and curtains with defensive fire. The bastion was designed to offer a full range on which to attack oncoming troops. Previous fortifications had been of little use within a certain range. The bastion solved this problem.

109 Defensive structure consisting of a movable obstacle composed of spikes attached to a (usually wooden) frame; used to obstruct cavalry.

110 This committee consisted of John Earl of Rutland, Theophilus Earl of Lincoln, Francis Lord Willoughby of Parham, Edward Lord Montague (members of the House of Peers), Mr William Pierepoint, Sir W. Armyn, Sir A. Heselrig, Sir E. Ascough, Sir C. Wray, Sir A. Irby, Mr T. Hatcher, and Mr Wm. Ellys (members of the House of Commons).

111 Dispatch of the Earl of Leven as reported to the House of Lords.

112 Perfect Diurnall, December 8–15 December 15–22; Perfect Occurrences, December 12–19.

113 Perfect Diurnall, January 5–12 states that Poyntz engaged the enemy with his sword, killed the first man to enter, and drove the remainder downstairs where he slew another of them. The Moderate Intelligencer, on the other hand, says that he had to run without his boots and that he lost his money and had his quarters ransacked.

114 Parliamentary History.

115 A pinnace describes two different sizes of marine craft. The first, smaller pinnace was a light boat, propelled by sails or oars, used as a 'tender' for guiding merchant and war vessels, to ferry messages between ships of the line, visit harbours ahead of the fleet to pick up mail, etc. Widely used during the 1600s, the Dutch used them as raiders, pirates frequently used them as scouts and for night attacks since they were small, reliable, and extremely quick, even against the wind. The second, larger type, of which this vessel appears to have been one, was developed by the Dutch during the early seventeenth century. She had a hull form resembling a small 'race built' galleon, and was usually square rigged on two or three masts. Pinnaces saw use as merchant vessels, pirate vessels and small warships, seeing widespread use in northern waters as they had a shallow draught.

116 Pamphlet extant, entitled, 'Orders from the Lord of Hosts, for regulating the Hosts of the Lord, set down in a sermon preached at the Leaguer before Newark, on Friday, 27th March, 1646, by order from, and by the desire of, the Committee of Lords and Commons, Commissioners from the Parliament of England, on the occasion of a Public Fast and Solemn humiliation appointed

to be kept that day throughout the English and Scottish armies before Newark, to seek a blessing from Heaven upon the proceedings of the said Forces in the present siege of that garrison, by Edward Reyner, Preacher of the Gospel in the City of Lincoln.'

117 Letter dated 28 March 1646 from Balderton, to the Honourable William Lenthal, Esquire, Speaker to the Honourable House of Commons, from the commissioners employed by parliament for reducing Newark, together with the summons, the commissioners of both Kingdoms to the governor to deliver up the town for the use of king and parliament, and the governor's answer, and signed, W. Pierrepont, Tho. Hatcher, W. Armyne, Edw. Ascoughe.

118 The different varieties are described thus: Coins were issued dated 1645 and 1646. Of the former year are pieces of the values of thirty, twelve, and nine pence whilst of the latter year there are in addition sixpences. The general design of these coins is the same, the obverse having within a pearled border the letters C R on each side of a crown, and the value expressed beneath in Roman numerals; whilst on the reverse is the legend OBS NEWARK, with the date beneath, in Arabic figures. All the coins issued from Newark are struck on lozenge-shaped flans, apparently cut direct from the dishes, trenchers, and other varieties of silver plate, in the town, or obtained from Royalist adherents in the neighbouring country districts. (Paper written by Dr Philip Nelson of Liverpool).

119 Memoirs of Montrose.

120 MSS of Frasers.

121 Stratherrick was last seen as the idyllic setting in 1642 for the young Master of Lovat's hunting diversions with his lady and retinue.

122 From 1643 the lieutenant-colonel of the regiment is recorded as having been William Crawford of Nether Skeldon, listed as having died in 1646, presumably earlier in January. Regimental records show Monro, the regiment's major from 1643, as lieutenant-colonel from 1646.

123 Moderate Intelligencer, May 7–14.

124 Brown, ii, p. 120. In Stoke 159 people died of the plague in 1646. In Balderton the burials for that year numbered 129 against nineteen in 1645.

125 Now the court.

126 Rushworth.

127 S. R. Gardiner, History of the Commonwealth and Protectorate, 1903.

Chapter 10

128 Obviate – to anticipate and dispose of effectively; render unnecessary. Synonyms – forfend, forestall, stave off.

129 John Cumming of Relugas to James Grant of Grant, 26 February 1649.

130 Hugh Fraser 7th Lord Lovat survived the master by two years, and was succeeded by his grandson, Hugh, a child of about two years of age. Sir James Fraser of Brae continued, as Tutor, to be the ruling spirit of the administration of all the Lovat interests. He was a staunch Presbyterian who took a prominent part in the business of Inverness Presbytery and the General Assembly of the Kirk, and was a leading Covenanter. Although the success of the Royalists was short-lived, the loss of Inverness Citadel during the struggle broke his heart and, after returning from the south, he died at Lovat in 1649.

131 A fever marked by chills and sweating that recur at regular intervals.

132 English folk belief of the 1600s.

133 Bezoar were also calculi found in the gut of Persian wild goats. You may think that it would be hard to tell these stones from other less exotic varieties. There must have been a big racket not only in bezoar but in the bones from a stag's heart or unicorn horn. Oriental bezoar was also administered to the dying Charles II.

134 Sovereign Remedies, A Critical Depreciation Of The 17th-Century London Pharmacopoeia by William Brockbank.

135 One such example was Lady Sedley's Receipt Book dated 1686. Successive prescriptions are 'to make almond gingerbread', 'For those that can't hold their water', 'To pott craw fish…' Her cure for those who can't hold their water includes: 'Take the claws of hogs, don't wash um, dry um in an oven, but be sure they are not burnt. Beat um to a powder, sift um. Take as much of the powder as will lie on a sixpence, morning and night till you are cured.'

136 From Dr Thomas Sydenham, Medical Observations on the History and Cure of Acute Illnesses, 1676.

137 Natural and artificial Directions for Health, derived from the best philosophers, as well modern as ancient (Vaughan, 1617).

138 The word 'physic' meaning 'laxative' or 'purgative' survived into American English through the late nineteenth century.

139 High Dutch was the language most commonly spoken within the gentry and the officer class on the continent during the Thirty Years' War.

140 Eythin settled in Sweden and was created Baron Sandshult in Kalmar. In 1650, Charles II commissioned him lieutenant-general under the Marquis of Montrose. He was expected to lead a force of mercenaries in Montrose's projected invasion of Scotland, but only a small advance party ever sailed and Eythin himself never left Sweden. He died in June 1652 and was buried at Stockholm.

141 Execution of Montrose by Richard Cavendish.

142 At 11.15 a.m. on 20 April 1653, Cromwell entered parliament to dissolve it. After listening to the debate for a time, then beginning to speak in calm tones, he changed to 'a furious manner', walking up and down the house, stamping the ground with his feet and shouting 'with so much passion and

discomposure of mind as if he had been distracted'. He said: 'It is time for me to put an end to your sitting in this place, which you have dishonoured by your contempt of all virtue and defiled by your practice of every vice. Ye are a factious crew, and enemies to all good government. Ye are a pack of mercenary wretches and would, like Esau, sell your country for a mess of pottage.' He pointed to individuals and called them 'whoremasters, drunkards, corrupt and unjust men', adding, 'Ye have no more religion than my horse. Ye are grown intolerably odious to the whole nation ... Perhaps ye think this is not parliamentary language. I confess it is not, neither are you to expect any such from me ... It is not fit that ye should sit as a parliament any longer. Ye have sat long enough unless you had done more good.' When Sir Peter Wentworth protested at such language from one they had 'so highly trusted and obliged', Cromwell retorted: 'Come, come, I will put an end to your prating. Ye are no parliament. I say ye are no parliament. I will put an end to your sitting.' He shouted to Thomas Harrison, 'Call them in', and the musketeers entered. He pointed to the Speaker: 'Fetch him down.' Harrison hesitated: 'The work is very great and dangerous', then obeyed. Sir Henry Vane protested: 'This is not honest, yea it is against morality and common honesty.' Cromwell: 'Oh, Sir Henry Vane, Sir Henry Vane, the Lord deliver me from Sir Henry Vane.' Then, turning to the mace: 'What shall we do with this bauble? Here, take it away.' Then, to the members: 'I command ye therefore, upon the peril of your lives, to depart immediately out of this place. Go, get ye out! Make haste! Ye venal slaves begone! Take away that shining bauble and lock up the doors.' By 11.40 the house was cleared and locked. Someone put up a poster: 'This House is to be Lett; now unfurnished.' S.R. Gardiner, History of the Commonwealth and Protectorate, 1903.

End Tables

143 Muskets fired a lead ball of between 10 & 20 to the pound:

Great Britain: Weight of Musket Balls

Weapon	Number per Pound	Diameter of Ball in Inches
Wall Piece	6 ¾	.89
Musket	14 ½	.68
Carbine	20	.60
Pistol	34	.51
7 Barrel Gun	46 ½	.46

'A musket required the half weight of her ball in fine powder and two thirds of common powder (1:1:7 Sulphur, charcoal, salt petre), i.e. one pound of fine powder to two pounds of lead, and two pounds of ordinary powder for three pounds of lead.

144 Taking 14.5 musket balls per pound of lead, this equates to nearly 60,000 musket balls.
145 Possibly for regimental colours?
146 Estimates a possible 461 dragouners.
147 Estimates a possible 497 dragouners.
148 Estimates over eight months pay for the regiment.
149 Estimates a possible 471 men & officers.
150 Estimates a possible 478 dragouners and officers. While many regiments seldom achieved the paper figures expected for their type of unit (i.e. 800–1,000 men for a foot regiment on paper, frequently only 500–600 men in reality); based upon the pay attributed to to Fraser's dragoons, this regiment appears to have consistently numbered between 461 and 478 dragouners plus its officers – Colonel Fraser, Lieutenant-Colonel Crawford, Major Jon Munro, Chaplain, Scrivener, Quartermaster etc. and the four company commanders – Captain Alexander Ferguson, Captain David Lumsden, Captain John Forrester and Captain Michael Bruce. It would seem that each company numbered 115–119, remarkably close to the 120–125 aspired to on paper for a dragoon regiment of 480–500.

Index